Activities for Successful Spelling

Activities for Successful Spelling

The essential guide

Philomena Ott

Routledge
Taylor & Francis Group

LONDON AND NEW YORK

To Georgina, Rhodri and Fredrick, with love

First published 2008
by Routledge
2 Park Square, Milton Park, Abingdon, Oxon, OX14 4RN

Simultaneously published in the USA and Canada
by Routledge
270 Madison Avenue, New York, NY 10016

Routledge is an imprint of the Taylor & Francis Group, an informa business

© 2008 Philomena Ott

Typeset in Palatino by
Keystroke, 28 High Street, Tettenhall, Wolverhampton
Printed and bound in Great Britain by
TJ International Ltd, Padstow, Cornwall

British Library Cataloguing in Publication Data
A catalogue record for this book is available from the British Library

Library of Congress Cataloging in Publication Data
A catalog record for this book has been requested.

ISBN10: 0–415–38574–1 (pbk)
ISBN10: 0–203–96608–2 (ebk)

ISBN13: 978–0–415–38574–9 (pbk)
ISBN13: 978–0–203–96608–2 (ebk)

Contents

Acknowledgements

I am grateful to those I have taught and from whom I have learned so much. My thanks to their parents and carers for their faith and fortitude. I have been inspired and influenced by many talented teaching colleagues.

My editor Gerard Hill has been generous with his time, encyclopaedic knowledge of language and readiness to contribute improvements to the content and presentation. Mike Jubb provided the verse and Steph Dix provided most of the illustrations. Maggie Lindsey-Jones's encouragement was invaluable throughout the production process.

Introduction

People learn in different ways. Different strategies and a variety of approaches will need to be used depending on preferred learning style. The 'learners' using these activities may be school pupils or children out of school, but they may also be people of any age improving their literacy, learning English for the first time or struggling with learning difficulties. Their 'learning partner' may be a teacher, parent, a classroom assistant or another learner.

Many dyslexic learners have difficulties with word retrieval and word naming, so teachers and learners must recall keywords before starting an activity. The teacher and learner can discuss the aim of each activity and revise key vocabulary, then use the checklists to look at given examples as well as the target words. Further words may be generated orally with the learners and these can be written on index cards, the board or an overhead transparency (OHT), or using an interactive whiteboard, for example during the Shared Reading of texts during the Literacy Hour. These words may be noted and included in a personal 'Spellofax.'

Keywords

Here are the keywords needed to understand and use phonemic and phonological strategies and techniques. The manual *How to Manage Spelling Successfully* has a glossary of over 200 terms that you may meet elsewhere.

The **vowels** are 'a' 'e' 'i' 'o' 'u'

'y' is sometimes a vowel as in: sky, lady, tyre

There are two kinds of vowels: **short vowels** say their sounds and **long vowels** say their names.

Diacritical marks are code marks or signs used to show whether a vowel is short or long. Short vowels are coded with a breve (˘): pĕt, cŭp, ăct. Long vowels are coded with a macron (¯): ōpen, drāīn, gō.

Digraphs are two letters making one sound: they may be two consonants (like ch) or two vowels (like ai), or one of each (like ar).

Diphthongs are two vowels found next to each other, which glide together when pronounced. They sound separately but quickly and retain their distinct sound.

Blends are letters found next to each other. They sound separately, but quickly blend.

Assimilations are sounds made down one's nose, involving the letters 'm' and 'n'.

Phonemes are the smallest units of sound in a word; they are the smallest part that changes the meaning of one spoken word to another. For example, /c/ /p/ /s/ before 'at' can make 'cat' 'pat' 'sat'.

Phonics means teaching reading and spelling by sounding out the letter sounds, then blending the sounds when learning to read. It can also be used to segment the sounds in the letters when spelling a word.

Synthetic phonics means sounding out each letter, then blending the letters to read the word: /d/ /o/ /g/ and segmenting the sounds to spell the word. **Analytic phonics** means the reader breaks the word into chunks – the initial consonant(s), called the 'onset', then the vowel sound and final consonant(s) together, called the 'rime': /d/ /og/.

Rhyme describes words that have the same ending sound(s).

Alliteration is when words have the same sound at the beginning.

Keywords are used to demonstrate a particular phoneme, to establish the letter–sound relationship.

Target words are the words used to demonstrate a spelling pattern and the rule or convention it shows.

Differentiated activities

All the activities apply and use multi-sensory learning strategies. There are different activities to match the individual's development and current level of literacy skills.

Section A

The pupil:

- Looks at the target word
- Says the target word
- Sounds out the letters in the word
- Writes the word while simultaneously saying the sound of each letter under his breath
- Reads what he has written

This utilises visual, oral, aural and kinaesthetic skills. It incorporates synthetic phonics to blend the sounds to read and to segment the sounds to spell.

Section B

Dictation

The teacher/learning partner:

- Says the sentence

The learner:

- Repeats the sentence aloud
- Writes the sentence while sub-vocalising the words as he writes them
- Reads what he has written

- Uses the proof-reading C-O-P-S (to check for the use of **C**apital letters, **O**missions, **P**unctuation and **S**pelling errors).

Dictation is valuable because it helps to develop auditory sequential memory, including short-term memory and working memory skills. It also helps to establish visual memory for spelling patterns.

Dictation can also be used by an individual without the help of a teacher/learning partner. In that case, the learner:

- Reads the sentences on to a cassette-tape recorder or MiniDisk recorder with a play-back facility – or he can use a computer package such as Dragon Naturally Speaking
- Plays it back, using headphones to listen to it sentence by sentence
- Writes it down
- Re-reads using the proof-reading C-O-P-S and checking with the original sentences.

These activities use different learning strategies, a variety of tactics and different skills to teach, rehearse and reinforce phonemic and phonological skills. They include differentiated levels of difficulty to match different spelling abilities. Some individuals will be able to tackle all the activities during the 20 minutes of the Literacy Hour that is to be used 'for group or independent work', whereas others may work on fewer sections. The keywords and strategies can be revised during the plenary session. Pupils can be asked to identify their 'best' strategy for remembering.

Section C: Crossword Puzzles

The learner:

- Re-reads the target words
- Reads the sentence with clues
- Fills in the missing word in the grid
- Reads the whole sentence

This utilises mainly oral, visual and auditory skills.

All the activities can also be used for one-to-one learning and teaching. An individual may do one item each day from the three activities for five consecutive days to maximise learning. Constant repetition and repeated exposure to print as well as the use of multi-sensory methods helps to develop mastery and automatic recall of sound/ symbol relationships and spelling patterns to manage phonics plainly and simply when reading and spelling.

These photocopiable activities are linked to the manual *How to Manage Spelling Successfully* and may be used to implement the spelling strategies and methods suggested. They can also be used to meet the National Curriculum and the National Literacy Strategy (NLS, 1998) objectives.

How these activities link to the National Literacy Strategy objectives

The NLS recommends that learners should be taught "alphabetic and phonic knowledge through: sound and naming each letter of the alphabet in lower and upper case. . . . To link sound and spelling patterns by using knowledge of rhyme to identify families of rhyming consonant-vowel-consonant (CVC) words e.g. hot, top, mop, fat, mat, pat . . . Discriminating 'onsets' from 'rimes' in speech and spelling. e.g. 'tip'. 'sip', 'skip', 'flip', chip. . . . Identifying alliteration in known and new or invented words." The Rose Review (2006) recommended that 'in practice this means teaching relatively short, discrete daily sessions, designed to progress from simple elements to the more complex aspects of phonic knowledge, skills and understanding'. These are included in Chapter 1, How to Manage Synthetic Phonics Plainly and Simply.

The NLS recommends that learners "should be taught to discriminate, orally, syllables in multi-syllabic words using children's names and from their reading , e.g. dinosaur, family, dinner, children [and to] extend to written forms and note syllable boundary in speech and writing." These are included in Chapter 2, How to Manage Syllables Successfully.

It recommends that learners should "investigate, collect and classify spelling patterns in pluralisation, construct rules for regular spellings, e.g. add 's' to most words; add 'es' to most words ending in 's', 'sh', 'ch'; change 'f' to 'ves'; when 'y' is a final consonant change to 'ies'." These are included in Chapter 3, How to Manage Plurals Painlessly.

Another recommendation of the NLS is that learners should be taught how "to distinguish between the spelling and meanings of common homophones, e.g. to/two/too; they're/their/there; peace/piece/piece [and] to distinguish between homophones, i.e. words with common pronunciation but different spellings, e.g. eight, ate; grate, great; rain, rein, reign." These are included in Chapter 4, How to Manage Homophones Happily.

Finally, the NLS recommends that learners should be taught "to spell words with common suffixes e.g. 'ful', 'ly' . . . to recognise and spell common prefixes and how these influence word meanings, e.g. un, de, dis, re, pre [and] to use their knowledge of prefixes to generate new words from root words, especially antonyms, happy/unhappy, appear/disappear". They should also be taught "how words change when er, est and y are added . . . to use their knowledge of suffixes to generate new words from root words, e.g. proud/proudly, hope/hopeless [and] to investigate spelling patterns and generate rules to govern the patterns". It also recommends that children should "collect/classify words with common roots, e.g. advent, invent, prevent, press, pressure, depress, phone, telephone, microphone [and] identify word roots, derivations and spelling patterns e.g. sign, signature, signal, bomb, bombastic, bombard, remit, permit, permission in order to extend keywords and provide support for spelling". These are included in Chapter 5, How to Manage Root Words, Prefixes and Suffixes Skilfully. The Rose Review pointed out that "high quality phonic work is not a 'strategy' so much as a body of knowledge" which is provided in the various Activities.

A structured, sequential and cumulative approach is used throughout, using multi-sensory teaching methodology. Consequently, as far as possible the words in the dictations use only the sounds and spelling patterns that have been specifically taught. This step-by-step approach develops confidence as well as skills. It prevents high levels of spelling errors, which otherwise lead to a sense of failure and frustration in those who struggle to master spelling conventions, often because of gaps in underlying knowledge.

Who can use these resources?

The activity pages in this book may only be photocopied for use within the purchasing establishment and by individual purchasers for use at home and in one-to-one teaching situations. These resources are appropriate for use at different stages of development and the activities can be chosen to match the individual's current skills. They are suitable for:

- Pupils in mainstream classrooms in line with the Rose Review recommendations that 'all maintained schools with primary aged pupils are required to teach phonics.'
- Pupils undertaking additional literacy support in small groups with a teaching assistant
- One-to-one teaching of individuals with specific learning difficulties including dyslexia
- Support and reinforcement by parents with homework
- English as a second language (ESL) students
- Adult basic literacy learners

For convenience, the learner is 'he' and the teacher is 'she' throughout this book, but 'she' and 'he' could be substituted in every case.

1 How to Manage Synthetic Phonics Plainly and Simply

Checklist of 44 phonemes and keywords

These are the 44 phonemes of English, with examples. Some authorities list more than 44 sounds; some say there are fewer. It depends how you define a 'sound' and whether you include sounds taken from other languages and dialects. One or two difficult sounds have been omitted or mentioned only briefly because they are used less frequently.

CONSONANTS (18)

/b/	bus	/n/	nut
/d/	dog	/p/	pot
/f/	fan, photo	/r/	rat
/g/	gun	/s/	sun, city
/h/	hat	/t/	tin
/j/	jam, gym	/v/	van
/k/	cat, kid, choir	/w/	wig
/l/	log	/y/	yak
/m/	man	/z/	zip

VOWELS

Short vowels (5) (these say their sounds)	Long vowels (5) (these say their names)			
ă ăpple	ā ācorn	brāin	plāy	cāke
ĕ ĕlephant	ē ēmu	trēē	trēat	Pēte
ĭ ĭnk	ī īron	fīght	tīe	crȳ wīne
ŏ ŏrange	ō ōpen	gōat	snōw	nōte
ŭ ŭmbrella	ū ūniform	glūe	stēw	tūne

CONSONANT DIGRAPHS (6), ALL WITH 'H'

/sh/	ship	/ph/	phone
/ch/	chin	/wh/	whip
/th/	that (voiced)	/gh/	laugh
/th/	thumb (unvoiced)		

VOWEL–CONSONANT DIGRAPHS (4), ALL WITH 'R'

/ar/	car
/er/, /ir/	herb, skirt
/or/	corn
/ur/	nurse

VOWEL DIGRAPHS (3)

'ai' saying	/ā/	train
'ea' saying	/ē/	seat
'oa' saying	/ō/	boat

VOWEL DIPHTHONGS (3)

'oo' saying	/oŏ/	cook
'oo' saying	/ōu/	pool
'ow' saying	/ow/	cow
'oy' saying	/oi/	coin

The aims of this chapter

To develop a basic understanding of the structure of language – including the anatomy of words – is a worthwhile investment in time and effort for all learners, but it is essential for those who struggle with developing literacy skills. Adams (1990) argued that "a deep and thorough knowledge of letters, spelling patterns, and words, and of phonological translations of all three, are of inescapable importance to both skilful reading and its acquisition".

Dissecting words by getting down to the bare bones – including saying the word aloud, identifying the phonemes (the individual sounds), then matching these to the letters that represent them – is indispensable for decoding words not instantly recognised when reading: "to establish the link between a letter and a sound, the learner must first establish a clear image of each" (Adams, 1990). Writing develops and reinforces word patterns and sound/symbol relationships.

People learn differently. Those with good visual skills can memorise word patterns. Those who are strong verbalisers with good language skills can learn by using and saying the individual letter/sound combinations and by understanding syllables. Those who are auditory learners will learn mostly from hearing and saying the letter/sound correspondences, as well as by dividing words into syllables. Those with good kinaesthetic skills will often learn best by handwriting and other physical activities involving the use of motor skills, such as the keyboard.

Most spellers need to know the contents of the checklist of phonics if they are to develop basic literacy skills. For most learners, this requires explicit teaching of phonics. There are 44 sounds in the English language and only 26 letters to represent them. The appearance of letters – including the printed uppercase, lowercase and handwritten forms of the letters – must be internalised to read and write. Letters have to be used in combination to represent some of these sounds, but these 44 sounds are the building blocks of the language and all learners need to have instant and automatic recall of them for reading and spelling. Later, spellers will need to learn and be familiar with over 140 letter combinations. The Rose Review showed that 'the systematic approach, which is generally understood as 'synthetic' phonics, offers the vast majority of young children the best and most direct route to becoming skilled readers and writers' and is also essential for the development 'especially [of] spelling'.

SHORT VOWELS

Aim: To learn the short vowels and use them for reading and spelling

The teacher/learning partner:

- explains the aim
- reviews the key words

Short vowels say their sounds. Short vowels are coded with a breve (˘). The short vowels and their keywords are:

ă	ăpple
ĕ	ĕgg
ĭ	ĭnk
ŏ	ŏrange
ŭ	ŭmbrella

The teacher/learning partner:

- demonstrates all the short vowels by segmenting the sounds and then blending them as /b/ /a/ /d/, /d/ /o/ /g/, /s/ /i/ /t/.

> bad   dog   sit   wet   pup

- generates further examples from discussion with the learner(s)

HANDY HINT

**Mnemonic: The short vowel men met Nellie an elephant in orange underwear
– a reminder that the short vowels are a e i o u**

Section A

Aim: To learn to read and spell words with the short vowel sound /ă/

The teacher/learning partner:

- explains the aim
- revises the keywords. Short vowels say their sounds and are coded with a breve (˘)
- demonstrates the target sound /ă/
- demonstrates the vowels with the (boxed) target words

Short vowel 'a' says /ă/

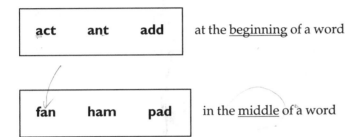

| act | ant | add | at the beginning of a word

| fan | ham | pad | in the middle of a word

The teacher/learning partner:

- demonstrates the vowels with the (boxed) target words
- demonstrates separating the sounds and then blending them as:

/a/ /n/ /t/   /p/ /a/ /d/

- generates further examples in discussion with the learner(s)

ACTIVITY

You:

- look at the target word /b/ /a/ /t/
- say the target sound /ă/
- sound out each letter in the word
- write the word while saying the sound of each letter
- read what you have written

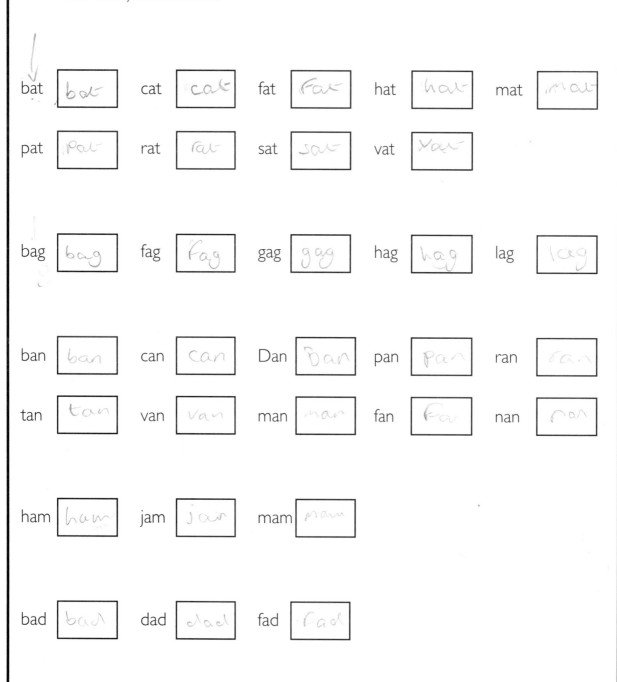

bat	bat	cat	cat	fat	fat	hat	hat	mat	mat
pat	pat	rat	rat	sat	sat	vat	vat		

bag	bag	fag	fag	gag	gag	hag	hag	lag	lag

ban	ban	can	can	Dan	Dan	pan	pan	ran	ran
tan	tan	van	van	man	man	fan	fan	nan	nan

ham	ham	jam	jam	mam	mam

bad	bad	dad	dad	fad	fad

Done

ACTIVITY

Aim: To find the odd-man-out in each line – the one that <u>begins</u> with a different sound

The teacher/learning partner:

- explains the aim
- revises the keywords
- demonstrates the activity using:

  sat   sad   **rat**   sag

- generates further examples in discussion with the learner(s)

You:

- look at the line of words
- find the odd-man-out, the one that begins with a different sound
- put a ring around it

bag   ban   bad   (pad)   (ram)   fat   fad   fag

fan   hat   had   (ham)   rat   rag   (van)   rap

mam   man   pan   (mat)

ACTIVITY

Aim: To find the odd-man-out in each line – the one that does not rhyme

The teacher/learning partner:

- explains the aim
- revises the keywords. Rhyme is when two words <u>end</u> with the same sound
- demonstrates the activity using:

fan   **pad**   tan

- generates further examples in discussion with the learner(s)

You:

- look at the words
- say the words
- find the one that <u>ends</u> in a different sound
- put a ring around the odd-man-out

van	pad	man		pat	bag	vat
ram	fad	jam		gag	rag	mat
tan	wag	rag		sag	mad	dad
bad	can	lad		bat	nag	tag
rat	hat	rag		tab	lag	dab

The proof-reading C-O-P-S

They remind us to check for errors, including:

C   **Capital Letters**

O   **Omissions**

P   **Punctuation**

S   **Spellings**

Section B

Dictation

The teacher/learning partner:

- says the sentence

The learner:

- repeats the sentence aloud
- writes the sentence while saying it under their breath
- reads what he has written
- uses the proof-reading C-O-P-S

1. Dan had a ram in a van.
2. Sam has a bat and a pad in his bag.
3. Pam had a hat and a fan.
4. The man had a cat in a bag.
5. The cat sat on a fat rat on the mat.
6. Sam had ham and jam in a bag.
7. The bag had a tag on it.
8. Sam had to gag the bad man.
9. The lad sat in the van.
10. Pat is mad, bad and sad.

Section A

Aim: To learn to read and spell words with the short vowel sound /ĕ/

The teacher/learning partner:

- explains the aim
- revises the keywords. Short vowels say their sounds and are coded with a breve (ˇ)
- demonstrates the target sound:

Short vowel 'e' says /ĕ/

| edit   egg   elf |

at the <u>beginning</u> of a word

| bed   hen   peg |

in the <u>middle</u> of a word

- demonstrates separating the sounds and then blending them as:

/b/ /ĕ/ /d/   /w/ /e/ /d/

- generates further examples in discussion with the learner(s)

ACTIVITY

You:

- look at the target word (start with 'bed') /b/ /e/ /d/
- say the target sound /ĕ/
- sound out the letters in the word
- write the word while saying the sound of each letter
- read what you have written

bed [bed]   fed [fed]   led [led]

beg [beg]   keg [keg]   leg [leg]

Ben [ber]   den [den]   hen [hen]

bet [bek]   jet [jet]   let [let]

ACTIVITY

Aim: To find the odd-man-out in each line – the one that <u>begins</u> with a different sound

The teacher/learning partner:

- explains the aim
- revises the keywords
- demonstrates the activity using:

    red   bed   beg   bet

- generates further examples in discussion with the learner(s)

CONTINUED

You:

- look at the line of words
- find the odd-man-out, the one that begins with a different sound
- put a ring around it

| pet | vet | peg | pen | | let | led | leg | met |
| men | Meg | jet | met | | bet | hen | bed | beg |

ACTIVITY

Aim: To find the odd-man-out in each line – the one that does not rhyme

The teacher/learning partner:

- explains the aim
- revises the keywords. Rhyme is when two words <u>end</u> with the same sound
- demonstrates the activity using:

    bet   **peg**   wet

- generates further examples in discussion with the learner(s)

You:

- look at the words
- say the words
- find the one that <u>ends</u> in a different sound
- put a ring around the odd-man-out

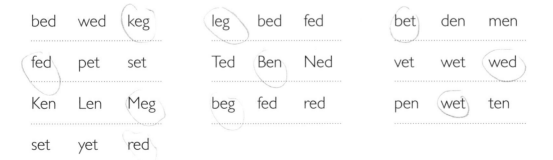

bed	wed	keg		leg	bed	fed		bet	den	men
fed	pet	set		Ted	Ben	Ned		vet	wet	wed
Ken	Len	Meg		beg	fed	red		pen	wet	ten
set	yet	red

Section B

Dictation

The teacher/learning partner:

- says the sentence

The learner:

- repeats the sentence aloud
- writes the sentence while saying it under their breath
- reads what he has written
- uses the proof-reading C-O-P-S

1. Len met ten men.
2. Ted fed the red hen.
3. He had a bed in his den.
4. Ben the vet got wet.
5. Meg let the pet hen sit on the bed.
6. Meg and Ted met in his den.
7. The leg of the bed had a peg in it.
8. Len and Meg met on a jet.
9. Let Ben get a pen.
10. Is the hen at the vet yet?

Section A

Aim: To learn to read and spell words with the short vowel sound /ĭ/

The teacher/learning partner:

- explains the aim
- revises the keywords. Short vowels say their sounds and are coded with a breve (˘)
- demonstrates the target sound:

Short vowel 'i' says /ĭ/

ink	imp	inn

at the <u>beginning</u> of a word

lid	pig	tin

in the <u>middle</u> of a word

- demonstrates separating the sounds and then blending them as:

/i/ /m/ /p/   /i/ /n/ /k/
/l/ /i/ /d/   /w/ /i/ /g/

- generates further examples in discussion with the learner(s)

ACTIVITY

You:

- look at the target word
- say the target sound /ĭ/
- sound out the letters in the word
- write the word while saying the sound of each letter
- read what you have written

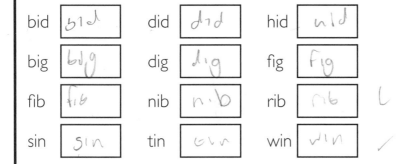

bid	bid	did	did	hid	hid
big	big	dig	dig	fig	fig
fib	fib	nib	nib	rib	rib
sin	sin	tin	tin	win	win

ACTIVITY

Aim: To find the odd-man-out in each line – the one that <u>begins</u> with a different sound

The teacher/learning partner:

- explains the aim
- revises the keywords
- demonstrates the activity using:

    dig   **pig**   din   did

- generates further examples in discussion with the learner(s)

You:

- look at the line of words
- find the odd-man-out, the one that begins with a different sound
- put a ring around it

(sin)	wit	win	wig		Sid	sin	sit	(nit)
pin	(kit)	pig	pit		(fig)	kit	kid	kin
bin	(gin)	big	bit					

ACTIVITY

Aim: To find the odd-man-out in each line – the one that does not rhyme

The teacher/learning partner:

- explains the aim
- revises the keywords. Rhyme is when two words <u>end</u> with the same sound
- demonstrates the activity using

     fit   **fig**   pit

- generates further examples in discussion with the learner(s)

You:

- look at the words
- say the words
- find the one that <u>ends</u> in a different sound
- put a ring round the odd-man-out

bid	rid	(rig)	kid	(kit)	lid
(win)	dig	rig	(wit)	gig	big
fin	(fig)	kin	din	(wig)	sin
bit	(tin)	sit	nit	hit	(hid)
sip	kip	(pig)	pip	(did)	lip

Section B

Dictation

The teacher/learning partner:

- Says the sentence

The learner:

- repeats the sentence aloud
- writes the sentence while saying it under their breath
- reads what he has written
- uses the proof-reading C-O-P-S

1. Sid hit the lid of the tin.
2. The fig hit the pig.
3. He hid the wig in the bin.
4. The big kid can sit on the lid of the bin.
5. Pin the kit on the kid.
6. Old Sid can dig a big pit.
7. He got rid of the bad zip.
8. Pam hit Sid on the leg.
9. The nits hid in the wig.
10. Sid hid the wig in his kit bag.

Section A

Aim: To learn to read and spell words with the short vowel sound /ŏ/

The teacher/learning partner:

- explains the aim
- revises the keywords. Short vowels say their sounds and are coded with a breve (˘)
- demonstrates the target sound:

Short vowel 'o' says /ŏ/

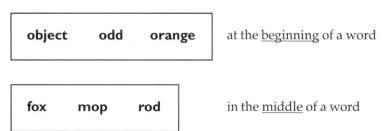

| object   odd   orange | at the <u>beginning</u> of a word

| fox   mop   rod | in the <u>middle</u> of a word

- demonstrates separating the sounds and then blending them as:

/o/ /d/ /d/ or /o/ /dd/
/m/ /o/ /p/ or /m/ /op/

- generates further examples in discussion with the learner(s)

ACTIVITY

You:

- look at the target word /b/ /o/ /d/
- say the target sound /ŏ/
- sound out the letters in the word
- write the word while saying the sound of each letter
- read what you have written

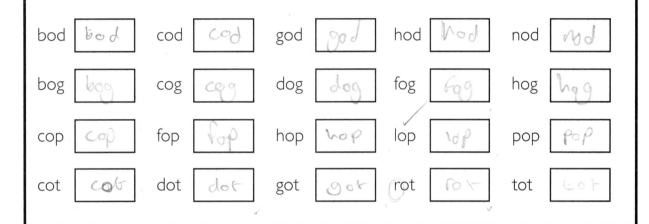

bod	bod	cod	cod	god	god	hod	hod	nod	nod
bog	bog	cog	cog	dog	dog	fog	fog	hog	hog
cop	cop	fop	fop	hop	hop	lop	lop	pop	pop
cot	cot	dot	dot	got	got	rot	rot	tot	tot

ACTIVITY

Aim: To find the odd-man-out in each line – the one that <u>begins</u> with a different sound

The teacher/learning partner:

- explains the aim
- revises the keywords
- demonstrates the activity using:

    jog   jot   **god**

- generates further examples in discussion with the learner(s)

You:

- look at the line of words
- find the odd-man-out, the one that begins with a different sound
- put a ring around him

sop   cog   cod   cot   pop   pot   pod   jot   pot

mop   top   tog   bog   lop   lot

ACTIVITY

Aim: To find the odd-man-out in each line – the one that does not rhyme

The teacher/learning partner:

- explains the aim
- revises the keywords. Rhyme is when two words <u>end</u> with the same sound
- demonstrates the activity using:

    cod   **cot**   rod

- generates further examples in discussion with the learner(s)

You:

- look at the words
- say the words
- find the one that <u>ends</u> in a different sound
- put a ring around the odd-man-out

bog	tog	pod	log	cod	jog
pot	sod	cod	tog	god	nod
hop	hod	top	pop	lop	fog
cot	lop	tot	dog	dot	jot
not	lop	sop	tog	hog	tot

Section B

Dictation

The teacher/learning partner:

- says the sentence

The learner:

- repeats the sentence aloud
- writes the sentence while saying it under their breath
- reads what he has written
- uses the proof-reading C-O-P-S

1. Pop the log in the hod.
2. The tot is in his cot.
3. Tom got a cod on his rod.
4. I can jog in fog but not a lot.
5. The pod had a lot of rot in it.
6. We got a hot dog.
7. Tom can hop and jog.
8. Bob has not got a job.
9. Pop the hot pot on top of the hob.
10. Can we jog in a wet bog?

Section A

Aim: To learn to read and spell words with the short vowel sound /ŭ/

The teacher/learning partner:

- explains the aim
- revises the keywords. Short vowels say their sounds and are coded with a breve (ˇ)
- demonstrates the target sound:

Short vowel 'u' says /ŭ/

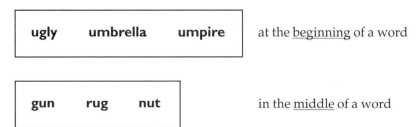

| ugly   umbrella   umpire | at the <u>beginning</u> of a word

| gun   rug   nut | in the <u>middle</u> of a word

- demonstrates separating the sounds and then blending them as:

  /u/ /p/   /g/ /u/ /n/   /r/ /u/ /g/

- generates further examples in discussion with the learner(s)

ACTIVITY

You:

- look at the target word /b/ /u/ /g/
- say the target sound /ŭ/
- sound out the letters in the word
- write the word while saying the sound of each letter
- read what you have written

bug *bug*	hug *hug*	jug *jug*	rug *rug*	tug *tug*
bun *bun*	fun *fun*	gun *gun*	nun *nun*	run *run*
gum *gum*	hum *hum*	mum *mum*	rum *rum*	sum *sum*
but *but*	cut *cut*	hut *hut*	nut *nut*	rut *rut*

ACTIVITY

Aim: To find the odd-man-out in each line – the one that <u>begins</u> with a different sound

The teacher/learning partner:

- explains the aim
- revises the keywords
- demonstrates the activity using

    hug   **gum**   hum   hut

- generates further examples in discussion with the learner(s)

You:

- look at the line of words
- find the odd-man-out, the one that begins with a different sound
- put a ring around him

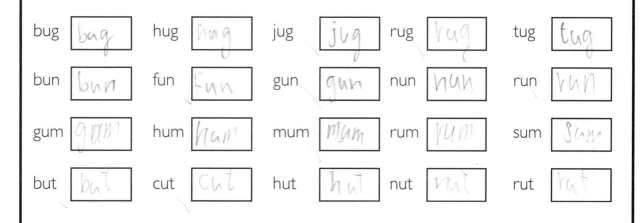

hut	rut	hum		hug	gut	but		bun	bug	gun
gum	gut	rum		rut	sun	run				

ACTIVITY

Aim: To find the odd-man-out in each line – the one that does not rhyme

The teacher / learning partner:

- explains the aim
- revises the keywords. Rhyme is when two words <u>end</u> with the same sound
- demonstrates the activity using:

    bun   gun   **rub**

- generates further examples in discussion with the learner(s)

You:

- look at the words
- say the words
- find the one that <u>ends</u> in a different sound
- put a ring around the odd-man-out

but	rut	tun		bug	hut	cut
....				....		
sum	hug	gum		pun	hum	run
....				....		
but	tug	hug		bug	jug	gum
....				....		
sun	hum	gun		bun	hug	run
....				....		
pug	mug	sun		sum	rut	gut

Section B

Dictation

The teacher/learning partner:

- Says the sentence

The learner:

- Repeats the sentence aloud
- Writes the sentence while saying it under their breath
- Reads what he has written
- Uses the proof-reading C-O-P-S

1. Do not tug the rug.
2. The pug cut his leg on a tin can.
3. Mum had rum at the pub.
4. The nun had fun in the sun.
5. He had a bug in his gut.
6. The rug had mud and gum on it.
7. He hid the gun in the hut.
8. The mug had a bug in it.
9. The jug is in the pub.
10. Can he run in the sun?

How much have you remembered about all the short vowel sounds?

- The teacher/learning partner reads each sentence. You write it down while saying it aloud quietly
- At the end, read what you have written
- Highlight the short vowels
- Use the proof-reading C-O-P-S

Hateful Henry and Horrid Harry's Pets

Hateful Henry is a big fat lad. He has a bad leg so he has to hop a lot. He has a dog called Rex. Rex can run a lot. He met a man and a pug dog at the pub. Rex ran and hid by a hut. The fat pug got a big bag of nuts. Rex had fun as he sat in the sun. He had a nap.

Horrid Harry has a cat called Max. He is mad and bad. He got at the pot of jam. He saw the ham on top of the hob. He sat and had the lot. Harry called Max names. The fat cat ran and hid in his bed.

LONG VOWELS

Aim: To learn the long vowels and use them for reading and spelling

The teacher/learning partner:

- Explains the aim
- Reviews the key terms

Long vowels say their names and are coded with a macron (‾). The long vowels and their keywords are:

ā   ācorn
ē   ēmu
ī   īvy
ō   ōpener
ū   ūniform

The teacher/learning partner:

- demonstrates all the long vowels by segmenting the sounds and then blending them as:

/ā/ /gent/   /ē/ /vil/   /pī/ /lot/   /pō/ /lō/   /fl/ /ū/

- generates further examples from discussion with the learner(s)

/ā/	a	apron	agent					
/ē/	be	he	me	we	evil	demon		
/ī/	I	by	my	try	why	pilot	hi-fi	
/ō/	go	no	so	ago	also	polo	solo	zero
/ū/	flu	music	guru	menu				

Checklist of consonant sounds and the different ways to spell them

'Name' and /sound/	at the beginning of words	in the middle of words	at the end of words
'b' says /b/	bag	ca**b**in	ni**b**
		dri**bb**le	
'c' – see k or s			
'd' says /d/	dog	bor**d**er	po**d**
		la**dd**er	

'Name' and /sound/	at the beginning of words	in the middle of words	at the end of words
'f' says /f/	fan	sofa	loaf
		coffee	cliff
'ph' can say /f/	phone	elephant	graph
'gh' can say /f/		laughter	laugh
'g' says /g/	gun	regard	pig
see also j		wiggle	egg
'gh' can say /g/	ghost		
'gu' can say /g/	guide	beguile	
'h' says /h/	hut	behave	
'j' says /j/	jam	major	hajj
'g' can say /j/	gem	magic	huge
'dg' can say /j/		badger	badge
'k' says /k/	king	baker	oak
'c' can say /k/	cup	local	mac
'ck' can say /k/		chicken	duck
'ch' can say /k/	chemist	anchor	stomach
'lk' can say /k/		walker	yolk
'que' can say /k/		chequered	mosque
'l' says /l/	lamp	below	feel
		pillow	bell
'm' says /m/	man	remind	foam
		common	
'lm' can say /m/		calmer	palm
'mb' can say /m/		thumbing	lamb
'gm' can say /m/			paradigm
'mn' can say /m/			autumn
'n' says /n/	net	tend	pin
		dinner	inn
'gn' can say /n/	gnat	designer	sign
'kn' can say /n/	knee		
'mn' can say /n/	mnemonic		
'pn' can say /n/	pneumonia		
'p' says /p/	pig	transport	cup
		apple	
'q' says /kw/	quick	equal	
see also k			
'r' says /r/	rat	moral	fur
		carrot	purr
'wr' can say /r/	wren	rewritten	
'rh' can say /r/	rhyme		
's' says /s/	sun	basin	bus
		missile	class
'st' can say /s/		castle	

'Name' and /sound/	at the beginning of words	in the middle of words	at the end of words
'c' can say /s/	city	pencil	fence
'sc' can say /s/	science	rescind	coalesce
'sw' can say /s/	sword		
'ps' can say /s/	psalm		
't' says /t/	tap	later	hat
		button	putt
'th' can say /t/	thyme		
'pt' can say /t/	ptarmigan		
'v' says /v/	van	vivid	love
'w' says /w/	witch	mower	show
'u' can say /w/		languid	
'x' says /ks/		taxi	annex
'x' can also say /gz/		exact	
'y' says /y/	yet	royal	
'y' can say /ē/			baby
'y' can say /ī/			cry
'z' says /z/	zebra	razor	quiz
		dazzle	jazz
's' can say /z/		cosy	cars
		scissors	James's

Aim: To learn to read and spell words with 'b' saying /b/

The teacher/learning partner:

- explains the aim
- demonstrates the target sound:

The consonant 'b' says /b/

| bat   beg   bun | /b/ at the <u>beginning</u> of words |

| cabin   robin   goblin | /b/ in the <u>middle</u> of words |

| cab   fib   rub | /b/ at the <u>end</u> of words |

- demonstrates separating the sounds and then blending them as:

/b/ /ă/ /t/ or /c/ /ă/ /b/

- generates further examples in discussion with the learners
- recites and/or mimes the following

> When a robin came bobbing along,
> To babble his bright morning song,
> Did I raise my bald head?
> Did I bounce out of bed?
> Or say "Clear off to where you belong!"

Dictation

The teacher/learning partner:

- says the sentence

The learner:

- repeats the sentence aloud
- writes the sentence while saying it under their breath
- reads what he has written
- uses the proofreading C-O-P-S

1. Bob put his bat in his bag.
2. Ben got a job on a bus.
3. The robin sat in the wet bog.
4. Bob got a big bag of buns.
5. Ben hid the bib in the bin.

Aim: To learn to read and spell words with 'c' saying /k/

The teacher/learning partner:

- explains the aim
- demonstrates the target sound:

The consonant 'c' says /k/

cat	cot	cup

'c' saying /k/ at the <u>beginning</u> of words

Arctic	picnic	piccolo

in the <u>middle</u> of words

music	tonic	topic

at the <u>end</u> of words

- demonstrates separating the sounds and then blending them as:

/c/ /ă/ /t/ or /m/ /ū/ /s/ /ĭ/ /c/

- generates further examples in discussion with the learners
- recites and/or mimes the following

> To a creepy old castle in Kent
> A courageous young captain was sent.
> When he came, he was cool,
> But the place had a ghoul;
> Now he's crazy and can't pay his rent.

Dictation

The teacher/learning partner:

- says the sentence

The learner:

- repeats the sentence aloud
- writes the sentence while saying it under their breath
- reads what he has written
- uses the proofreading C-O-P-S

1. The fox fed his cub.
2. The cat can get cod.
3. He has a tin can and a coffee cup.
4. We had fun at the picnic.
5. We did a topic on cats.

Aim: To learn to read and spell words with 'd' saying /d/

The teacher/learning partner:

- explains the aim
- demonstrates the target sound:

The consonant 'd' says /d/

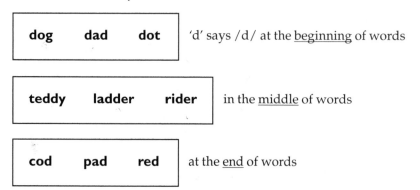

dog	**dad**	**dot**	'd' says /d/ at the <u>beginning</u> of words
teddy	**ladder**	**rider**	in the <u>middle</u> of words
cod	**pad**	**red**	at the <u>end</u> of words

- demonstrates separating the sounds and then blending them as:

/d/ /ŏ/ /g/ or /c/ /ŏ/ /d/

- generates further examples in discussion with the learners
- recites and/or mimes the following

When David from Dudley got mad,
He decided to do something bad.
This decision delighted
And made him excited,
Till he wound up in jail like his dad.

Dictation

The teacher/learning partner:

- says the sentence

The learner:

- repeats the sentence aloud
- writes the sentence while saying it under their breath
- reads what he has written
- uses the proofreading C-O-P-S

1. I met a mad adder and I hid.
2. Dad got a ladder to mend the shed.
3. This red pen is a dud.
4. Dan had a lot of cod in his net.
5. He put a red ink dot on the pad.

Aim: To learn to read and spell words with 'f' saying /f/

The teacher/learning partner:

- explains the aim
- demonstrates the target sound:

The consonant 'f' says /f/

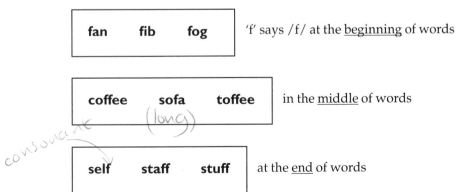

| fan   fib   fog | 'f' says /f/ at the <u>beginning</u> of words |

| coffee   sofa   toffee | in the <u>middle</u> of words |

| self   staff   stuff | at the <u>end</u> of words |

- demonstrates separating the sounds and then blending them as:

/f/ /ă/ /n/ or /s/ /t/ /ă/ /f/ /f/

- generates further examples in discussion with the learners
- recites and/or mimes the following

> A farmer from Frinton called Fred
> Really fancied a florist, who said:
> "In fair or foul weather
> I'll carry a feather
> And tickle poor Fred till he's dead".

Dictation

The teacher/learning partner:

- says the sentence

The learner:

- repeats the sentence aloud
- writes the sentence while saying it under their breath
- reads what he has written
- uses the proofreading C-O-P-S

1. Find a fan. I feel hot.
2. It is a big, bad fib.
3. We had fine fun in the sun.
4. The fog is thick.
5. Fred and Philip are big fans.

Aim: To learn to read and spell words with 'g' saying /g/

The teacher/learning partner:

- explains the aim
- demonstrates the target sound:

Hard 'g' says /g/

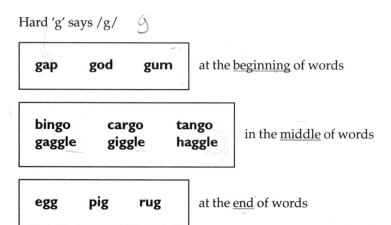

gap	**god**	**gum**	at the <u>beginning</u> of words

bingo	**cargo**	**tango**	
gaggle	**giggle**	**haggle**	in the <u>middle</u> of words

egg	**pig**	**rug**	at the <u>end</u> of words

- demonstrates separating the sounds and then blending them as:

/g/ /ă/ /p/ or /ĕ/ /g/ /g/

- generates further examples in discussion with the learners

'gh' can say /g/ in a few words

ghost	**ghoul**	**ghastly**

'gu' can say /g/ in a few words

guide	**guild**	**beguile**	**league**

- recites and/or mimes the following

A greedy old grandad called Jerry
Gobbled seventeen glasses of sherry.
Beginning to boast,
He gave up the ghost;
Now he groans in his grave, not so merry.

Dictation

The teacher/learning partner:

- says the sentence

The learner:

- repeats the sentence aloud
- writes the sentence while saying it under their breath
- reads what he has written
- uses the proofreading C-O-P-S (see p. 00)

1. The fat pig can dig a lot.
2. His gran had a red wig.
3. The dog ran into the gap.
4. Dad cut the twigs off the log.
5. The girl had a gun.

Aim: To learn to read and spell words with 'h' saying /h/

'h' says /h/

ham	**hog**	**hut**

at the <u>beginning</u> of words

behave	**behold**	**inhale**

in the <u>middle</u> of words

- demonstrates separating the sounds and then blending them as:

/h/ /ă/ /m/ or /b/ /ē/ /h/ /ō/ /l/ /d/

- generates further examples in discussion with the learners
- recites and/or mimes the following

A horrible hog from Redruth
Had a habit of being uncouth;
He happily stood
With each hoof in the mud.
"I'm a horrid old hog, that's the truth".

Dictation

The teacher/learning partner:

- says the sentence

The learner:

- repeats the sentence aloud
- writes the sentence while saying it under their breath
- reads what he has written
- uses the proofreading C-O-P-S

1. He had ham and eggs.
2. Harry hid the hat in the hut.
3. The hag hums happily.
4. He hit the hog and ran to the hut.
5. Harry! Behave!

Aim: To learn to read and spell words with 'j' saying /j/

The teacher/learning partner:

- explains the aim
- demonstrates the target sound:

'j' says /j/

| jam   job   jug | mostly at the <u>beginning</u> of words

- demonstrates separating the sounds and then blending them as:

/j/ /ă/ /m/ or /j/ /ŏ/ /b/

- generates further examples in discussion with the learners

- recites and/or mimes the following

A jolly old jester named Jack
Could juggle while riding a yak;
But, just as he joked
"I'm a jovial bloke",
It jolted him right off its back.

Aim: To learn to read and spell words with 'k' saying /k/

The teacher/learning partner:

- explains the aim
- demonstrates the target sound:

'k' says /k/

key	king	kit

at the <u>beginning</u> of words

baker	making	woken

in the <u>middle</u> of words

ask	milk	monk

at the <u>end</u> of words with a <u>consonant</u> before the /k/ sound

- demonstrates separating the sounds and then blending them as:

/k/ /ĭ/ /t/ or /b/ /ā/ /k/ /e/ /r/ or /a/ /s/ /k/

- generates further examples in discussion with the learner(s)

back	neck	pick	clock	duck

at the <u>end</u> of words with a short vowel, /k/ is spelt 'ck'

at the end of words with a long vowel, /k/ is spelt 'k'

oak	cheek	peak

after a <u>vowel digraph</u>

bike	cake	duke

between a long vowel and Magic 'e'

HANDY HINT

/k/ is spelt 'k' before 'e' or 'i'

key king kit

/k/ is spelt 'k' after a long vowel

baker bike oak

/k/ is spelt 'k' after a consonant

ask pink milk

/k/ is spelt 'c' before 'a' 'o' 'u'

cat cod cup

/k/ is spelt 'c' before a consonant

act crop include

- recites and/or mimes the following

> When a kindly old lady from Kent
> Sneaked a kiss with an elderly gent,
> He exclaimed "That's a crime
> If you're just killing time:
> Now kiss me again, with consent".

Dictation

including 'k' and 'c' spellings for /k/ sound

The teacher/learning partner:

- says the sentence

The learner:

- repeats the sentence aloud
- writes the sentence while saying it under their breath
- reads what he has written
- uses the proofreading C-O-P-S

1. Colin and Jake met in a bank.
2. Her kit is in her case.
3. Do not wink at the king.
4. Ken had a kip in his cot.
5. Kate got pink ink on her kit.

Dictation

including 'ck' and 'ke' spellings for /k/ sound

The teacher/learning partner:

• says the sentence

The learner:

• repeats the sentence aloud
• writes the sentence while saying it under their breath
• reads what he has written
• uses the proof-reading C-O-P-S

1. The duke has six black ducks on his lake.
2. Jack's black jacket went up in smoke.
3. Dick had a cricket bat in the back of the car.
4. Her bus ticket fell out of her pocket.
5. I like that pink frock and black hat.

Copy out and complete the following sentences by inserting 'k', 'ck' or 'k-e'

1. The Du _____ of Kent has six pairs of bla _____ so _____ s.
2. We had chi _____ en and chips in a bas _____ et for lunch.
3. Quic ——! Get a bu —— et. He is about to be si _____ !
4. That blo _____ went for a sm _____ behind the shed.
5. Pam had a glass of cup of mil _____ and a pa _____ et of nuts.

Aim: To learn to read and spell words with 'l' saying /l/

The teacher/learning partner:

• explains the aim
• demonstrates the target sound:

'l' says /l/

| leg   log   lump | at the <u>beginning</u> of words |

| pillow   pilot   hollow | in the <u>middle</u> of words |

| feel   meal   wheel | at the <u>end</u> of words |

- demonstrates separating the sounds and then blending them as:

/l/ /ĕ/ /g/ or /f/ /ēē/ /l/

- generates further examples in discussion with the learners
- recites and/or mimes the following

Lady Lucinda la Fay
Loves playing lacrosse every day;
Let loose with a racket,
She's liable to whack it
At each little lass in her way.

Dictation

The teacher/learning partner:

- says the sentence

The learner:

- repeats the sentence aloud
- writes the sentence while saying it under their breath
- reads what he has written
- uses the proofreading C-O-P-S

1. The cat sat on her lap.
2. He cut his leg on the tin lid.
3. We had to lag the loft.
4. I lit the lamp and left well alone.
5. The pilot got lost in the fog.

Aim: To learn to read and spell words with 'm' saying /m/

The teacher/learning partner:

- explains the aim
- demonstrates the target sound:

'm' says /m/

| man   mat   mug | at the <u>beginning</u> of words |

| combat   comet   comic | in the <u>middle</u> of words |

foam	ram	zoom

at the <u>end</u> of words

game	home	time

at the end of words with long vowel and Magic 'e'

- demonstrates separating the sounds and then blending them as:

  /m/ /ă/ /n/ or /f/ /oa/ /m/

- generates further examples in discussion with the learners
- recites and/or mimes the following

> Miss Miriam Mimi Malcreep
> Asked Minnie and Maggie to sleep
> But she made a mistake
> When she kept them awake,
> Madly muttering 'I'm Little Bo-Peep'.

Dictation

The teacher/learning partner:

- says the sentence

The learner:

- repeats the sentence aloud
- writes the sentence while saying it under their breath
- reads what he has written
- uses the proofreading C-O-P-S

1. Tom had a big mat for his lamp.
2. Meg met Pam and mum.
3. The man is in combat with Matt.
4. The mug has a mark on it.
5. Pam has the most comics.

Aim: To learn to read and spell words with 'n' saying /n/

The teacher/learning partner:

- explains the aim
- demonstrates the target sound:

'n' says /n/

net	nits	nut

at the <u>beginning</u> of words

end	land	minor
manners	sinner	winter

in the <u>middle</u> of words

pin	sun	win

at the <u>end</u> of words

dine	line	wine

at the end of words with a long vowel and Magic 'e'

- demonstrates separating the sounds and then blending them as:

/n/ /ĕ/ /t/ or /p/ /ĭ/ /n/

- generates further examples in discussion with the learners
- recites and/or mimes the following

> When Old Nick invites Nancy to dine,
> They drink nettle-and-blackberry wine;
> And he says as he pours
> "May I drink half of yours?
> For I'm over the limit on mine".

Dictation

The teacher/learning partner:

- says the sentence

The learner:

- repeats the sentence aloud
- writes the sentence while saying it under their breath
- reads what he has written
- uses the proofreading C-O-P-S

1. Ann has lots of fine wine.
2. I had to pin up the hem.
3. Did you send them the nuts?
4. Adam can wine and dine in the sun.
5. Put the china cup in the bin as it is in bits.

Aim: To learn to read and spell words with 'p' saying /p/

The teacher/learning partner:

- explains the aim
- demonstrates the target sound:

'p' says /p/

pan	**pig**	**pup**

at the <u>beginning</u> of words

chapel	**apple**	**apron**

in the <u>middle</u> of words

tip	**hop**	**cap**

at the <u>end</u> of words

cape	**rope**	**wipe**

at the end of words with a long vowel and Magic 'e'

- demonstrates separating the sounds and then blending them as:

/p/ /ă/ /n/ or /t/ /ĭ/ /p/

- generates further examples in discussion with the learners
- recites and/or mimes the following

> Whenever the Pied Piper played,
> All the rats soon appeared on parade.
> They plunged in the waters
> With sons and with daughters;
> Yet the Pied Piper never got paid.

Dictation

The teacher/learning partner:

- says the sentence

The learner:

- repeats the sentence aloud
- writes the sentence while saying it under their breath
- reads what he has written
- uses the proofreading C-O-P-S

1. Pat pops into the pub for a pint.
2. Get a bit of tape to mend the pipe.
3. Bob had a top hat and a cape.
4. Put the map in the box.
5. The bad pup nips Pam on the leg.

Aim: To learn to read and spell words with 'qu' saying /kw/

The teacher/learning partner:

- explains the aim
- demonstrates the target sound:

'qu' says /kw/

| quill   quit   quiz | at the <u>beginning</u> of words

| equal   liquid   squash | in the <u>middle</u> of words

- demonstrates separating the sounds and then blending them as:

  /k/ /w/ /ĭ/ /t/ or /l/ /ĭ/ /k/ /w/ /ĭ/ /d/

- generates further examples in discussion with the learners

| cheque   mosque   unique | at the <u>end</u> of words derived from French it uses 'que'

HANDY HINT

'q' and 'u' always go together

Mnemonic: Like conjoined twins, they stick together.

- recites and/or mimes the following

  > A quiet young duck from Quebec
  > Cannot quack, for his nerves are a wreck;
  > He just quivers and quakes,
  > Then he shivers and shakes,
  > But's quite safe on the *Queen Mary*'s deck.

Dictation

The teacher/learning partner:

- says the sentence

The learner:

- repeats the sentence aloud
- writes the sentence while saying it under their breath
- reads what he has written
- uses the proofreading C-O-P-S

1. Tim had a quick mug of squash.
2. Ann won the quiz.
3. Be quick! The quiz is on.
4. Tom has a quill pen.
5. He is in the rugby squad.

Aim: To learn to read and spell words with 'r' saying /r/

The teacher/learning partner:

- explains the aim
- demonstrates the target sound:

'r' says /r/

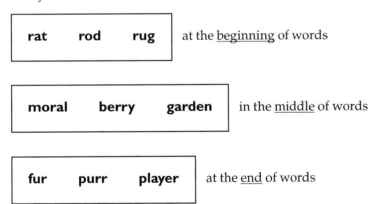

| rat   rod   rug | at the beginning of words

| moral   berry   garden | in the middle of words

| fur   purr   player | at the end of words

- demonstrates separating the sounds and then blending them as:

  /r/ /ă/ /t/ or /f/ /ŭ/ /r/

- generates further examples in discussion with the learners

- recites and/or mimes the following

> A robber from Richmond called Rich
> Robbed the house of a rather rich witch.
> He ran off with her rings
> And some other fine things;
> So she cursed him to live in a ditch.

Dictation

The teacher/learning partner:

- says the sentence

The learner:

- repeats the sentence aloud
- writes the sentence while saying it under their breath
- reads what he has written
- uses the proofreading C-O-P-S

1. The cat left a rat on the rug.
2. Tom hit Rod in the ribs.
3. Cats purr, dogs bark.
4. The rug is a rag; it has lots of rips in it.
5. The moral is rats can kill.

Aim: To learn to read and spell words with 's' saying /s/

The teacher/learning partner:

- explains the aim
- demonstrates the target sound:

's' says /s/

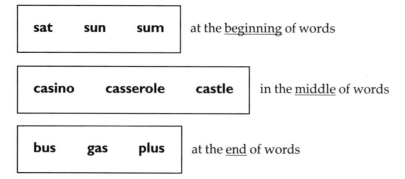

| sat   sun   sum | at the <u>beginning</u> of words

| casino   casserole   castle | in the <u>middle</u> of words

| bus   gas   plus | at the <u>end</u> of words

- demonstrates separating the sounds and then blending them as:

  /s/ /ă/ /t/ or /b/ /ŭ/ /s/

- generates further examples in discussion with the learners

HANDY HINT

'c' says /s/ before 'e', 'i', 'y'

cent   city   cycle   dice   fence   icy

- recites and/or mimes the following

> A salty old sailor called Shane
> Sailed the seas from Sumatra to Spain;
> But the sun, sea and sand
> Seemed the same in each land,
> So he turned round and sailed home again.

Dictation

The teacher/learning partner:

- says the sentence

The learner:

- repeats the sentence aloud
- writes the sentence while saying it under their breath
- reads what he has written
- uses the proofreading C-O-P-S

1. It is not a sin to sit and sob.
2. Sam met the gas man on the bus.
3. Sid lost a big sum.
4. He sat in the sun and got red.
5. The sand is hot in the sun.

Aim: To learn to read and spell words with 't' saying /t/

The teacher/learning partner:

- explains the aim
- demonstrates the target sound:

't' says /t/

tap   tin   tub

at the <u>beginning</u> of words

butler   metal   cotton

in the <u>middle</u> of words

hat	**pit**	**hut**	

at the <u>end</u> of words

- demonstrates separating the sounds and then blending them as:

/t/ /ă/ /p/ or /h/ /ă/ /t/

- generates further examples in discussion with the learners
- recites and/or mimes the following

A tiresome teacher from Tring
Tried to teach twenty tigers to sing.
Only two got the trick,
While the eighteen were sick
After eating that teacher from Tring.

Dictation

The teacher/learning partner:

- says the sentence

The learner:

- repeats the sentence aloud
- writes the sentence while saying it under their breath
- reads what he has written
- uses the proofreading C-O-P-S

1. Tom left the tap on in the hut.
2. Tina cannot fit nuts in the tin.
3. Sam sat in a hot tub.
4. Pat had a hat on in the sun.
5. Pam got a tub of nuts.

Aim: To learn to read and spell words with 'v' saying /v/

The teacher/learning partner:

- explains the aim
- demonstrates the target sound:

'v' says /v/

van	**velvet**	**vet**	

at the <u>beginning</u> of words

cover	oven	vivid

in the <u>middle</u> of words

five	glove	love

at the <u>end</u> of words with a long vowel and Magic 'e'

- demonstrates separating the sounds and then blending them as:

  /v/ /ă/ /n/ or /v/ /ī/ /v/ /i/ /d/

- generates further examples in discussion with the learners

HANDY HINT

No English words end in 'v'. We always add an 'e' on the end.

- recites and/or mimes the following

  A vivacious young vampire from Tyne
  Thought her white velvet gloves were divine.
  Vegetarians vexed her
  And victims would text her:
  "We never wear gloves when we dine."

Dictation

The teacher/learning partner:

- says the sentence

The learner:

- repeats the sentence aloud
- writes the sentence while saying it under their breath
- reads what he has written
- uses the proofreading C-O-P-S

1. The vet had five dogs in his van.
2. I love my velvet dress.
3. Cover the pan and pop it in the oven.
4. He left his glove on the bus.
5. This is a vivid red velvet.

Aim: To learn to read and spell words with 'w' saying /w/

The teacher/learning partner:

- explains the aim
- demonstrates the target sound:

'w' says /w/

wax **wig** **wolf**	at the <u>beginning</u> of words

coward **power** **rewind**	in the <u>middle</u> of words

new **now** **slow**	at the <u>end</u> of words

- demonstrates separating the sounds and then blending them as:

  /w/ /ĭ/ /g/ or /w/ /e/ /t/

- generates further examples in discussion with the learners
- recites and/or mimes the following

> When a weary old woman called Win
> Wandered down to a well and jumped in,
> She found with surprise,
> When she opened her eyes,
> That the well water tasted of gin.

Dictation

The teacher/learning partner:

- says the sentence

The learner:

- repeats the sentence aloud
- writes the sentence while saying it under their breath
- reads what he has written
- uses the proofreading C-O-P-S

1. My mum has a red wig.
2. That wolf is wet.
3. Dan went into a wigwam.
4. Is that a cobweb?
5. Can Pam get rid of the wax?

Aim: To learn to read and spell words with 'x' saying /ks/ or /gz/

The teacher/learning partner:

- explains the aim
- demonstrates the target sound:

'x' says /ks/

| x-ray | at the <u>beginning</u> of words |

| extra   luxury   taxi | in the <u>middle</u> of words |

| mix   box   tax | at the <u>end</u> of words |

'x' can also say /gz/

| exact   exam   luxurious | in the <u>middle</u> of words |

- demonstrates separating the sounds and then blending them as:

  /e/ /ks/ /t/ /r/ /ă/ or /t/ /a/ /ks/ /ē/

  and

  /e/ /gz/ /ă/ /k/ /t/ or /e/ /gz/ /ă/ /m/

- generates further examples in discussion with the learners
- recites and/or mimes the following

  A Mexican fox known as Max
  Was exceptionally good on the sax.
  For an extra six pounds
  He would mix in the sounds
  Of an ox in a box with an axe.

Dictation

The teacher/learning partner:

- says the sentence

The learner:

- repeats the sentence aloud
- writes the sentence while saying it under their breath

- reads what he has written
- uses the proofreading C-O-P-S

1. Tim got a fax from Texas.
2. We ran for the exit.
3. This is the exact cash for the bus.
4. This is a horrid exam.
5. To exist we must have oxygen.

Aim: To learn to read and spell words with 'y' saying /y/, /ī/ or /ē/

The teacher/learning partner:

- explains the aim
- demonstrates the target sound:

'y' can be a consonant or a vowel
'y' as a consonant says /y/

yap	yell	yak

at the <u>beginning</u> of words

eye	rye	yo-yo

in the <u>middle</u> of words

- demonstrates separating the sounds and then blending them as:

/y/ /ă/ /p/ or /y/ /a/ /m/

- generates further examples in discussion with the learners

'y' as a vowel can say /ē/

baby	copy	pony

at the <u>end</u> of words

mummy	daddy	happy

'y' as a vowel can say /ī/

type	pyre	tyre

in the <u>middle</u> of words

cry deny try	at the <u>end</u> of words

- demonstrates separating the sounds and then blending them as:

/t/ /ī/ /p/ or /k/ /r/ /ī/

- generates further examples in discussion with the learners

HANDY HINT
No English word ends in 'i' – we use 'y' instead.

Dictation on 'y' saying /ī/ sound

The teacher/learning partner:

- says the sentence

The learner:

- repeats the sentence aloud
- writes the sentence while saying it under their breath
- reads what he has written
- uses the proofreading C-O-P-S

1. Try not to cry yet.
2. The shy pig is in his sty.
3. Why did Amy pry and spy on Tony?
4. The baby wet the mat so Mum had to dry it.
5. I deny I had a fry-up.

Dictation on 'y' saying /ē/ sound

1. His daddy is in the army.
2. That lady had a baby and is so happy.
3. Mummy and Daddy had fun at yoga.
4. That puppy is so lazy it is funny.
5. Try not to copy that silly bully.

- recites and/or mimes the following

When a hungry young yeti said "Mum!
There's a yawning great hole in my tum",
She replied "Here's a yak
You can have for a snack".
So he opened his mouth and said "Yum!"

Aim: To learn to read and spell words with 'z' saying /z/

The teacher/learning partner:

* explains the aim
* demonstrates the target sound:

'z' says /z/

zebra	**zinc**	**zip**

at the <u>beginning</u> of words

dozen	**razor**	**wizard**

in the <u>middle</u> of words

jazz	**maze**	**quiz**

at the <u>end</u> of words

* demonstrates separating the sounds and then blending them as:

/z/ /ĭ/ /p/ or /j/ /ă/ /z/

* generates further examples in discussion with the learners

's' can say /z/

cars	**has**	**dishes**

at the <u>end</u> of words

At the end of a word the suffix 'ize' is sometimes used instead of 'ise' – 'ize' is used in American English spelling

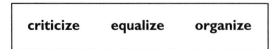

criticize	**equalize**	**organize**

British English mostly uses 'ise'

criticise	**equalise**	**organise**

Dictation

The teacher/learning partner:

- says the sentence

The learner:

- repeats the sentence aloud
- writes the sentence while saying it under their breath
- reads what he has written
- uses the proofreading C-O-P-S

1. The zoo had a big zebra.
2. Zoe is so zany.
3. Zack got zero in the exam.
4. He had to zip up his bag.
5. That is made of zinc.

- recites and/or mimes the following

  A zebra called Zebedee Zed
  Getting ready to snooze in his bed,
  When his stripes were unzipped,
  He was totally stripped
  And wore zigzag pyjamas instead.

CONSONANT DIGRAPHS

Aim: To learn to read and spell words with consonant digraphs

The teacher/learning partner:

- explains the aim
- reviews the keywords:

  - Digraphs are two letters making one sound
  - Consonant digraphs are two consonants making one sound
  - Consonant digraphs occur at the beginning, middle and ends of words

- gives, as an example, 'sh' in

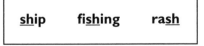

| ship | fi<u>sh</u>ing | ra<u>sh</u> |

- generates further examples of consonant digraphs from the learners

  The most common consonant digraphs are:

  'ch' 'sh' 'th' 'wh' 'ph' 'gh'

Aim: To learn to read and spell words with 'ch' saying /ch/

The teacher/learning partner:

* explains the aim
* demonstrates the target sound:

'ch' says /ch/

chip   **chop**   **chum**

at the <u>beginning</u> of words

tea<u>ch</u>er   **crou<u>ch</u>ing**   **lun<u>ch</u>es**

in the <u>middle</u> of words

in<u>ch</u>   **mu<u>ch</u>**   **ri<u>ch</u>**

at the <u>end</u> of words

* demonstrates separating the sounds and then blending them as:

  /ch/ /ĭ/ /p/ and /r/ /ĭ/ /ch/

* generates further examples in discussion with the learners

If there is a long vowel or a consonant before the /ch/ sound, it is always spelt 'ch'

   bench   church   munch

If there is a short vowel before the /ch/ sound, it can be spelt 'tch'

   catch   fetch   notch   clutch

Crossword Puzzle No. 1

'ch' saying /ch/

How good a detective are you?

- read the clues (below)
- fill in the crossword

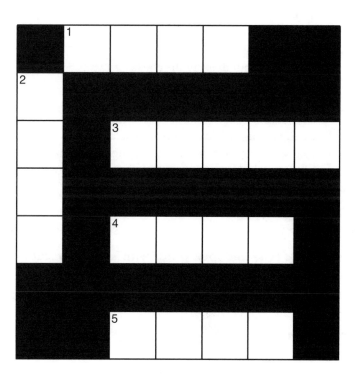

1. He went to the fish and . . . . shop.
2. How . . . . is the doggie in the window?
3. Soldiers . . . . . on parade.
4. Lottery winners are . . . . people.
5. An . . . . is 2.4 cm long.

Dictation for 'ch' spellings

The teacher/learning partner:

- says the sentence

The learner:

- repeats the sentence aloud
- writes the sentence while saying it under their breath
- reads what he has written
- uses the proofreading C-O-P-S

1. Ben cut his chin on the bench.
2. That chap had a long chat to his chum.
3. Can he pinch an inch of it?
4. Jim had egg and chips for lunch.
5. Chop the logs and put them in the chest.

Dictation for 'ch' and 'tch' spellings

1. That chap must not pinch and punch my chum.
2. I had a chat with Pat when we went to watch the match.
3. They had to switch the match to the pitch by the church.
4. Do not snatch my chunk of cheese.
5. Pam can stitch a patch on this dress before church.

Aim: To learn to read and spell words with 'sh' saying /sh/

'sh' says /sh/

| shed ship shop | at the <u>beginning</u> of words |

| crashed fishing wishes | in the <u>middle</u> of words |

| cash dish rash | at the <u>end</u> of words |

Crossword Puzzle No. 2

'sh' saying /sh/

How good a detective are you?

- read the clues (below)
- fill in the crossword

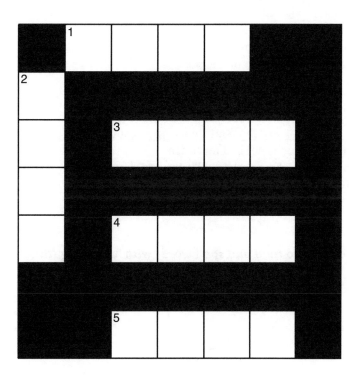

1. Len had a bad .... on his arms.
2. I like to eat .... and chips.
3. I must .... for the last bus.
4. He was in such a .... to get home.
5. He lost all his .... in the robbery.

Dictation for 'sh' spellings

The teacher/learning partner:

- says the sentence

The learner:

- repeats the sentence aloud
- writes the sentence while saying it under their breath
- reads what he has written
- uses the proofreading C-O-P-S

1. I wish to get rid of the rats in the shed.
2. Mash up this dish of fish for the cat.
3. He shut the dog in the shed.
4. I must dash to get the cash.
5. Mel is rushing to get on the bus.

Dictation for the confusable 'sh' and 'ch' spellings

1. I had a cut on my chin and a gash on my shin.
2. The chip shop is not bad for lunch.
3. That chap had the cash for his chum to shop.
4. My chum Sam shot the rat.
5. I must dash to get fish and chips.

Aim: To learn to read and spell words with 'th' saying /th/

The teacher/learning partner:

- explains the aim
- demonstrates the target sound:

'th' says /th/

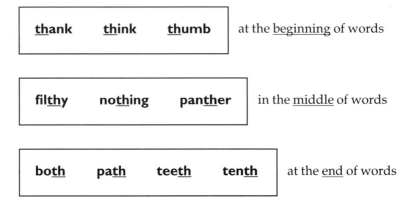

| **thank** **think** **thumb** | at the <u>beginning</u> of words |

| **fil<u>th</u>y** **no<u>th</u>ing** **pan<u>th</u>er** | in the <u>middle</u> of words |

| **bo<u>th</u>** **pa<u>th</u>** **tee<u>th</u>** **ten<u>th</u>** | at the <u>end</u> of words |

Aim: To learn to read and spell words with 'th' saying hard /th/

The teacher/learning partner:

- explains the aim
- demonstrates the target sound:

'th' says /*th*/:

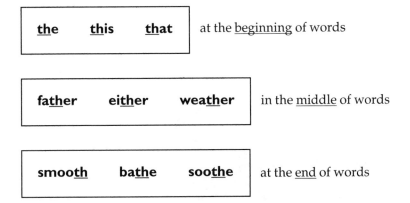

the   this   that   at the <u>beginning</u> of words

father   either   wea**ther**   in the <u>middle</u> of words

smoo**th**   ba**the**   soo**the**   at the <u>end</u> of words

The teacher/learning partner generates further examples of /th/ and /*th*/ in discussion with the learners

Crossword Puzzle No. 3

'th' saying /th/

How good a detective are you?

- read the clues (below)
- fill in the crossword

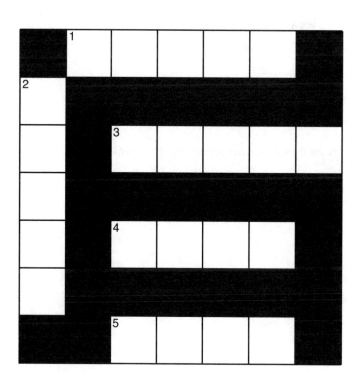

1. Do not suck your . . . . . .
2. You need to . . . . . to work out the answer.
3. People like to get a . . . . . you letter.
4. She led him up the garden . . . . .
5. I hate finding spiders in the . . . . .

Dictation for 'th' spellings

The teacher/learning partner:

- says the sentence

The learner:

- repeats the sentence aloud
- writes the sentence while saying it under their breath
- reads what he has written
- uses the proofreading C-O-P-S

1. The thin man had fish but no chips.
2. Jean had a hot bath and a long think.
3. That moth is a pest: it made holes in the cloth.
4. My father thinks it must be either this or that.
5. Ali must thank both his chums.

Dictation for the confusable /f/, /v/ and /th/ spellings

1. Jim the fat vet had a thin dog.
2. The moth fell into a vat of hot suds.
3. That fish has a big fin.
4. This man has a van of wet fish.
5. I need a fan as I got so hot in the bath.

Aim: To learn to read and spell words with 'wh' saying /wh/, and 'ph' and 'gh' saying /f/

'wh' says /wh/

| **whale**   **wheel**   **whip** | at the <u>beginning</u> of words |

'ph' can say /f/

| **phone**   **phobia**   **phrase** | at the <u>beginning</u> of words |

| **alphabet**   **prophet**   **dolphin** | in the <u>middle</u> of words |

| **autograph**   **paragraph**   **photograph** | at the <u>end</u> of words |

'gh' can also say /f/

| **coughing**   **laughter**   **roughness** | in the <u>middle</u> of words |

| **cough**   **laugh**   **enough** | at the <u>end</u> of words |

Crossword Puzzle No. 4

'wh', 'ph', 'gh' saying /wh/ and /f/

How good a detective are you?

- read the clues (below)
- fill in the crossword

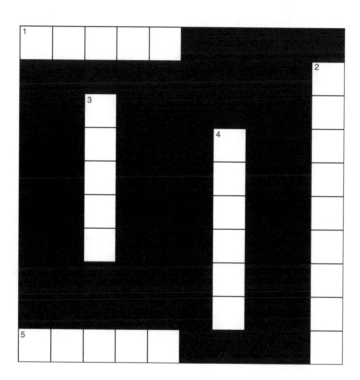

1. The cook . . . . . the cream for the pudding.
2. . . . . have long trunks.
3. Did you hear the . . . . . ring?
4. The . . . . . . on the bus go round and round.
5. That joke always makes me . . . . . .

Dictation for 'gh', 'wh', 'ph' spellings

The teacher/learning partner:

- says the sentence

The learner:

- repeats the sentence aloud
- writes the sentence while saying it under their breath
- reads what he has written
- uses the proofreading C-O-P-S

1. Philip ran to pick up the phone.
2. I used graph paper in class.
3. Tom whacks the top with a whip.
4. When did you learn to say the alphabet?
5. Moby Dick was a big whale.

Aim: To learn to read and spell words with 'g' or 'dg' saying /j/

The teacher/learning partner:

- explains the aim
- demonstrates the target sound:

Soft 'g' says /j/ when the <u>next</u> letter is 'e', 'i' or 'y'

gem **gin** **gym**	at the <u>beginning</u> of words

angel **magic** **imagine**	in the <u>middle</u> of words

Soft 'g' or 'dg' says /j/ when the <u>next</u> letter is 'e'

stage **badger** **gadget**	in the <u>middle</u> of words

cage **hinge** **judge**	at the <u>end</u> of words

Soft 'g' or 'dg' says /j/ before 'i' or 'y'

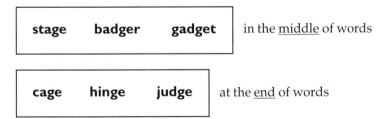

cartridge **edging** **sledging**	in the <u>middle</u> of words

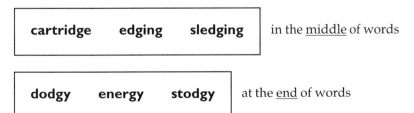

dodgy **energy** **stodgy**	at the <u>end</u> of words

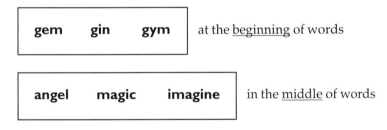

Dictation

The teacher/learning partner:

- says the sentence

The learner:

- repeats the sentence aloud
- writes the sentence while saying it under their breath
- reads what he has written
- uses the proofreading C-O-P-S

1. Jim had lots of gin at the pub.
2. We go to the gym to get fit.
3. Bob robs a big bag of gems.
4. The gents is by the gym.
5. Tim is no angel.

Dictation including 'j' and 'ge' spellings saying /j/

The teacher/learning partner:

- says the sentence

The learner:

- repeats the sentence aloud
- writes the sentence while saying it under their breath
- reads what he has written
- uses the proofreading C-O-P-S

1. Jeff got into a rage when his barge hit a log.
2. He had red jam on the bun.
3. Jane had to have a flu jab.
4. We can jog gently even if it is wet.
5. Jim is a big jazz fan.

Dictation including 'dge' spellings saying /j/

The teacher/learning partner:

- says the sentence

The learner:

- repeats the sentence aloud
- writes the sentence while saying it under their breath
- reads what he has written
- uses the proofreading C-O-P-S

1.   The barge hit the bridge.
2.   The badger slept under a hedge.
3.   The judge told Bob to get a job.
4.   Jack kept the fudge in the fridge.
5.   The lodger had to trudge up to the attic to bed.

CONSONANT BLENDS

Aim: *To learn to read and spell words with consonant blends*

The teacher/learning partner:

*   explains the aim
*   reviews the keywords:

The consonant blends are letters found next to each other. They sound separately but quickly, and so they blend.

*   demonstrates how blends (for example, 'st' – /s/ /t/ say /st/) are found

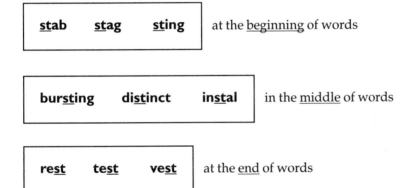

stab stag sting	at the <u>beginning</u> of words
bursting distinct instal	in the <u>middle</u> of words
rest test vest	at the <u>end</u> of words

*   generates further examples of consonant blends with the learner(s)

Consonant blends at the beginning of words

bl, br, cl, cr, dr, dw, fl, fr, gl, gr, pl, pr, sc, scr, sk, sl, sm, sn, sp, spl, spr, squ, str, sw, tr, tw, thr, shr

Consonant blends at the end of words

ld, lf, ng, lk, sk, lp, mp, sp, ct, ft, lt, pt, st, xt, lth

Dictation

The teacher/learning partner:

*   says the sentence

The learner:

- repeats the sentence aloud
- writes the sentence while saying it under their breath
- reads what he has written
- uses the proof-reading C-O-P-S

1. It is sad she has a red ink blot on her best dress.
2. Do not spit on the mat or the cat.
3. That slug is slim and slimy; this chap is fat and flabby.
4. We had a glut of red plums.
5. Tom had a British flag on top of his flat.
6. He had a splint on his leg and a sling on his arm.
7. Plop it went, with a big splash.
8. Pam felt glum when a fox got her pet cat.
9. We plan to meet at the club disco.
10. Tom split the logs and cut them up for Gran.

Dictation

The teacher/learning partner:

- says the sentence

The learner:

- repeats the sentence aloud
- writes the sentence while saying it under their breath
- reads what he has written
- uses the proof-reading C-O-P-S

1. I must get a trap to catch the rats.
2. My gran has a big old pram in the shed.
3. He bent the prong of the fork.
4. She bent the brim of her hat.
5. Dan has a big set of drums.
6. We went on a trip in an old trap.
7. I can grip the trunk and drag it.
8. The frog can grab the crab.
9. I do not trust Pam not to prod the dog.
10. He hid the drugs in a bin.

Dictation

The teacher/learning partner:

- says the sentence

The learner:

- repeats the sentence aloud
- writes the sentence while saying it under their breath
- reads what he has written
- uses the proof-reading C-O-P-S

1. His cash began to dwindle as he spent it.
2. The twin dwells in that hut.
3. Tim will snap the twigs and cut the logs.
4. The swell made the boat swing.
5. A dwarf is a small man.
6. That chap is such a twit he forgot the map.
7. When Ann got on the swing, Jan gave her a big push.
8. Dilly had a bad rash on her skin.
9. The black swan swam on the pond.
10. Did gran slip when she went for a swim?

Aim: To learn to read and spell words, using onset and rime, with the initial blends 'sc', 'sk', 'squ'

The teacher/learning partner:

- explains the aim
- reviews the keywords:

Onset is the initial consonant(s) in a word

f/an   **gr**/ip   **str**/ap

Rime is the vowel and final consonant(s) in a word

d/**ump**   cr/**isp**   th/**ick**

ACTIVITY

Blending to read, segmenting to spell

You:

- look at the initial letters
- say the onset sound
- look at the end of the word and say the rime sound
- read the whole word
- copy out the word in the box
- use the word in a sentence

sc ____
ab
an
um

shr ____
ed
ub
ink

sk ____
ill
in
ip

squ ____
ash
id
irt

str ____
ap
ip
ing

Dictation

The teacher/learning partner:

- says the sentence

The learner:

- repeats the sentence aloud
- writes the sentence while saying it under their breath
- reads what he has written
- uses the proof-reading C-O-P-S

1. She had a scab on her right hand.
2. I must not slip when I skip.
3. Be careful or you will squash it.
4. There was scum on the water.
5. Fry the squid and then try it.
6. Pam went for a check-up and a scan.
7. He is good at his job; he has skill.
8. Do not squirt me with that squash.
9. There is a scab on my skin.
10. Why did you squirt ink at me?

Dictation

The teacher/learning partner:

- says the sentence

The learner

- repeats the sentence aloud
- writes the sentence while saying it under their breath
- reads what he has written
- uses the proof-reading C-O-P-S

1. Jim is smart, but such a lazy chap.
2. Meg cannot stand it when I sniff.
3. I felt sick with the smell of bad fish.
4. This shop is spick and span.
5. The smart cat can sniff the rat.
6. She had a long, black smock.
7. The spark fell on the rug.
8. Raj dug up lots of shrubs.
9. Do not squirt ink at Pam.
10. Sam had to shred it and put it in the bin.

Dictation

The teacher/learning partner:

- says the sentence

The learner:

- repeats the sentence aloud
- writes the sentence while saying it under their breath
- reads what he has written
- uses the proof-reading C-O-P-S

1. Scram, you bad dog!
2. He left the script on top of the bus.
3. He had a big strap on his trunk.
4. Pam got such a thrill when she won the sprint.
5. My vest will shrink in a hot wash.
6. Scrub the shelf and wash it with hot suds.
7. The dog did not have a scrap of fat in his dish.
8. That thrush sang a shrill song.
9. Dad has lots of shrubs in big tubs.
10. He had a lot of stress in his job at the club.

Dictation

The teacher/learning partner:

- says the sentence

The learner:

- repeats the sentence aloud
- writes the sentence while saying it under their breath
- reads what he has written
- uses the proof-reading C-O-P-S

1. Tim had a bad gash on his scalp.
2. Fill up this shelf with lots of pots of jam.
3. When the dog cut his leg, Megan ran to get help.
4. He has a smart felt hat and an old black jacket.
5. I have not yet met an elf.
6. He got lots of fresh milk at the shop.
7. A silk vest is warm in winter.
8. He must not cry and sulk.
9. This will melt in the sun.
10. Can we get a plot of land for golf?

Dictation

The teacher/learning partner:

- says the sentence

The learner:

- repeats the sentence aloud
- writes the sentence while saying it under their breath
- reads what he has written
- uses the proof-reading C-O-P-S

1. It is a fact that Tim lost his car in the car park.
2. I felt nothing as I slept.
3. He made a pact not to tell on his chum.
4. The text did not cost a lot.
5. His next gift was a plant.
6. He got a lift from the pub with Jim.
7. Pat kept mum and did not tell.
8. It is too cold for it to melt.
9. We crept into the tent.
10. He left his best gift in the shop.

Dictation

The teacher/learning partner:

- says the sentence

The learner:

- repeats the sentence aloud
- writes the sentence while saying it under their breath
- reads what he was written
- uses the proof-reading C-O-P-S

1. The sun sets in the west at dusk.
2. The cat crept up to the nest in the bush.
3. He did ask, but he did not grasp it.
4. Test me on my sums.
5. The dust in the desk made her gasp.
6. Is that an ant in your vest?
7. The robber wore a mask.
8. Ask the way if you are lost.
9. Grasp my hand and I will lift you up.
10. The last crisp was the best

Dictation

The teacher/learning partner:

- says the sentence

The learner:

- repeats the sentence aloud
- writes the sentence while saying it under their breath
- reads what he has written
- uses the proof-reading C-O-P-S

1. Ben will punch that man if he robs his cash.
2. We had a long lunch with mum and dad in a pub.
3. The bandstand was old and rusty.
4. I got a bunch of mint in the garden.
5. Can Sam mend this sink?
6. He had a tent on the sand.
7. I will camp on this land.
8. He lent me the cash for my rent.
9. The lamp is on the top shelf.
10. Can he lend me a stamp for this?

LONG VOWELS AND MAGIC 'e'

Aim: To learn to read and spell words with long vowels and Magic 'e'

> Note: To prevent confusion, avoid using homophones at first, until the spelling pattern is well established

The teacher/learning partner:

- explains the aim
- reviews the key terms:

> Magic 'e' makes the vowel say its name, but it keeps quiet.
> Magic 'e' is usually found at the end of words.

- demonstrates the target words with and without Magic 'e':

'a'	hăt	hāt**e**
'e'	pĕt	Pēt**e**
'i'	pĭp	pīp**e**
'o'	cŏd	cōd**e**
'u'	tŭb	tūb**e**

- discusses the Handy Hint

HANDY HINT: MNEMONIC

Magic Mrs 'e' comes knocking at the back door of the Long Vowel Men's house and says, "Who's there?"

The Vowel Men are polite and say their names

/Ā/ Abel   /Ē/ Enoch   /Ī/ Ivan   /Ō/ Owen   /Ū/ Uri

but Magic Mrs 'e' keeps quiet and doesn't say a thing.

- generates further examples of Magic 'e' with the learner(s)

Aim: To learn to read and spell words with long /ā/ sound and Magic 'e'

The teacher/learning partner:

- explains the aim
- reviews the keywords:

> Magic 'e' makes the vowel say its name, but it keeps quiet.
> Magic 'e' is usually found at the end of words.

- demonstrates the target words with and without Magic 'e':

hăt   hāte

ACTIVITY

Choose long or short 'a'

How good a detective are you?

- read the sentence
- fill in the missing letters
- copy out the sentence
- use the proof-reading C-O-P-S

1. My n_m_ is the s_m_ as his.

2. I h_t_ that noisy t_p_.

3. The old man did a t_p dance with his c_n_.

4. I am gl_d there is sh_d_ under the tree.

5. That m__t is the s__m_ as Pam's.

6. I hat_ it when mum is l_t_.

7. K_t_ was l_t_ for her d_t_.

8. My m_t_ has a m_t by the door.

9. He got in such a st_t_ by the school g_t_.

10. Scr_p_ that scr_p of mud off his leg.

_____

_____

_____

_____

_____

_____

_____

_____

_____

_____

Dictation

The teacher/learning partner:

- says the sentence

The learner:

- repeats the sentence aloud
- writes the sentence while saying it under their breath
- reads what he has written
- uses the proof-reading C-O-P-S

1. I hate to swim in that lake: it has water snakes.
2. All he did in the exam was to stare at the page.
3. Ali had to scrape the pan to get rid of the fat.
4. I hate stale buns and cake.
5. The whale made a big splash on the lake.

Aim: To learn to read and spell words with long /ē/ sound and Magic 'e'

The teacher/learning partner:

- explains the aim
- reviews the keywords:
- demonstrates the target words with and without Magic 'e':

pĕt   Pēte

ACTIVITY

Choose long or short 'e'

How good a detective are you?

- read the sentence
- fill in the missing letters
- copy out the sentence
- use the proof-reading C-O-P-S

1. On Christmas _v_ children hang up their stockings.

2. P_t keeps his p_t snake in a box under his b_d.

3. The farmer fed each sheep one sw_d_ each day in winter.

4. That athl_t_ is a good runner.

5. What was the th_m_ of your project?

6. Adam and _v_ ate the forbidden apple.

7. The farmer chopped up the sw_d_ for his cattle.

8. Rita had to _k_ out a living selling newspapers.

9. I had to compl_t_ my homework before I went to bed.

10. Jeans for G_n_s is the name of a children's charity.

_____

_____

_____

_____

_____

_____

_____

_____

_____

_____

Dictation

The teacher/learning partner:

• says the sentence

The learner:

• repeats the sentence aloud
• writes the sentence while saying it under their breath
• reads what he has written
• uses the proof-reading C-O-P-S

1. Mum will mete out the fish and chips for lunch.
2. The scheme will work well next term.
3. The farmer had turnips and swedes in his van for the pigs.
4. The athlete was a good sport.
5. Eve and Pete compete in running races.

Aim: To learn to read and spell words with long /ī/ sound and Magic 'e'

The teacher/learning partner:

• explains the aim
• reviews the keywords:

   Magic 'e' makes the vowel say its name, but it keeps quiet.
   Magic 'e' is usually found at the end of words.

• demonstrates the target words with and without Magic 'e':

   pĭp   pīpe

ACTIVITY

Choose long or short 'i'

How good a detective are you?

- read the sentence
- fill in the missing letters
- copy out the sentence
- use the proof-reading C-O-P-S

1. It is t_m_ to find my b_k_ and to r_d_ home.

2. The pr_z_ is a bottle of f_n_ w_n_.

3. F_v_ bees flew out of the h_v_.

4. The fish's f_n has f_n_ colours.

5. Steve won a pr_z_ at the k_t inspection.

6. S_d sat on the left s_d_.

7. Let's get r_d of the dog and we can r_d_ our b_k_s.

8. I got a b_t of a fright when I got a mosquito b_t_.

9. What a d_n that child made when we went to d_n_ with the boss.

10. He h_d the k_t_ in his k_t bag.

_____

_____

_____

_____

_____

_____

_____

_____

_____

_____

Dictation

The teacher/learning partner:

- says the sentence

The learner:

- repeats the sentence aloud
- writes the sentence while saying it under their breath
- reads what he has written
- uses the proof-reading C-O-P-S

1. Jack and Jill like to wine and dine well.
2. I hate grime and slime in the sink or in the bath.
3. The tile fell on the car a mile from the shops and made a big dent in it.
4. Pat did not go down the slide, but he fell off it.
5. Grandad put his pipe on the side and lost it.

Aim: To learn to read and spell words with long /ō/ sound and Magic 'e'

The teacher/learning partner:

- explains the aim
- reviews the keywords:

    Magic 'e' makes the vowel say its name, but it keeps quiet.
    Magic 'e' is usually found at the end of words.

- demonstrates the target words with and without Magic 'e':

    hŏp   hōpe

ACTIVITY

Choose long or short 'o'

How good a detective are you?

- read the sentence
- fill in the missing letters
- copy out the sentence
- use the proof-reading C-O-P-S

1. I h_p_ he can h_p on one leg in the hop, skip and jump race.

2. Tim sent Ben a n_t_ about the trip but he did n_t get it in t_m_.

3. Can you hear the dialling t_n_ on the mobile ph_n_?

4. The sm_k_ went up my n_s_ and made me ch_k_.

5. Have you seen the film H_m_ Al_n_?

6. This n_t_ is n_t written in c_d_.

7. The m_l_ made a huge h_l_ on our lawn.

8. I h_p_ to h_p on a bus and get h_m_ soon.

9. Don't m_p_! Get a m_p, and clean this up quick!

10. There is a large st_n_ under the Queen's thr_n_.

_____

_____

_____

_____

_____

_____

_____

_____

_____

_____

_____

Dictation

The teacher/learning partner:

- says the sentence

The learner:

- repeats the sentence aloud
- writes the sentence while saying it under their breath
- reads what he has written
- uses the proof-reading C-O-P-S

1. Do not mope over spilt milk: get a mop and wipe it up before Jane comes home.
2. He has a black cock and a red hen in the chicken run.
3. Can you cope in the hop, skip and jump race?
4. That bloke fell and cut his nose on his way home.
5. Rose went to smoke behind the garden shed.

Aim: To learn to read and spell words with long /ū/ sound and Magic 'e'

The teacher/learning partner:

- explains the aim
- reviews the keywords:

  Magic 'e' makes the vowel say its name, but it keeps quiet.
  Magic 'e' is usually found at the end of words.

- demonstrates the target words with and without Magic 'e':

  cŭb   cūbe

ACTIVITY

Choose long or short 'u'

How good a detective are you?

- read the sentence
- fill in the missing letters
- copy out the sentence
- use the proof-reading C-O-P-S

1. The Grand Old D_k_ of York, he had ten thousand men.

2. Amos played a t_n_ on his fl_t_.

3. In France the T_b_ is called the Metro.

4. He is a very r_d_ and cr_d_ man with no manners.

5. He left the t_b_ of toothpaste by the bath t_b.

6. J_n_ is often r_d_ to Milo.

7. He can play six t_n_s on the fl_t_.

8. That joke was not funny, it was cr_d_.

9. They say J_n_ is the month of roses.

10. The ship had a cargo of cr_d_ oil.

_____

_____

_____

_____

_____

_____

_____

_____

_____

_____

Dictation

The teacher/learning partner:

- says the sentence

The learner:

- repeats the sentence aloud
- writes the sentence while saying it under their breath
- reads what he has written
- uses the proof-reading C-O-P-S

1. He made lots of ice cubes and put them in a bag.
2. The black smoke made horrid fumes in my flat.
3. That flute is not in tune.
4. I refuse to eat hard plums. I like mine ripe.
5. It is a rule, so we must obey.

VOWELS WITH THE CONSONANT 'R'

The teaching/learning partner:

- explains the aim – to learn to read and spell words with 'ar', 'er', 'ir', 'or', 'ur'
- reviews the keywords
- demonstrates the target sound:

    car   verb   bird   cork   burn

- generates further examples in discussion with the learner(s)

Aim: To learn to read and spell words with the vowel 'a' and the consonant 'r' – the digraph 'ar'

The teaching/learning partner:

- explains the aim – to learn to read and spell words with 'ar'
- reviews the keywords:

    - The vowels are a e i o u.
    - Consonants are all the other letters in the alphabet.
    - Digraphs are pairs of letters that together make one sound.

- demonstrates the target sound:

    /ar/ is spelt 'ar' at the beginning, middle and end of words

    art   park   car

- generates further words with 'ar' in discussion with the learner(s)

ACTIVITY

'ar' saying /ar/

Mix and Match

- look at the sentence
- read the words in brackets aloud
- choose the words that make the best sense
- copy out the sentence with the words you chose

1. Can we (mar, star, park) the (jar, car, far) here?

2. Tina ate (part, farm, ark) of the jam (dart, tar, tart).

3. How (star, far, dart) is it to the (farm, jar, arm) shop?

4. Tom fell in the (tar, dark, ark) and broke his (arm, charm, bar).

5. Dad will (mark, harm, dart) into the (car, bar, harm) for a quick drink.

1. _____

2. _____

3. _____

4. _____

5. _____

Dictation

The teacher/learning partner:

- says the sentence

The learner:

- repeats the sentence aloud
- writes the sentence while saying it under their breath
- reads what he has written
- uses the proof-reading C-O-P-S

1. Jim has a bad scar on his left arm.
2. I must start to mark my star chart.
3. It will do no harm if we park on the grass.
4. Mum must start to make the plum tart for lunch.
5. Tom gets mad when the dog barks in the dark barn.

Aim: To learn to read and spell words with the vowel 'e' and the consonant 'r' – the digraph 'er' – saying /ur/

The teaching/learning partner:

- explains the aim
- reviews the keywords:

    - The vowels are a e i o u.
    - Consonants are all the other letters in the alphabet.
    - Digraphs are pairs of letters that together make one sound.

- demonstrates the target sound:

    /ur/ can be spelt 'er' at the beginning, middle and end of words

    verb   refer

- generates further words with 'er' in discussion with the learner(s)

ACTIVITY

'er' saying /ur/

Mix and Match

- look at the sentence
- read the words in brackets aloud
- choose the words that make the best sense
- copy out the sentence with the words you chose

1. The (term, herd, reverse) of cows was eating the patch of (germs, hers, herbs).

2. Last (fern, kerb, term), my (deter, gerbil, verb) was ill with a (merchant, stern, germ).

3. The (stern, mermaid, herd) swam to the rock to get (alert, her, herb) comb.

4. There were a lot of (herbs, germs, verbs) at school last (reverse, infer, term).

5. She had some dried (verbs, herbs, germs) in the larder.

1. _____

2. _____

3. _____

4. _____

5. _____

Dictation

The teacher/learning partner:

- says the sentence

The learner:

- repeats the sentence aloud
- writes the sentence while saying it under their breath
- reads what he has written
- uses the proof-reading C-O-P-S

1. Is that a mermaid on the rock?
2. Dad put the car in reverse.
3. Tom had lots of bad germs.
4. Ted is such a stern man.
5. This has been a long term.

Aim: To learn to read and spell words with the vowel 'i' and the consonant 'r' – the digraph 'ir' – saying /ur/

The teaching/learning partner:

- explains the aim
- reviews the keywords:

    - The vowels are a e i o u.
    - Consonants are all the other letters in the alphabet
    - Digraphs are pairs of letters that together make one sound.

- demonstrates the target sound:

    /ur/ can be spelt 'ir' at the beginning, middle and end of words

    irk   shirt   fir

- generates further words with 'ir' in discussion with the learner(s)

ACTIVITY

'ir' saying /ur/

Mix and Match

- look at the sentence
- read the words in brackets aloud
- choose the word that makes the best sense
- copy out the sentence with the words you chose

1. In Scotland, a church is called a (circle, skirt, kirk).

2. Some (shirts, firms, girls) like a short (bird, skirt, dirt); some prefer a long one.

3. At Billy Smart's (whirl, first, circus), the horses gallop in a (kirk, firm, circle).

4. A baker's dozen is not twelve, but (first, thirteen, shirt).

5. The boy fell in the (birch, bird, dirt) and got mud on his (flirt, first, shirt).

1. _____

2. _____

3. _____

4. _____

5. _____

Dictation

The teacher/learning partner:

- says the sentence

The learner:

- repeats the sentence aloud
- writes the sentence while saying it under their breath
- reads what he has written
- uses the proof-reading C-O-P-S

1. The birth of a baby girl gave them such a thrill.
2. Tom is such a flirt.
3. Pam gave me a firm handshake.
4. Turn round and make that skirt whirl.
5. Is there a bird in that nest?

Aim: To learn to read and spell words with the vowel 'o' and the consonant 'r' – the digraph 'or' saying /or/

The teaching/learning partner:

- explains the aim
- reviews the keywords:

  - The vowels are a e i o u.
  - Consonants are all the other letters in the alphabet.
  - Digraphs are pairs of letters that together make one sound

- demonstrates the target sound:

  /or/ can be spelt 'or' at the beginning and middle of words

  ornament   born

- generates further words with 'or' in discussion with the learner(s)

ACTIVITY

'or' saying /or/

Mix and Match

- look at the sentence
- read the words in brackets aloud
- choose the words that make the best sense
- copy out the sentence with the words you chose

1. We are (lord, short, born) of (forks, snort, fort).

2. The water in the (ford, born, stork) is very deep because of the (worn, port, storm).

3. The (snort, lord, fort) has a very (worn, corn, morning) jacket.

4. Pass the (horn, born, port) – we are (short, cork, torn) of it at this end of table.

5. The farmer cut the (lord, pork, corn) early in the (morning, shorn, form).

1. _____

2. _____

3. _____

4. _____

5. _____

Dictation

The teacher/learning partner:

- says the sentence

The learner:

- repeats the sentence aloud
- writes the sentence while saying it under their breath
- reads what he has written
- uses the proof-reading C-O-P-S

1. Turn left at the church gate to find the house.
2. We like to surf when we go to Cornwall.
3. That bad burn hurt her a lot.
4. We had to send for help when we had a burst pipe.
5. The church bells rang on the morning of my wedding.

Aim: To learn to read and spell words with the vowel 'u' and consonant 'r' – the digraph 'ur' saying /ur/

The teaching/learning partner:

- explains the aim
- reviews the keywords:

  - The vowels are a e i o u.
  - Consonants are all the other letters in the alphabet.
  - Digraphs are pairs of letters that together make one sound.

- demonstrates the target sound:

  /ur/ is spelt 'ur' at the beginning, middle and end of words

  urge   church   blur

- generates further words with 'ur' in discussion with the learner(s)

ACTIVITY

'ur' saying /ur/

Mix and Match

- look at the sentence
- read the words in brackets aloud
- choose the word that makes the best sense
- copy out the sentence with the word you chose

1. Jane must (turn, curl, surf) her hair before the party.

2. The nurse (curb, burst, hurl) the blister on my hand.

3. Knit one, (blur, purl, burst) one, is an instruction used in knitting patterns.

4. Peat used on fires is called (surf, turf, churn) in Ireland.

5. Butter was made in a (spur, churn, turn) on farms in olden days.

1. _____

2. _____

3. _____

4. _____

5. _____

Dictation

The teacher/learning partner:

- says the sentence

The learner:

- repeats the sentence aloud
- writes the sentence while saying it under their breath
- reads what he has written
- uses the proof-reading C-O-P-S

1. This fork is old and very worn.
2. The army had to storm the fort to get into the port.
3. Uncork the port and let's have some fun at the party.
4. The lord got on his horse this morning.
5. The storm will harm the corn on the farm.

VOWEL DIGRAPHS

The teacher/learning partner:

- explains the aim – to learn to read and spell words with digraphs that make vowel sounds
- reviews the keywords:
- demonstrates the target sounds:

rail   day   read   high   boat   moon

Aim: To learn to read and spell words with the vowel digraph 'ai' saying /ā/

The teacher/learning partner:

- explains the aim
- reviews the keywords:

  - The vowels are a e i o u.
  - Long vowels say their names and are coded with a macron (ā).
  - Digraphs are pairs of letters that together make one sound.
  - Vowel digraphs are two vowels side-by-side making one sound.

- demonstrates the target sound:

  The /ā/ sound can be spelt 'ai' at the beginning and in the middle of words

  aid   brain

- generates further words in discussion with the learner(s)
- discusses the Handy Hint on the next page.

HANDY HINT

There are several common homophones for the long /ā/ sound:

maid/made   main/mane   pain/pane   pail/pale   tail/tale

fair/fare   hair/hare   stairs/stares

For further practice see Chapter 4, How to Manage Homophones Happily.

Dictation

The teacher/learning partner:

- says the sentence

The learner:

- repeats the sentence aloud
- writes the sentence while saying it under their breath
- reads what he has written
- uses the proof-reading C-O-P-S

1. They met in Spain on a train.
2. Tom must not fail the test again.
3. The bottom fell out of the chair when he sat on it.
4. He put a nail in the lid of the box.
5. Hang this jacket up on the rail.
6. Aim for the target if you want to win a prize.
7. Jim paid for the drinks in the pub.
8. Jack and Jill must not raid my tuck box.
9. Tom drains the last drop of wine from the glass.
10. Pam has a very good brain.

Crossword Puzzle No. 5

'ai' saying /ā/

How good a detective are you?

- read the clues (below)
- fill in the crossword

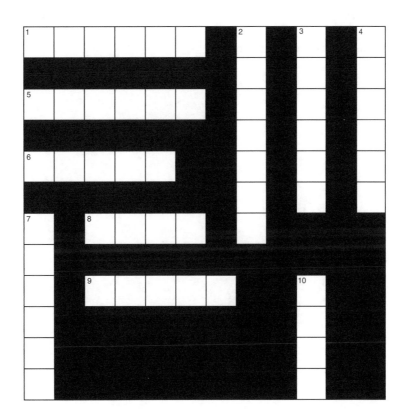

1. Red wine . . . . . . are difficult to remove.
2. Can you . . . . how to work the video?
3. The . . . . . . were blocked by leaves.
4. The . . . . . . were not on time.
5. '. . . . . . in your seats, please!'
6. The dog left a . . . . . of mud on the carpet.
7. The child is . . . . . . of the dark.
8. The hungry baby began to . . . . .
9. The kitchen . . . . . is blocked.
10. The judge sent him to . . . . .

Aim: To learn to read and spell words with the vowel digraph 'ay' saying /ā/ at the end of words

The teacher/learning partner:

- explains the aim
- reviews the keywords:

    - The vowels are a e i o u.
    - Long vowels say their names and are coded with a macron.
    - Digraphs are pairs of letters that together make one sound.
    - Vowel digraphs are two vowels side-by-side making one sound.

- demonstrates the target sound:

    s<u>ay</u>   pl<u>ay</u>   holid<u>ay</u>

Crossword Puzzle No. 6

'ay' saying /ā/

How good a detective are you?

- read the clues (below)
- fill in the crossword

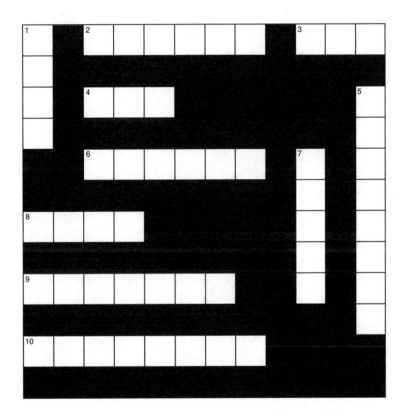

1. Donkeys . . . . loudly.
2. Do not . . . . . . the secret code.
3. A . . . is a very brightly coloured woodland bird.
4. Farmers make . . . when the sun shines.
5. The . . . . was blocked by a delivery lorry.
6. The fog caused . . . . . . at the airport.
7. That boy . . . . . with his train set all day long.
8. Pottery is made from . . . . .
9. Shops . . . . goods in their windows.
10. She had candles on her . . . . cake.

Dictation

The teacher/learning partner:

- says the sentence

The learner:

- repeats the sentence aloud
- writes the sentence while saying it under their breath
- reads what he has written
- uses the proof-reading C-O-P-S

1. The captain told us to please stay seated.
2. She had her breakfast on a tray.
3. I always blow out the candles when I leave the room.
4. Last May we fed that stray cat every day.
5. Do not delay me or I will be late for my train.
6. The model was made of clay.
7. His flat is next to the railway.
8. The fox cubs play in the moonlight.
9. Did he finish the essay on time?
10. Jane had a big party on her birthday.

Aim: To learn to read and spell words with the vowel digraph 'ea' saying /ē/

The teacher/learning partner:

- explains the aim
- reviews the keywords:

    - The vowels are a e i o u.
    - Long vowels say their names and are coded with a macron (ā).
    - Digraphs are pairs of letters that together make one sound.
    - Vowel digraphs are two vowels side-by-side making one sound – train, boat.

- demonstrates the target sound:

    The /ē/ sound is spelt 'ea' at the beginning, middle and end of words

    ear   cream   tea

HANDY HINT

There are several common homophones for the long /ē/ sound:

bean/been   beach/beech   dear/deer   leak/leek   meat/meet   sea/see

(For further practice see Chapter 4, How to Manage Homophones Happily.)

Crossword Puzzle No. 7

'ea' saying /ē/

How good a detective are you?

- read the clues (below)
- fill in the crossword

1. Polite people always say . . . . . . and thank you.
2. Salmon can . . . . out of the water.
3. You must change . . . . to get the car up the hill.
4. Flour is made from . . . . . .
5. Martin Luther King said 'I have a . . . . .'.
6. Please . . . . me how to make a cake.
7. The child sat in the . . . . seat; Mum and Dad sat in the front.
8. 'Remain in your . . . . , please!'
9. Strawberries and . . . . . go well together.
10. We had champagne as a special . . . . . to celebrate.

Dictation

The teacher/learning partner:

- says the sentence

The learner:

- repeats the sentence aloud
- writes the sentence while saying it under their breath
- reads what he has written
- uses the proof-reading C-O-P-S

1. Can you read this to me, please?
2. We had a cream tea every day in Devon.
3. Can you teach Amy how to swim?
4. They must beat that team to stay on top.
5. Clean the seat, please, before I sit on it.
6. I fear I may not speak to Gran for some time.
7. Last year we were near a beach when camping.
8. We had a cheap meal in that pub.
9. Can we have some wine for lunch as a treat?
10. I like the farmer's golden wheat.

Aim: To learn to read and spell words with the vowel 'i' and consonants 'gh' – 'igh' saying /ī/

The teacher/learning partner:

- explains the aim
- reviews the keywords:

    - The vowels are a e i o u.
    - Long vowels say their names and are coded with a macron (ā).

- demonstrates the target sound:

    Long /ī/ sound is spelt 'igh' in the middle and at the end of words

    fight   mighty   sigh

- generates further words in discussion with the learner(s)

Crossword Puzzle No. 8

'igh' saying /ī/

How good a detective are you?

- read the clues (below)
- fill in the crossword

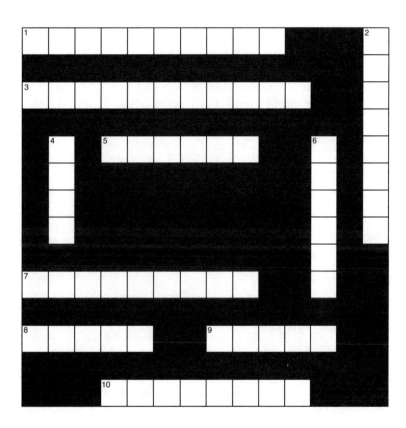

1. In Spain they watch . . . .
2. The Jack Russell terrier was in a . . . .
3. The . . . . were turned on at night for all the football games.
4. He gave a . . . . of relief.
5. . . . . . . is a disease that rots potatoes.
6. The tiger gave me a big . . . .
7. The visit to the Eiffel Tower was the . . . . of their trip.
8. Turn off the . . . . . , please.
9. I must go on a diet, my skirts are too . . . . .
10. London streets were lit by . . . . in Victorian times.

Dictation

The teacher/learning partner:

- says the sentence

The learner:

- repeats the sentence aloud
- writes the sentence while saying it under their breath
- reads what he has written
- uses the proof-reading C-O-P-S

1. The bright sunshine made the flowers bloom.
2. Can you highlight the main points please?
3. That boss is very high and mighty with his staff.
4. Thigh-high skirts are banned at this school.
5. There was a gunfight outside the night club.
6. You gave me a fright when you jumped out.
7. Cats and dogs often fight.
8. I might have a curry tonight for supper.
9. Moonlight and roses can be romantic.
10. I draw the curtains when twilight comes.

Aim: To learn to read and spell words with the vowel digraph 'oa' saying /ō/

The teacher/learning partner:

- explains the aim
- reviews the keywords:

  - The vowels are a e i o u.
  - Long vowels say their names and are coded with a macron (ā).
  - Digraphs are pairs of letters that together make one sound.
  - Vowel digraphs are two vowels side-by-side making one sound – train, boat.

- demonstrates the target sound:

  Long /ō/ sound is spelt 'oa' at the beginning and in the middle of words

  oak   coat   soap

- generates further words in discussion with the learner(s)

HANDY HINT

There are some common homophones for the long /ō/ sound:

road/rode, loan/lone

For further practice see Chapter 4, How to Manage Homophones Happily.

Crossword Puzzle No. 9

'oa' saying /ō/

How good a detective are you?

- read the clues
- fill in the missing words

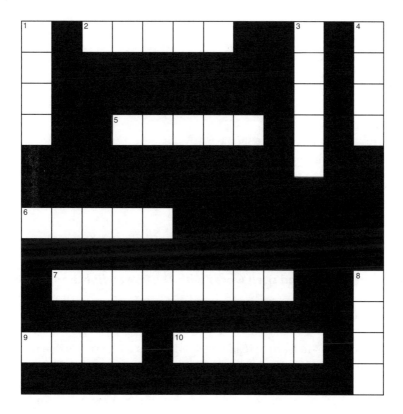

1. '. . . . in the hole' was on the menu.
2. The detective book cover had a picture of a . . . . . and dagger.
3. The . . . . . guards rescued the climbers on the cliff.
4. The bomb scare was a . . . . .
5. I like marmalade on . . . . . .
6. We had . . . . . . beef for Sunday lunch.
7. Her . . . . kept her at work late.
8. He had to swear an . . . . . in court.
9. The castle had fish in the . . . . . around it.
10. The . . . . . . of frogs kept me awake at night.

Dictation

The teacher/learning partner:

- says the sentence

The learner:

- repeats the sentence aloud
- writes the sentence while saying it under their breath
- reads what he has written
- uses the proof-reading C-O-P-S

1. The ship is afloat on the sea.
2. The old toad lives under the garden shed.
3. Load the goat into the back of the truck.
4. He began to croak after eating the fishbone.
5. I love to soak in a long hot bath.
6. Jan has a red coat and hat.
7. He swore on oath that this was the truth.
8. The frogs croak in the pond all day long.
9. Is the coast clear so I can escape?
10. That boat cannot float: it is overloaded.

DIPTHONGS

Aim: To learn to read and spell words with the vowel diphthong 'oo' saying /o͞o/

The teacher/learning partner:

- explains the aim – to learn to read and spell words with vowels that make diphthongs
- reviews the keywords:

  - Vowel digraphs are two vowels side-by-side making one sound – train, boat.
  - Diphthongs are two vowels that glide together when said, but still keep their separate sounds – book, house, cow, boil, boy

- demonstrates the target sound:

  The /ou/ sound is spelt 'oo' at the beginning, middle and end of words

  oops   food   igloo

- generates further words in discussion with the learner(s)

Crossword Puzzle No. 10

'oo' saying /o͞o/

How good a detective are you?

- read the clues
- fill in the missing words

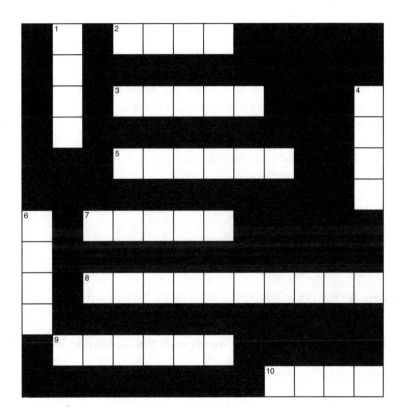

1. We kept the picnic . . . . in a lunch box.
2. Weavers work at a . . . . .
3. He sat at the bar on a . . . . . .
4. I put the shopping in the . . . . . of the car
5. The song of the . . . . . . tells us that spring has begun and it will soon be summer.
6. They say a . . . . and his money are soon parted.
7. The roses began to . . . . . in the warm sunshine.
8. The witch sat on her . . . .
9. The panda eats . . . . . . shoots and leaves.
10. The dining . . . . looked lovely in candlelight.

Dictation

The teacher/learning partner:

- says the sentence

The learner:

- repeats the sentence aloud
- writes the sentence while saying it under their breath
- reads what he has written
- uses the proof-reading C-O-P-S

1. He left his football boots on the coach.
2. Shoot for the goal post!
3. Try not to fall off that tall stool in the bar.
4. I will cool off in that pool with a long swim.
5. The moon was full last night so we could see the badgers.
6. The fox got into the chicken coop and ate the lot.
7. They say a bad workman blames his tools.
8. Jim had a tattoo on his arm and on his back.
9. Ali had some bamboo chairs in the garden.
10. Does an igloo ever melt?

The teacher/learning partner:

- demonstrates the target sounds:

    w<u>oo</u>d   c<u>ow</u>   b<u>oy</u>

- generates further words in discussion with the learner(s)

Aim: To learn to read and spell words with the diphthong 'oo' saying /o͝o/

The teacher/learning partner:

- explains the aim
- demonstrates the target sound:

    The /o͝o/ sound is spelt 'oo' in the middle of words

    w<u>oo</u>d   noteb<u>oo</u>k   c<u>oo</u>k

Crossword Puzzle No. 11

'oo' saying /o͝o/

How good a detective are you?

- read the clues
- fill in the missing words

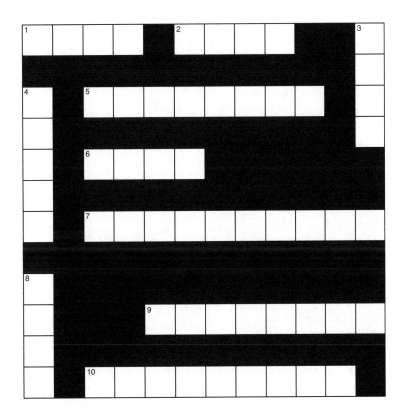

1. *Treasure Island* is a great . . . . .
2. Delia Smith is a famous . . . . .
3. He . . . . the wrong exit off the M6 motorway.
4. He . . . . . his head to mean 'no'.
5. He . . . . the lorry in the outside lane.
6. An old saying is '. . . . before you leap'.
7. He left his . . . . in the bank.
8. The . . . . is a member of the crow family.
9. The instructions were in the . . . .
10. The old cottage had an . . . . fireplace.

Dictation

The teacher/learning partner:

- says the sentence

The learner:

- repeats the sentence aloud
- writes the sentence while saying it under their breath
- reads what he has written
- uses the proofreading C-O-P-S

1. Tamara did her homework in her copybook.
2. The logbook gave a history of the car.
3. The brook was flooded because of the heavy rainfall.
4. I can book a room in a hotel.
5. A spider built a web in a tiny nook under the shelf.
6. Hang the herbs on a hook to dry in the larder.
7. He took a good look at the garden.
8. The flat will overlook the river.
9. She shook with rage.
10. She mistook him for his twin brother.

Aim: To learn to read and spell words with the diphthong 'ow' saying /ow/

The teacher/learning partner:

- explains the aim
- reviews the keywords:

  - Digraphs are pairs of letters that together make one sound.
  - Vowel digraphs are two vowels side-by-side making one sound – tr<u>ai</u>n, b<u>oa</u>t.
  - Diphthongs are two vowels that glide together when said, but still keep their separate sounds – b<u>oo</u>k, h<u>ou</u>se, c<u>ow</u>, b<u>oi</u>l, b<u>oy</u>

- demonstrates the target sound:

  The /ow/ sound can be spelt 'ow' at the beginning, middle and end of words

  <u>ow</u>l   t<u>ow</u>n   c<u>ow</u>

- generates further words in discussion with the learner(s)

Crossword Puzzle No. 12

'ow' saying /ow/

How good a detective are you?

- read the clues
- fill in the missing words

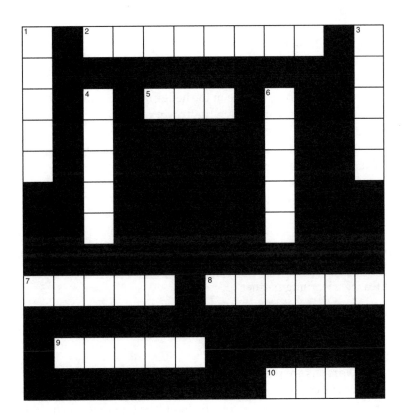

1. The Prime Minister has great political . . . . . .
2. He raised his . . . . in surprise.
3. The dog will . . . . . at strangers.
4. Every word must have a . . . . . in it.
5. 'I . . . to thee, my country' is a line from a well-known hymn.
6. The Leaning . . . . . of Pisa is very old.
7. She was as . . . . . as a berry.
8. The daffodil is the national . . . . . . of Wales.
9. The queen wore a . . . . . at her Coronation.
10. We get milk from a . . . .

Dictation

The teacher/learning partner:

- says the sentence

The learner:

- repeats the sentence aloud
- writes the sentence while saying it under their breath
- reads what he has written
- uses the proofreading C-O-P-S

1. How now, brown cow?
2. We have a power shower in the bathroom.
3. David Beckham had a row with Sir Alex Ferguson.
4. The cow got through a hole in the hedge and ate some flowers.
5. The Crown Jewels are kept in the Tower of London.
6. 'The Talk of the Town' was the name of a nightclub.
7. He will drown if the lifeboat does not reach him soon.
8. You will get lines if you frown a lot.
9. I met Brown Owl in town.
10. Brown horses are often a bay colour.

Aim: To learn to read and spell words with the diphthong 'oy' saying /oy/

The teacher/learning partner:

- explains the aim
- reviews the keywords:

  - Digraphs are pairs of letters that together make one sound.
  - Vowel digraphs are two vowels side-by-side making one sound – tr<u>ai</u>n, b<u>oa</u>t.
  - Diphthongs are two vowels that glide together when said, but still keep their separate sounds – b<u>oo</u>k, h<u>ou</u>se, c<u>ow</u>, b<u>oi</u>l, b<u>oy</u>

- demonstrates the target sound:

  'oy' says /oy/ at the beginning, middle and end of words

  <u>oy</u>ster   l<u>oy</u>al   t<u>oy</u>

- generates further words in discussion with the learner(s)

Crossword Puzzle No. 13

'oy' saying /oy/

How good a detective are you?

- read the clues
- fill in the missing words

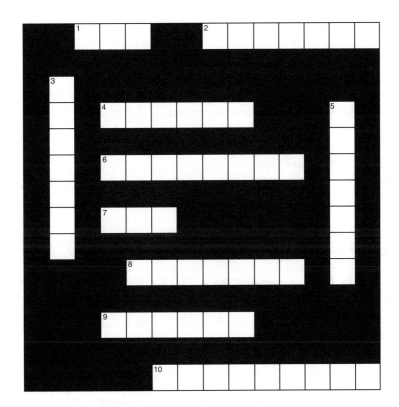

1. Little .... blue, come blow your horn.
2. .... and Indians was a children's game.
3. The shop .... six people.
4. The cars at the funeral travelled in ....
5. Pearls are found in ....
6. The bride had two .... at her wedding.
7. Lego is a popular children's ....
8. The king wanted to .... his enemies once and for all.
9. Tina is such a .... that she likes to play with boys.
10. The .... left his satchel on the coach.

Dictation

The teacher/learning partner:

- says the sentence

The learner:

- repeats the sentence aloud
- writes the sentence while saying it under their breath
- reads what he has written
- uses the proofreading C-O-P-S

1. They employ a nanny to look after the children.
2. Do not destroy the hedges in the countryside.
3. During the war, ships often sailed in convoy.
4. Roy Rogers was a well-known cowboy in old films.
5. The queen has many loyal royal servants.
6. Joy was coy about how much she had won in the Lottery.
7. The boy plays the piano and the violin.
8. Brass is an alloy of copper and zinc.
9. Barbie is a toy for girls.
10. The schoolboy did a newspaper round before school.

Crossword Puzzle Solutions

Crossword No. 1

1 chip
2 much
3 march
4 rich
5 inch

Crossword No. 2

1 gash
2 fish
3 dash or rush
4 rush
5 cash

Crossword No. 3

1 thumb
2 think
3 thank
4 path
5 bath

Crossword No. 4

1 whips
2 elephants
3 phone
4 wheels
5 laugh

Crossword No. 5

1 stains
2 explain
3 drains
4 trains
5 remain
6 trail
7 afraid
8 wail
9 drain
10 jail

Crossword No. 6

1 bray
2 betray
3 jay
4 hay
5 driveway
6 delays
7 plays
8 clay
9 display
10 birthday

Crossword No. 7

1 please
2 leap
3 gear
4 wheat
5 dream
6 teach
7 rear
8 seat
9 cream
10 treat

Crossword No. 8

1 bullfights
2 dogfight
3 floodlights
4 sigh
5 blight
6 fright
7 highlight
8 light
9 tight
10 gaslight

Crossword No. 9

1 toad
2 cloak
3 coast
4 hoax
5 toast
6 roast
7 workload
8 oath
9 moat
10 croak

Crossword No. 10

1 food
2 loom
3 stool
4 boot
5 cuckoo
6 fool
7 bloom
8 broomstick
9 bamboo
10 room

Crossword No. 11

1 book
2 cook
3 took
4 shook
5 overtook
6 look
7 chequebook
8 rook
9 handbook
10 inglenook

Crossword No. 12

1 power
2 eyebrows
3 growl
4 vowel
5 vow
6 tower
7 brown
8 flower
9 crown
10 cow

Crossword No. 13

1 boy
2 cowboys
3 employs
4 convoy
5 oysters
6 pageboys
7 toy
8 destroy
9 tomboy
10 schoolboy.

Synthetic Phonics Diagnostic and Attainment Test

This has many possible uses, including:

- screening to establish current skills
- monitoring progress
- revision and reinforcement
- target-setting for Individual Education Plans
- for diagnostic purposes, to establish an appropriate starting point for teaching
- identifying weaknesses, such as poor phonemic or phonological skills, by making an analysis of errors.

The test can be administered in sections or as a whole. Later, a miscue analysis of the errors can be made and noted in the boxes below. It can later be used to monitor progress or identify specific weaknesses, which could be included in individual education plans (IEPs).

The teacher/learning partner:

- asks the learner(s) to write their name on the Synthetic Phonics Test sheet
- explains how the test works:

  - I will read a word and then repeat it
  - you write the word only once, in the box
  - if you cannot spell it, just do your best
  - try not to leave the box blank

- reads each word slowly and clearly, twice
- pauses for a few seconds before reading the next word

Test questions

1. **Initial letters**

fan	kip	gum	cap	hug
vat	jet	wag	zip	yap

2. **Final letters**

mix	yak	cots	jog	my
pens	pip	kid	pod	jugs

3. **Short vowels**

peg	act	bin	job	yet
cut	fax	pop	hum	fig

4. **Consonant digraphs**

rash	whip	graph	such	then
rough	thin	shin	chit	throb

5. **Consonant blends**

brim	crisp	trust	risk	twin
split	scrub	shrimp	strap	shrub

6. **Assimilations**

crunch	length	stump	blunt	grind
shrink	thump	blond	trench	sprung

7. **Magic 'e'**

scrape	stripe	clothe	prize	tube
eve	rude	nine	square	use

8. **Vowel consonant 'r'**

alarm	bird	term	form	born
girl	churn	hurt	stern	park

9. **Vowel digraphs**

again	delay	dream	air	gloat
fleet	fright	mood	igloo	hoax

10. **Diphthongs**

notebook	put	oil	took	royal
crowd	loud	book	shower	employ

SYNTHETIC PHONICS TEST

You will hear each word twice. Write it in the box just once.

1. Initial letters

2. Final letters

3. Short vowels

4. Consonant digraphs

5. Consonant blends

6. Assimilations

7. Magic 'e'

8. Vowel consonant 'r'

9. **Vowel digraphs**

10. **Diphthongs**

2 How to Manage Syllables Successfully

The aims of this chapter

To help learn and understand the principles and processes involved in using syllables. Long words are often seen as difficult and challenging and can be hard to read and spell. People with phonological difficulties may tend to omit 'parts' of words – 'rember' for 'remember'. Awareness can be developed by counting or tapping out syllables, and by saying the individual syllables aloud and synthesising these to make whole words (initially in spoken words, later in writing). This can ultimately be done as a spelling activity.

Those who are stronger visually may find it helpful to practise identifying and using common spelling patterns – such as 'ai', 'ee', 'ie', 'oa' or 'oo' – and common suffixes – such as 'ful', 'ly' or 'less' – and also common roots such as 'vent', 'press' or 'phone', as recommended by the NLS (1998). Kinaesthetic learners with good motor memory skills will find it helpful if they are taught to clap, beat out or count syllables as well as copy out and insert the syllable division line.

Multi-sensory teaching of spelling has been found to be the most effective means of teaching spelling for all learners including those with special educational needs. When all the senses are used at once, they utilise all the pathways to the brain and activate different areas. Multi-sensory teaching can also be adapted to match and enhance individual learning styles.

Critics of multi-sensory teaching methods frequently derided what they called 'drill and skill' methods, accusing teachers of inducing 'death by workbook'. The criticism was valid when learners were given worksheets and just asked to fill in or copy out missing words on the page. The current text includes explanation of multi-sensory strategies for learning.

Recall and understanding of the keywords are fundamental factors for successful work on syllables. They can be established by using different strategies and a variety of tactics depending on preferred learning style. Many dyslexic learners have difficulties with word retrieval and word naming, so it is essential that teacher/learning partner revise and rehearse keywords, such as short and long vowel, consonant, blend, digraph, prefix, root word and suffix. The teacher/learning partner can discuss the aim of each activity, then use the list of keywords and look at the examples given. Further examples may be generated and written on the board, on an overhead transparency (OHT) or on an interactive whiteboard to provide a computer printout. They may also be recorded in a personal spellofax for reference and revision.

Keywords

These are the keywords needed to understand and use syllable division strategies and techniques. Revise and rehearse the following orally:

> The vowels are 'a''e''i''o''u'
> 'y' is sometimes a vowel, as in: sky, lady, tyre

There are two kinds of vowels: short vowels say their sounds; long vowels say their names. Digraphs are two letters making one sound and include consonant digraphs and vowel digraphs. Diphthongs are two vowels side by side, which glide together when pronounced in rapid succession. Blends are letters found next to each other; they sound separately but quickly to make the sound. Assimilations are nasal sounds (made down one's nose) and involve the letters 'm' and 'n'.

Diacritical marks are the code marks used in dictionaries above, below or beside a letter, showing pronunciation, stress, word-division and syllabification. Short vowels are coded with a breve (˘)

> căt   cŏd   cŭp

Long vowels are coded with a macron (‾)

> hē   grāī n   w ēē d

Slash marks are used to denote letter phonemes /c/ /a/ /t/.
Quote marks are used to denote letter names 'c' 'a' 't'.

Differentiated activities

The learner reads the target words. This helps those who are strong visualisers to remember the visual features, such as spelling patterns, as well as the code marks on the vowel and the syllable division line. Those who are stronger auditorially will be helped to learn by remembering the individual syllables when they are said aloud.

The simultaneous use of seeing, saying, tapping out, listening and writing individual syllables applies multi-sensory principles to segmenting words and is an effective method for learning and remembering spelling.

Most topics have three sections, with different levels of activities to match the individual's development and skills.

Section A: Quiz questions

The learner:

- re-reads the target words
- reads the clues
- fills in the missing word in the quiz
- reads the whole sentence
- underlines the target word

Practising with target words helps to reinforce meaning for auditory learners as well as reinforcing spelling patterns.

Section B: Wordsearches

The learner:

- reads the target word
- finds the word, which is either horizontal or vertical on the page
- puts a ring round the word
- highlights it
- reads the word

The wordsearch is useful because it allows further reinforcement of the spelling of individual words. This is particularly useful for strong visualisers.

Section C: Seeing and hearing syllables

The teacher and learner read the passage through, to practise seeing and hearing the polysyllabic words in context.
　　The learner:

- re-reads the passage, sentence by sentence (longer sentences may need to be broken into shorter, meaningful phrases)
- copies out the passage.
- uses the passage for dictation
- re-reads the passage using the proof-reading C-O-P-S
- highlights the polysyllabic target words

Dictation can also be used by an individual without the help of a teacher/parent, as follows:
　　The learner:

- reads the passage onto a cassette tape recorder or a Minidisk recorder with a playback facility
- plays it back using headphones to listen to it sentence by sentence
- writes it in dictation
- re-reads using the proof-reading C-O-P-S and by checking with the original passage

Dictation helps to reinforce the strategy or technique being taught by applying it in meaningful contexts. It also helps to develop short-term and working memory skills.

How you can use these activities

These three sections use different learning strategies, a variety of tactics and different skills to teach, learn, reinforce and rehearse syllabification skills. They represent differentiated levels of difficulty to match different spelling abilities.

Some learners will be able to tackle all the activities during the 20-minute segment of The Literacy Hour used 'for group or independent work', whereas others may work just on section A, or A and B. The keywords and strategies can be revised during the plenary session. Pupils can be asked to identify their 'best' strategy for remembering. Further examples can be noted during shared and guided text activities and added to individual's personal 'Spellofax'.

The various activities can also be used for one-to-one learning and teaching. An individual may do one part from each section of the three activities every day, thereby reinforcing syllabification skills for five consecutive days to maximise learning. Constant repetition and repeated exposure to the target words can act as a trigger to memorising words. The use of multi-sensory means helps to develop mastery and automatic recall to manage syllables successfully when reading and doing independent writing.

How to count syllables orally

Aim: To learn to count syllables orally

Keywords for review:

A syllable is a beat
A syllable must have one vowel sound

> **cat**
> cat/nap
> cat/a/pult
> cat/er/pill/ar

ACTIVITY

- look at the word
- say the word
- repeat it while tapping out the syllables
- count the syllables

Ben	Dan	Pat	Sam	Raj
Bill	Jill	Pam	Jim	Tom

How many syllables are there in each word? ☐

Amy	Billy	Dodi	Jimmy	Susy
Ali	Betty	Davy	Jenny	Sammy

How many syllables are there in each word? ☐

Benjamin	Diana	Oliver	Lucinda	Cameron
Fatima	Anthony	Caroline	Timothy	Melanie

How many syllables are there in each word? ☐

Angelina	Juliana	Philomena	Antonio	Elizabeth
Victoria	Felicity	Jeremiah	Alexander	Tiziano

How many syllables are there in each word? ☐

Aim: To use chin-to-hand clapping to help count syllables in polysyllabic words

The teacher/learning partner models this first and:

- puts the back of the outstretched hand directly under the chin
- keeps the forearm straight
- says the target word
- counts the number of times the hand touches the chin to find the number of syllables

ACTIVITY

- look at each word
- say the word aloud
- repeat the word and count the number of times your chin touches your hand

Try it with these words – they have two, three or four syllables

attic	comic	escalator
goblet	magnet	rhinoceros
button	damson	technology

Aim: To use hand-to-thigh clapping to help count syllables in polysyllabic words

ACTIVITY

- look at each word
- say the word aloud
- repeat the word slowly while clapping out the syllables on your thigh

Try it with the months of the year and the days of the week

January	July	Monday	Saturday
February	August	Tuesday	Sunday
March	September	Wednesday	
April	October	Thursday	
May	November	Friday	
June	December		

How to code vowels and consonants

Aim: To code short vowels

Keywords to review:

The short vowels a e i o u say their sounds
A breve is a code mark placed over the short vowel

bŭt
bŭt/tĕr
bŭt/tĕr/cŭp

ACTIVITY

- look at each word
- say the word aloud
- code the short vowel by adding a breve above it
- read the word again

h i m	f a t	c u t	f i t	y a m
r u n	w i g	m a t	r u t	z i p
d i d	p u b	b e d	d i p	a n t

Complete the following sentence:

Short vowels say their _____

and are coded with a _____.

Aim: To code long vowels

Keywords to review:

The long vowels a e i o u say their names
A macron is a code mark placed over the long vowels

ī
/ī/ /ō/ /tā/

ACTIVITY

- look at each word
- say the word aloud
- code the long vowel by adding a macron above it
- read the word again

h e	h i	m e	n o	b y
n o	J o	a	s o	I
b e	m y	w h y	g o	w e

Complete the following sentence:

Long vowels say their _____

and are coded with a _____.

Aim: To code short and long vowels

ACTIVITY

- look at each word
- say the word aloud
- code the vowel by adding a breve or a macron above it
- read the word again

h a s	h a d	p i n	t i n	p o l o
a c t	b y	b a d	c a n	h e r o
n o	b e	p i p	p a d	z e r o

Aim: To identify consonant blend words

Keywords to review:

Consonant blends are two or more consonants found next to each other; they sound separately but quickly to make one sound.

They can occur at the beginning, middle or ends of words.

s<u>k</u>in
ba<u>sk</u>et
ru<u>sk</u>

ACTIVITY

Consonant blends at the <u>beginning</u> of words

bl	br	cl	cr	dr	dw	fl	fr	gl	gr	pl	pr
sc	scr	sk	sl	sm	sn	sp	spl	spr	squ		
st	str	sw	tr	tw	thr	shr					

Consonant blends at the <u>end</u> of words

ld	lk	sk	lp	sp	ct	ft
lt	pt	st	xt	lf	lth	

- Look at each word
- Say the word aloud
- Highlight the consonant blend(s)
- Read the word again

skin	plan	frog	string	crust	desk
slab	skin	scrap	split	grub	crisp
twin	clap	clog	prim	vest	crust

HANDY HINT

The blends are like twins: they always stay together in a syllable

Aim: To identify consonant digraph words

Keywords to review:

Consonant digraphs are two consonants next to each other that make one sound.

They can occur at the beginning, middle or ends of words.

<u>th</u>umb
ba<u>th</u>er
pa<u>th</u>

ACTIVITY

Consonant digraphs

> sh   ch   wh   th   ph   gh

- look at each word
- say the word aloud
- circle the consonant digraph
- read the word again

shin	chap	whisk	rich	chum
cough	phone	dash	bath	thin

HANDY HINT

Digraphs always stay together in a syllable.
Mnemonic: The digraphs are inseparable, like conjoined twins.

Aim: To identify assimilation words

Keywords to review:

Assimilations are sounds made down one's nose including the letters 'm' and 'n'

The assimilations are:

ng   nk   nd   nt   nch   ngth   mp

song
le<u>ng</u>th

ACTIVITY

- look at each word
- say the word aloud
- highlight the assimilation
- read the word again

strong	blink	dump	pong	song	thing
vamp	tend	wing	length	band	bend

Aim: To underline the blends and assimilations, circle the digraphs and code the vowels

ACTIVITY

- look at each word
- say the word
- code the vowel
- highlight the consonant blends and assimilations
- circle the consonant digraphs
- read the word

lump	grand	strum	crash	string
stump	thrust	flash	crisp	strength

Further practice

ACTIVITY

- look at each word
- say the word
- code the vowel
- highlight the consonant blends and assimilations
- circle the consonant digraphs
- read the word

h a n g	g l u m	t r y
s w i m	cold	s h y
r a s h	i t c h	b y
d e s k	c r i s p	t a n g o
t w i n	s h r i m p	s h e

How to divide words into syllables

Guidelines for multi-sensory strategies for syllable division:

- Say the word aloud
- Copy out the word
- Beat, clap or use the hand-to-chin method to count out the syllables
- Code the vowels
- Underline blends, prefixes or suffixes
- Circle the digraphs
- Insert the syllable division line
- Read the word again

Aim: To learn to divide words into syllables with a syllable division line

Keywords to review:

A syllable division line is a vertical line placed between syllables to show where a word can be divided to help with pronunciation and spelling.

e/mu   ze/ro   pup/pet   fan/tas/tic   non/re/turn/able

ACTIVITY

- underline the vowels

  r a̲b b i̲t

- put the index finger of each hand on the lines under the marked vowels
- divide the word with a syllable division line between the two consonants
- code the vowels
- say the syllables
- read the whole word

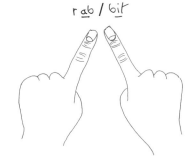

c a n d i d	s u b m i t	h u s b a n d
p e l l e t	h a p p e n	i n v e s t
h e c t i c	c o b w e b	k i p p e r
h o r r i d	f u n n e l	n a p k i n

HANDY HINT

The syllable division line usually comes between two consonants

Further practice

ACTIVITY

- underline the vowels

  b a̲n d i̲t   c o̲b w e̲b

- put the index finger of each hand on the lines under the marked vowels
- divide the word with a syllable division line between the two consonants
- code the vowels
- say the syllables
- read the whole word

V u l c a n	e s c o r t	d i s c u s	m o r t a l	v i c t i m
v e s s e l	c o r n e t	a n v i l	o r b i t	m o r b i d

HANDY HINT AND USEFUL TIP

Every syllable must have a vowel. Some syllables have only one letter, which must be a vowel:

   a / corn   i / de/ a   ver / y

HANDY HINT

When there are two consonants of the same letter, only one consonant is sounded and it is usually in the accented syllable.

(Accent is the emphasis or stress given to a letter or a syllable.)

   cŏt/tŏn   pŏp/pĕt   tŭn/nĕl

Aim: *To learn the six major types of syllables*

1. Closed syllables
2. Open syllables
3. Vowel–consonant–'e' syllables (Magic 'e' syllables)
4. Vowel digraph/diphthong syllables
5. Consonant 'le' syllables
6. 'R' combination syllables

How to be in C – L – O – V -E – R by using it as a mnemonic to remember the six syllable types; see *How to Manage Spelling Successfully* (Ott, 2007).

C	C losed syllables	cot	map	tap
L	Le syllables	ta/ble	ap/ple	ri/fle
O	O pen syllables	be	po/lo	i/de/a
V	V owel teams (digraphs/diphthongs)	train	speed/ing	play/ed
E	E Silent-e (Magic 'e')	gate	pipe	rope
R	R-controlled vowels	col/lar	act/or	paint/er

HANDY HINT

The vowel and the letters after it help decide the type of syllable

Aim: To code and read words with closed syllables

Keywords to review:

Closed syllables have a short vowel and end in a consonant

This can be taught by using this Closed Syllable Room illustration as a mnemonic

cŭt
vĕl/vĕt
iň/hăb/ĭt

Closed Syllable Room

Mr Consonant closes the back door. The vowel men are shut in and we can only hear the sounds they make; see *How to Manage Spelling Successfully*, chapter 12 (Ott, 2007).

ACTIVITY

- look at each word and say it under your breath
- code the vowel
- highlight the consonant that ends the word
- read the word again

c u d	p o d
d u d	b a d
c a d	b i d
d a n	b e d
p i n	b o d
p a n	b u d
p o d	a p t
i m p	e g g
m e t	p i n
b o x	a c t

Complete the sentences:

Closed syllables end in a _____.

The vowel is _____ and says its _____.

Aim: To learn to divide words with closed syllables and consonant digraphs

Keywords to review:

Consonant digraphs are two consonants making one sound

mĕth/ŏd

ACTIVITY

- look at each word
- highlight the digraph
- code the vowels
- divide the word with a syllable-division line
- place the index finger of each hand under each vowel, on either side of the syllable-division line
- read the word

dolphin	shamrock	ethnic	hatchet
orchid	panther	worship	marshal
prophet	graphic	sulphur	pamphlet
urchin	snapshot	anthem	chevron
sandwich	shipment	channel	punish

HANDY HINT

Remember! Digraphs, like conjoined twins are inseparable and always stay together in the same syllable

Section A – Quiz No. 1

- re-read the target words on page 137
- read the clues
- fill in the missing words in the quiz
- read the whole sentence
- highlight the target word

1. Jon Snow is a presenter on . . . . 4 News.

2. The UN sent a . . . . of food to the starving people in Liberia.

3. They say a . . . . is often not listened to by his own people.

4. . . . . . . minorities exist in many countries with many refugees.

5. The . . . . . . of Liverpool football supporters is 'You'll never walk alone'.

6. Desert . . . . . . was regarded as one of the best horses in racing history.

7. A . . . . has three leaves and one stem and is often confused with clover.

8. My granny always used to say that we should bury the . . . . and be friendly with our neighbours.

9. Field . . . . Montgomery was a great general during World War Two.

10. Read this little . . . . : it explains the rules for playing cricket.

Section B – Wordsearch

How good a detective are you?

- find these words
  (some go across, some go down)
- put a ring round each word in the Wordsearch
- highlight it
- read the word

g	s	t	p	c	i	n	w	l	c	d
r	c	s	a	n	d	w	i	c	h	f
a	i	d	n	w	n	i	l	m	a	u
p	h	a	t	c	h	e	t	m	n	r
h	p	p	h	g	y	e	z	a	n	h
i	a	r	e	c	b	j	k	r	e	f
c	r	o	r	c	h	i	d	s	l	e
e	g	p	u	n	i	s	h	h	c	d
d	s	h	j	z	y	q	l	a	u	i
a	b	e	t	h	n	i	c	l	j	p
x	e	t	j	e	a	h	f	u	k	m

marshal	prophet
ethnic	orchid
graphic	hatchet
channel	panther
punish	sandwich

Section C

- read the passage
- copy it out
- write the passage to dictation
- highlight target words with closed syllables and consonant digraphs

Evening Classes

Horrible Harry and Hateful Henry decided last September to go to evening classes. They both enrolled on a computer course. Horrible Harry did a project about deep-sea diving. He took lots of snapshots of dolphins and sharks with his digital camera. One day when he was filming he trod on a sea urchin. He yelled in agony as the prickly spikes stuck into his foot. 'Get me out of here quickly!' he groaned into his mobile phone.

Hateful Henry smirked as he cut up wood with a hatchet in an apple orchard at home. 'I'll come and cut off the bad leg if you want. I must go now and finish the pamphlet to include in my project. I found a great package of graphics on the Internet with panthers and lions and other wildlife. You need not have bothered with your camera at all,' he said as he smugly switched off his mobile phone.

_____
_____
_____
_____
_____
_____
_____
_____
_____
_____
_____
_____
_____
_____
_____
_____
_____
_____
_____
_____
_____
_____
_____
_____

Aim: To learn to divide words with closed syllables and consonant blends

Keywords to review:

The blends are letters found next to each other; they sound separately, but quickly, and so they blend

Closed syllables have a short vowel and end in a consonant

stŏ<u>ck</u>/pŏt
dĕ<u>sk</u>/tŏp
em/<u>pr</u>ĕss

ACTIVITY

- look at the word
- highlight the blends
- code the vowels
- divide the word with a syllable-division line
- place the index fingers of each hand under each vowel on either side of the syllable-division line
- read the word

impress	pilgrim	instant	suntrap
entrust	misspell	emblem	postbag
entrant	monster	instil	entrust
humdrum	construct	doldrums	mistress
dandruff	instruct	catnap	hamlet

HANDY HINT

Remember! The blends are like non-identical twins who hold hands and usually stick together in the same syllable

ACTIVITY

Aim: To learn to divide words with three closed syllables

con/un/drum

- look at the word
- code the vowels
- divide the word with a syllable-division line
- place the index fingers and third finger of one hand under each vowel on either side of the syllable-division line
- read the word

immortal	interest	annulment	expectant
sarcastic	September	consultant	internal
bombastic	indignant	cosmetic	forgotten
commandant	important	interrupt	gymnastics
fantastic	inhabit	Atlantic	

Section A – Quiz No. 2

- re-read the target words above
- read the clues
- fill in the missing words in the quiz
- read the whole sentence
- highlight the target word

1. Wild pigs . . . . mountainous parts of Italy.

2. The . . . . ocean separates America from Europe.

3. . . . . is a spectacular event in the Olympic Games.

4. In England, learners return to school in . . . . after the summer holidays.

5. The doctor sent the man to a . . . . for a second opinion about his illness.

6. Some music of great composers such as Mozart is . . . .

7. The Not . . . . Association looks after veteran soldiers.

8. She said she admired my hair style but she was being . . . .

9. The . . . . took the salute at the Sandhurst army parade.

Section B – Wordsearch

How good a detective are you?

- find the following words, some go horizontally some vertically
- put a ring round the word
- highlight it
- read the word

monster
indignant
consultant
pilgrim
mistress
inhabit
gymnastics
attendant
sarcastic
important

i	c	t	p	g	i	a	i	l	i	o
n	a	s	a	y	d	t	m	c	n	r
h	s	s	c	m	m	p	p	c	d	m
a	a	e	m	n	h	p	o	g	i	i
b	r	t	o	a	y	i	r	h	g	s
i	c	o	n	s	u	l	t	a	n	t
t	a	n	s	t	h	g	a	t	a	r
p	s	e	t	i	c	r	n	t	n	e
u	t	m	e	c	y	i	t	o	t	s
s	i	e	r	s	r	m	v	e	r	s
x	c	a	t	t	e	n	d	a	n	t

Section C

- read the passage
- copy it out
- write the passage to dictation
- highlight words with two closed syllables and consonant digraphs

Don't let your boss get in your hair

Hateful Henry had a new boss whom he wanted to impress with his smart appearance. He chuckled as he said, 'I will entrust my golden locks to my long-time barber, Tom, and instruct him to give me an instant make-over.' He sat in the chair reading a magazine and forgot to say that he hated short hair. When he looked up he saw in the mirror that all he had left was a short stubble. He leapt up and stormed out of the barber shop. He went to see a hair consultant at the cosmetic counter in a big shop. He was indignant when she said that she had no magic cures for short hair. 'Serves you right,' smirked Horrible Harry, when he got home.

Next day the new boss sent an e-mail to Horrible Harry to come instantly to a meeting. She said, 'It is important that you do something about the dandruff in your hair. It falls all over your work and mine, ' she said in a sarcastic manner. 'You twins get in my hair.'

_____

_____

_____

_____

_____

_____

_____

_____

_____

_____

_____

_____

_____

_____

_____

_____

_____

_____

_____

_____

_____

Aim: To code, read and spell words with open syllables

Keywords to review:

- Open syllables end in a vowel
- The vowel is long and says its name

This can be taught by using an illustration such as this:

nō
bī/rō
ī/dē/ā

Open Syllable Room

Mr Long Vowel opens the door. When he looks in he can see the Vowel Men and he can call them by their names. Open syllables therefore end in a vowel and say their names; see *How to Manage Spelling Successfully* (Ott, 2007).

ACTIVITY

Aim: To learn to divide, code, read and spell words with open syllables

- look at the word
- code the vowels
- divide the word with a syllable-division line
- place the index fingers of each hand under each vowel on either side of the syllable-division line
- read the word

s o f a	g y r o	j u d o	b a b y
s a g o	h a l o	l u d o	l a z y
l a d y	c r a z y	y o y o	z e r o
p o l o	e g o	s o l o	t i d y
g r a v y	n a v y	d o d o	q u o t a

Complete the sentences:

Open syllables end in a _____. The vowel is _____ and says its _____.

ACTIVITY

Aim: To learn to divide, read and spell words with open and closed syllables

- look at the word
- code the vowels
- divide the word with a syllable division line
- place the index fingers of each hand under each vowel on either side of the syllable-division line
- read the word

> pī/lŏt
> 'o' 'c'

unit	human	scampi	cargo	grotto
tiger	bingo	dingo	ghetto	hero
banjo	hippo	jumbo	ditto	veto
motto	mango	tango	hello	lotto
tempo				

HANDY HINT

Words of two syllables can have a mixture of closed and open syllables, which can occur in either order.

Aim: To learn to divide, read and spell words with closed–open–closed syllables

- look at the word
- code the vowels
- divide the word with a syllable division line
- place the index fingers of each hand under each vowel on either side of the syllable division line
- indicate type of syllable such as closed 'c'; open 'o'; vowel–consonant 'e' – 'v c e'
- read the word

> pŏpp/ā/dŏm
> 'c' 'o' 'c'

diplomat	daffodil
instrument	arrogant
octopus	competent
comprehend	pendulum
parasol	democrat
ornament	mandolin
acrobat	succulent
alcohol	turbulent
innocent	abdomen
aristocrat	extrovert

Section A – Quiz No. 3

- re-read the target words on pages 144 and 145
- read the clues
- fill in the missing words in the quiz
- read the whole sentence
- highlight the target word

1. They sat in the shade under a . . . .

2. . . . . is a game played on horseback with a ball and wooden mallet.

3. The . . . . became extinct hundreds of years ago.

4. Argentina is the home of . . . . . dancing.

5. The UN put a . . . . on trade with Libya.

6. The . . . . performed on a tight wire at the circus.

7. That man is an . . . . fool: he is such a know-all.

8. It was William Wordsworth who wrote a famous poem about the . . . . , the yellow flower that blooms in the spring.

9. Actors need to be . . . . when they perform.

10. The clock . . . . swung backwards and forwards.

Section B – Wordsearch

How good a detective are you?

- find the following words, some go horizontally some vertically
- put a ring round the word
- highlight it
- read the word

mango	octopus
alcohol	diplomat
ghetto	disco
democrat	ornament
scampi	extrovert

r	d	t	p	t	i	a	w	l	c	o
s	i	s	a	n	d	t	i	c	o	r
s	p	s	c	a	m	p	i	c	n	n
o	l	e	o	l	h	e	m	g	s	a
c	o	t	g	c	y	n	p	h	u	m
t	m	s	n	o	b	d	o	e	l	e
o	a	n	a	h	h	a	r	t	t	n
p	t	e	m	o	c	r	a	t	a	t
u	s	m	r	l	y	t	a	o	n	i
s	b	e	x	t	r	o	v	e	r	t
m	a	n	g	o	d	i	s	c	o	s

Section C

- read the passage
- copy it out
- write the passage to dictation
- highlight words with open and closed syllables

A no-fun day at the seaside

Hateful Henry decided that they should go to Brighton for the day. 'Don't forget to pack the parasol – it's a hot day,' insisted Horrible Harry. They forgot to calculate how long the journey would take. They were stuck in a long traffic jam and were late for lunch. 'I am innocent,' said Horrible Harry. 'You were the driver and if you were competent you would have found out how long it takes.'

He opened the sunroof of the car and began to strum 'I'm Going on a Summer Holiday' on his banjo. The woman in the car beside them rolled down her window and said, 'You are driving me crazy and you will wake my baby'. Just then they saw a signpost saying 'Circus'.

They forgot about the seaside. They went and bought tickets and later saw a tiger and a hippo in the ring. Then an acrobat started to perform. He had taken alcohol before the show to steady his nerves, but it made him dizzy. He began to wobble and he fell off the tight wire. Hateful Henry said, 'Serves him right: that silly man had too much beer in his abdomen'.

_____

_____

_____

_____

_____

_____

_____

_____

_____

_____

_____

_____

_____

_____

_____

_____

_____

_____

_____

_____

_____

_____

Aim: To code, read and spell words with syllables and Magic 'e'

Keywords to review:

Magic 'e' makes the vowel say its name, but Magic 'e' does not say a thing

When Magic Mrs 'e' comes knocking at the back door of the Vowel Men's room, she says, "Who's there?" The Vowel Men are polite and say their names, but she keeps quiet.

cāke
mīle/āge

ACTIVITY

- look at the word
- code the vowels
- read the word

cap	cape	cub	cube	fire
mat	mate	rat	rate	dress
pop	pope	gap	gape	pure
lop	lope	hire	ate	flat

HANDY HINT

Magic Mrs 'e' makes the vowel say its name, but she keeps quiet and does not make a sound

ACTIVITY

- look at the word
- code the vowels
- read the word

us	use	pet	Pete	fin	fine	not	note
pan	pane	hop	hope	rob	robe	fuss	fuse
wad	wade	Sid	side	rip	ripe	smock	smoke
hid	hide	tub	tube	slop	slope		
bid	bide	hat	hate	hop	hope		

ACTIVITY

Further practice

- look at the word
- code the vowels
- read the word

mutt	mute
shut	chute
mop	mope

Aim: To code and read words with closed syllables and Magic 'e'

ACTIVITY

- look at the word
- code the vowels
- divide the word with a syllable-division line
- place the index fingers of each hand under each vowel on either side of the syllable-division line
- read the word

măr/găr/īne

membrane	impede	sincere
astute	immune	advice
textile	entice	compete
ignore	capsule	include
conclude	sublime	invade
pancake	exile	baptise
confuse	empire	escape
reptile	combine	capsize
backbone	endure	produce
sunrise	invite	retire

Section A – Quiz No. 4

- re-read the target words on page 149
- read the clues
- fill in the missing words in the quiz
- read the whole sentence
- highlight the target word

1. She did a . . . . and design course at college.
2. Sailing boats can . . . . in rough weather.
3. Astronauts go to the moon in a sealed . . . . on board a spacecraft.
4. Men often . . . . . . at 65, women at 60.
5. Napoleon was sent into . . . . . on the island of St Helena.
6. You can . . . . a baby by pouring water on his head.
7. Queen Victoria ruled over an . . . .
8. Farmers' markets sell home-grown . . . .
9. *The Great . . . . . . is a popular war film.*
10. There is a . . . . race in Olney in Buckinghamshire on Shrove Tuesday.

Section B – Wordsearch

How good a detective are you?

- find these words
  (some go across, some down)
- put a ring round each word in the Wordsearch
- highlight it
- read the word

revive	insane
immune	invade
backbone	excuse
endure	promote
alcove	profile

e	c	t	p	p	r	o	f	i	l	e
x	a	s	a	y	d	t	m	r	n	r
c	s	s	i	m	m	u	n	e	d	m
u	a	e	m	n	h	e	o	v	i	i
s	r	t	a	a	y	n	r	i	g	s
e	c	o	l	s	u	l	e	v	n	i
t	b	a	c	k	b	o	n	e	a	n
p	s	e	o	i	c	r	d	t	n	s
u	i	n	v	a	d	e	u	o	t	a
s	i	e	e	s	r	o	r	e	r	n
x	p	r	o	m	o	t	e	a	n	e

Section C

- read the passage
- copy it out
- write the passage to dictation
- highlight words with closed syllables and Magic 'e'

A strange encounter on the way to the winter sales

Hateful Henry said, 'We must combine a trip to the sales with a chance to explore London'. They got up at sunrise to escape the traffic before the rush hour on the M25. They had to revise the plan when they saw a lorry capsize. It had a tank on the back with a large reptile, which escaped along the carriageway. The driver tried to entice the creature back into the tank. Meanwhile the lorry was blocking two lanes of the motorway. They both yelled out of the window at the driver as they drove past, 'You are insane to chase a live crocodile down the M25'.

Horrible Harry wailed, 'Hurry up! I must buy that bespoke suit in the Savile Row sale'.

'Don't be so obstinate,' yelled Hateful Henry, 'I am driving as fast as I can'. A police car came up behind and began to overtake them. What a lucky escape from a speeding fine!

ACTIVITY

Aim: To code, read and spell words with open syllables and Magic 'e'

- look at the word
- code the vowels
- divide the word with a syllable-division line
- place the index fingers of each hand under each vowel on either side of the syllable-division line
- read the word

bē/fōre

retire	decide	profile	demure
promote	require	profuse	deplore
retake	denote	before	revise
provoke	revive	escape	defile
remake	overtake	bespoke	female

Aim: To code, read and spell words with vowel digraphs and diphthongs

Keywords to review:

Vowel digraphs are two vowels making one sound
Diphthongs are two vowels that, when found side-by-side, glide together when pronounced

s t r ā̄i gh/tĕn   b o͞y/ho͞od   t o͞i l/ĭng

ACTIVITY

- look at the word
- highlight the diphthong or vowel digraph
- code the vowels
- divide the word with a syllable-division line
- place the index fingers of each hand under each vowel on either side of the syllable-division line
- read the word

house	prowler	crow	blew	clause	screw
daughters	wait	powder	train	roomy	Spain
float	soap	might	night	clown	new
childhood	mood	thousand	mischief	week	food
loans	laundry	complaint	fountain	beastly	

HANDY HINT

Vowel digraphs and diphthongs are regarded as single vowel sounds, and stay together in a syllable.

Section A – Quiz No. 5

- re-read the target words on p. 152
- read the clues
- fill in the missing words in the quiz
- read the whole sentence
- highlight the target word

1. Mothers and . . . . are often close friends.
2. Laurie Lee wrote about his . . . . in *Cider with Rosie*.
3. Some people like to . . . . their hair.
4. He made a . . . . about the poor service in the restaurant.
5. A millennium is a . . . . years.
6. The hotel sends tablecloths and sheets to a . . . .
7. . . . . pens nowadays mostly use ink cartridges.
8. Student . . . . . are widely available from banks.
9. The policeman arrested the . . . .
10. They have a holiday house in . . . . . .

Section B – Wordsearch

How good a detective are you?

- find these words
  (some go across, some down)
- put a ring round the word
- highlight it
- read the word

might
clown
house
screw
powder
float
beastly
roomy
mischief
daughter

e	c	t	b	e	a	s	t	l	y	e
x	l	s	a	y	d	t	m	r	m	r
h	o	u	s	e	m	m	n	e	o	m
u	w	e	m	n	h	i	o	v	o	i
s	n	t	a	a	y	g	r	s	r	s
e	c	o	l	s	u	h	e	c	n	i
t	d	a	u	g	h	t	e	r	a	f
p	s	e	o	i	c	r	d	e	n	l
m	i	s	c	h	i	e	f	w	t	o
s	p	o	w	d	e	r	r	e	r	a
x	p	r	o	o	m	y	e	a	n	t

Section C

- read the passage
- copy it out
- write the passage to dictation
- highlight words with vowel digraphs and diphthongs

An unforeseen delay on the painting holiday in Spain

Hateful Henry had been a keen artist from early childhood. 'Now that I am grown up, I might go to Spain and do a course at that place I saw advertised on the Internet,' he said to Horrible Harry. He wanted to improve his drawing.

The daughter of the artist met them at the airport. She told them to wait by the exit sign while she paid for the car park ticket. When she got to the cash desk she found she had no change for the ticket. She dashed back to borrow some cash from the twins.

Hateful Henry launched into a complaint and said, 'I should be toiling at my easel by now, painting in the sunlight'. 'Don't be such a moaner,' said Horrible Harry, 'you have all week to make a beastly mess on those canvases'.

ACTIVITY

Aim: To code and read words with 'le' syllables

Consonant-'le' syllables found at the end of words:

'ble'   'cle'   'fle'   'gle'   'kle'   'ple'   'stle'   'tle'   'zle'

| cā/<u>ble</u> |
| cŏb/<u>ble</u> |

Mnemonic

Tom-Tom the piper's son saw Greedy Myr<u>tle</u> at the ta<u>ble</u> ready to gob<u>ble</u> the whole ap<u>ple</u> pie. She was struck dumb when his dog grabbed her an<u>kle</u> and ran off with the pie.

- look at the word
- highlight 'le' and the consonant next to it
- code the vowels
- divide the word with a syllable-division line
- place the index fingers of each hand under each vowel on either side of the syllable-division line
- read the word

bubble	table
castle	candle
bible	whistle
rattle	jingle
scribble	ankle
maple	handle
jungle	bangle
kettle	apple
poodle	rifle
drizzle	treacle

HANDY HINT

Remember the fable of Greedy Myrtle and Tom-Tom the piper's son, which shows that 'e' at the end of 'le' letter clusters is dumb and does not say a thing.

Section A – Quiz No. 6

- re-read the target words on p. 155
- read the clues
- fill in the missing words in the quiz
- read the whole sentence
- highlight the target word

1. The kind of writing people do in a hurry is often a . . . .
2. It was once a fashion to have a French . . . . . . as a pet.
3. The Queen lives in a palace in London and in a . . . . . . in Windsor.
4. Michael's favourite pudding is . . . . tart and custard.
5. My granny used to say that eating an . . . . . a day keeps the doctor away.
6. Mum makes '. . . . . . and squeak' with left-over cabbage and mashed potatoes.
7. . . . . . syrup goes well with pancakes.
8. Chef Jamie Oliver loves to . . . . olive oil over cooked pasta.
9. A . . . . is useful when there is a power cut.
10. The referee blew the . . . . at the end of the match.

Section B – Wordsearch

How good a detective are you?

- find the following words
- put a ring round the word
- highlight it
- read the word

sizzle
rubble
rifle
rattle
feeble
muzzle
article
pebble
candle

e	c	a	n	d	l	e	t	l	y	e
x	l	s	a	y	d	t	r	r	m	r
r	o	n	s	e	m	m	u	e	o	m
u	w	a	f	f	e	e	b	l	e	i
s	n	r	r	y	g	b	s	r	s	
e	c	t	s	i	z	z	l	e	n	m
t	d	i	p	f	h	t	e	r	a	u
p	s	c	l	l	c	r	d	e	n	z
m	i	l	a	e	i	e	f	w	t	z
s	p	e	b	b	l	e	r	e	r	l
x	p	r	o	m	r	a	t	t	l	e

Section C

- read the passage
- copy it out
- write the passage to dictation
- highlight words with 'le' syllables

Old George hits the jackpot

Horrible Harry and Hateful Henry had an old uncle, who knocked on their door one day. To their surprise he shoved a bundle of cash into their hands. He won it, he said, playing bingo. He said that they could have a share of his winnings provided they spent it on a kitchen and invited him to stay for Christmas.

Hateful Henry said, 'Let me handle this; the kitchen is a mess. First we need new units with doors, cupboards with handles, a table that does not wobble and a kettle that can whistle. Let's get cracking on this now'.

Horrible Harry ran out of the door to a kitchen shop. On his way back he and fell off his bicycle and landed in a patch of thistles and nettles. He twisted his ankle. 'Serves you right,' muttered Hateful Henry as he picked up the bottle of wine his brother had dashed out to buy to celebrate. Then they drank a little toast to the new kitchen and Uncle George's winning streak.

ACTIVITY

Aim: To code, read and spell 'r'-combination syllables

The 'r'-combination syllables are made by adding 'r' to the vowels:

'ar'   'er'   'ir'   'or'   'ur'

These syllables can be at the beginning, middle or end of words:

ăr/rōw
ĕr/rŏr
mĭr/rŏr
ăn/gĕr
tēach/ĕr
ĭn/tĕr/ĕst

* look at the word
* highlight the vowel combined with 'r'
* code the vowels
* divide the word with a syllable-division line
* place the index fingers of each hand under each vowel on either side of the syllable-division line
* read the word

'ar'

archer	dollar
garden	arrest
arrow	artist
carpet	target
calendar	regular
smartly	startle
farmer	charter
harming	burglar
collar	altar
cellar	beggar

HANDY HINT

The vowel sounds can be long or short, depending on what letter comes after 'r'

HANDY HINT

The suffixes 'ar' 'er' 'or' say /ŏr/

Remember the mnemonic 'Mother Super<u>ior</u>, a super<u>ior</u> schol<u>ar</u> met a horrible murder<u>er</u> who got rid of h<u>er</u>'.

ACTIVITY

- look at the word
- highlight the vowel combined with 'r'
- code the vowels
- divide the word with a syllable-division line
- place the index fingers of each hand under each vowel on either side of the syllable-division line
- read the word

'or'

morning	organ
sword	orphan
actor	doctor
opportunity	performance
orchard	forget
mayor	born
decorate	motorway
absorb	storyboard
story	tractor
equator	storage

ACTIVITY

- look at the word
- highlight the vowel combined with 'r'
- code the vowels
- divide the word with a syllable-division line
- place the index fingers of each hand under each vowel on either side of the syllable-division line
- read the word

'ur'

urchin	urgent	occur	turkey
burst	hurt	absurd	hurdle
surprise	purpose	Saturday	turnip
curler	furnishings	disturb	murder
suburb	turban	survey	surname

Section A – Quiz No. 7

- re-read the target words on pp. 158 and 159
- read the clues
- fill in the missing words in the quiz
- read the whole sentence
- highlight the target word

1. Farmers use this vehicle: a . . . . to plough their land.
2. A line called the . . . . . . runs round the centre of the earth.
3. A bird traditionally eaten at Thanksgiving and on Christmas Day is a . . . .
4. The shipwrecked sailor sent an . . . . . message asking for rescue.
5. A . . . . gives the day and date, with important dates and events.
6. The . . . . traffic is very noisy.
7. A person who throws a polished stone when playing this Scottish game is a . . . .
8. A child whose parents are both dead is an . . . .
9. The policeman arrested the . . . . . with his bag of swag.
10. Many towns have a . . . . . who represents the town at civic events.

Section B – Wordsearch

How good a detective are you?

- find the following words
- put a ring round the word
- highlight it
- read the word

dollar
charter
erupt
kerb
irrigate
swerve
border
equator
tractor
born

e	i	s	n	d	l	e	t	l	y	e
q	l	s	b	o	r	n	r	r	m	r
u	o	n	s	l	m	m	u	e	o	m
a	w	a	f	l	e	e	b	l	e	s
t	n	c	h	a	r	t	e	r	r	w
o	c	t	i	r	r	i	g	a	t	e
r	k	i	p	f	h	t	e	r	a	r
p	e	r	u	p	t	r	d	e	n	v
t	r	a	c	t	o	r	f	w	t	e
s	b	o	r	d	e	r	r	e	r	l
x	p	r	o	m	w	a	t	u	l	o

Section C

- read the passage
- copy it out
- write the passage to dictation
- highlight words with 'r' combination syllables

Ned the inquisitive neighbour

Horrible Harry and Hateful Henry decided to decorate their house. They had an opportunity to do this one Saturday morning in June. Hateful Henry rolled up the carpet smartly and put it in the corner. He put the furnishings in the garden shed. As he moved the armchair, a girl driver stopped her car and had a long chat as she asked for directions to number thirty-four. Meanwhile, Horrible Harry was stuck up in the loft: a rung on the ladder had broken. 'Get me out of here,' he moaned pitifully, but in vain.

Eventually Hateful Henry went next door to borrow a ladder. Their neighbour Ned answered the door. When he was asked for the ladder, he said, 'I'd better come and have a look for myself and see what you two are up to now'. 'It's none of your business! Just lend me the ladder,' snapped Horrible Harry. 'Not unless I come and survey the job myself'. 'Don't be absurd, this is an emergency! Just let me have your ladder,' screamed Horrible Harry, stamping his foot in rage.

_____
_____
_____
_____
_____
_____
_____
_____
_____
_____
_____
_____
_____
_____
_____
_____
_____
_____
_____
_____
_____
_____
_____
_____

Prefixes

Aim: To code, read and spell words with prefixes

Keywords to review:

- A prefix is a letter or group of letters that go at the beginning of a word
- A prefix changes the meaning of a word
- Prefixes are (one or more) syllables and their letters always stay together

ā/pĕx   mĭs/tāke   aērō/plāne
o c   c vce   o vce

ACTIVITY

- look at the following prefixes
- code the vowels
- mark the type of syllable
- read the syllable

il	com	over	mini
non	maxi	inter	out
post	retro	di	quad
aero	hyper	un	omni
self	tele	ultra	mis

ACTIVITY

Aim: To divide, read and spell words with prefixes

- look at the word
- highlight the prefix
- code the vowel
- divide the word with a syllable-division line
- place the index fingers and middle fingers under each vowel
- read the word

distrust	cohabit	unisex	submarine
abandon	antenatal	hypermarket	photocopy
perfomance	recapture	television	explosive
internet	postscript	mistaken	pentagon
recycle	aerosol	withdraw	commandments

Further practice

ACTIVITY

- look at the word
- highlight the prefix
- code the vowel
- divide the word with a syllable-division line
- place the index fingers and middle fingers under each vowel
- read the word

convert	unafraid	interrupt	intake
comprehend	repaired	misinterpret	accelerate
forgetful	dislocate	resurface	devalue
premature	proposal	coeducate	postgraduate
experiment	important	discover	contraflow

HANDY HINT

The most commonly used prefixes are: 'com' 'con' 'de' 'dis' 'ex' 'im' 'in' 'pre' 'pro' 're' 'un'

Section A – Quiz No. 8

- re-read the target words on p. 163
- read the clues
- fill in the missing words in the quiz
- read the whole sentence
- highlight the target word

1. He . . . . the bicycle puncture.
2. The child was . . . . of the bull terrier, as they had one at home.
3. The traffic on the M6 had to use a . . . . system
4. They use . . . . to blast rock in quarries.
5. Many hairdressers have . . . . . . salons nowadays.
6. We went to watch the Rolling Stones in a live . . . . at Wembley Stadium.
7. My granny became very . . . . after she reached her 90s.
8. There was an . . . . meeting at the UN headquarters in New York.
9. The Beatles sang a famous song about a yellow . . . .
10. Moses was given the Ten . . . . on Mount Sinai.

Section B – Wordsearch

How good a detective are you?

- find the following words, some go horizontally some vertically
- put a ring round the word
- highlight it
- read the word

teacher
creative
aimless
devalue
recycle
feminine
aerosol
internet
forgetful
organic

i	i	s	o	r	g	a	n	i	c	e
n	l	s	b	o	r	i	r	r	m	f
t	o	c	s	l	m	m	u	e	o	o
e	w	r	f	l	e	l	b	l	f	r
r	t	e	a	c	h	e	r	r	e	g
n	c	a	i	r	r	s	g	a	m	e
e	k	t	p	f	h	s	e	r	i	t
t	e	i	u	p	t	r	d	e	n	f
d	e	v	a	l	u	e	f	w	i	u
s	r	e	c	y	c	l	e	e	n	l
a	e	r	o	s	o	l	z	u	e	o

Section C

- read the passage
- copy it out
- write the passage to dictation
- highlight words with prefixes

The consequences when motor did not give way to sail

Horrible Harry wanted to do a postgraduate course to accelerate his learning and to improve his promotion prospects. He looked up courses on the Internet that offered co-educational classes in naval history. He had to do an essay about World War One and the submerged wreckage of submarines.

He hired a cabin cruiser to look at abandoned wrecks in the English Channel. As he got near the site, he was so excited that he began to accelerate and did not notice that he was in a busy shipping lane. Suddenly he was in a collision with a sailing boat, which sank because the cabin cruiser had become uncontrollable.

There was wreckage everywhere. Luckily the sailor was picked up alive. Horrible Harry groaned and moaned and whispered, 'It was not my fault that the other boat just sailed into my path'. 'Don't be so stupid,' said Hateful Henry, 'Everyone knows that motor gives way to sail'.

_____

_____

_____

_____

_____

_____

_____

_____

_____

_____

_____

_____

_____

_____

_____

_____

_____

_____

_____

_____

_____

_____

_____

Suffixes

Aim: To code, read and spell words with suffixes

Keywords to review:

> A suffix is a letter or a group of letters that goes at the end of a word
>
> It changes the use of a word
>
> Suffixes are (one or more) syllables and their letters always stay together

look/s
look/ed
look/er
look/ing

ACTIVITY

- look at the following suffixes
- code the vowel
- mark the type of syllable
- read the syllable

en	er	ed	ist	ite	ful	ly
ive	less	ment	ing	ess	ate	ic
ble	age	ism	like	hood	ship	

HANDY HINT

**The most commonly used suffixes are: 'al' 'ble' 'ate' 'ant' 'ed' 'en' 'er' 'ent' 'ise' [or 'ize']
'ist' 'ing' 'ive' 'ition' 'ic' 'ful' 'ly' 'less' 'ment' 'ness' 'ous' 'y'**

ACTIVITY

Aim: To learn to divide, read and spell words with suffixes

- look at the word
- highlight the suffix
- code the vowel
- divide the word with a syllable-division line
- place the index fingers of both hands and a middle finger under each vowel
- read the word

homeward	scholarship	childhood	controllable
aimless	mended	mistress	running
decorate	redundant	education	gelignite
terrorist	advantageous	inventory	payable
wreckage	alcoholism	creative	forgetful

ACTIVITY

Further practice

- look at the word
- highlight the suffix/prefix
- code the vowel
- divide the word with a syllable-division line
- place the index fingers of both hands and a middle finger under each vowel
- read the word

misdirected	immortal	pendulum
transferable	thoughtless	inspector
anticlockwise	interrupt	competent
disestablished	freedom	importing
revolting	forgotten	homeopath
hyperactive	retainer	forementioned
misdirected	unconstitutional	disentangled
overtaken	annulment	decreasing
displeasure	unbreakable	instrument
vandalism	bombastic	pretender
tonsillitis	misdirected	dumbfound
fluorine	unseeing	rainbow
conductor	snowboarding	ashtray
unreliable	attendant	birthday
unforgotten	abdomen	groundsman
information	reinvented	chieftain
unfriendliness	comprehend	highland
subverting	nonpayment	tailwind
misinterpreted	vegetarianism	heartburn

Section A – Quiz No. 9

- re-read the target words on p. 167
- read the clues
- fill in the missing words in the quiz
- read the whole sentence on
- highlight the target word

1. A . . . . is the head of a tribe or clan.
2. A reaction to a shock or surprise can . . . . some people.
3. Cigarette butts should be left in an . . . .
4. If you walk in a circle from right to left, you are walking in an . . . . direction.
5. This seat is made of cast iron and is completely . . . .
6. Nelson Mandela was given his . . . . after years of imprisonment.
7. Trooping the Colour is held in June to celebrate the Queen's official . . . .
8. The . . . . is in charge of maintenance of a rugby pitch or cricket ground.
9. Bonny Prince Charlie was a . . . . to the throne.
10. After the kitten had tangled up the wool, I had to . . . . it.

Section B – Wordsearch

How good a detective are you?

- find the following words, some go horizontally some vertically
- put a ring round the word
- highlight it
- read the word

toiling
boyhood
fluorine
highland
moisture
tarpaulin
rainbow
beastly
roomy
sustainable

i	i	s	o	r	r	o	o	m	y	e
n	b	o	y	h	o	o	d	r	m	r
t	o	t	a	r	p	a	u	l	i	n
m	w	r	f	l	e	l	b	l	t	s
o	b	e	a	s	t	l	y	r	o	w
i	c	a	i	r	r	s	g	a	i	e
s	u	s	t	a	i	n	a	b	l	e
t	e	i	u	p	t	r	d	e	i	v
u	e	v	h	i	g	h	l	a	n	d
r	a	i	n	b	o	w	e	e	g	l
e	e	f	l	u	o	r	i	n	e	o

Section C

- read the passage
- copy it out
- write the passage to dictation
- highlight words with suffixes

The garden shed mystery

Hateful Henry kept poultry in a shed near some woodland at the bottom of their garden. The hens and chickens had freedom to roam. The only complaint they had was from their neighbour Nosy Ned about the cockerel crowing at six in the morning. One day they saw a suspicious chap on a nearby footpath. What was he up to?

Next day, Horrible Harry came to let the hens out. He was dumbfounded when the shed was empty. He ran back to the house yelling, 'You silly ass, you forgot to shut the door of the shed!'

'Let me straighten this out with you straight away,' declared Hateful Henry, 'I am innocent. I locked the birds up at ten o'clock last night', he proclaimed in a loud voice, 'I shall launch a campaign in the newspaper to close the footpath to keep prowlers away from our garden shed'. Nosy Ned had gone to bed and had not seen a thing. 'Much use he is', muttered the twins.

ACTIVITY

How much have you remembered?

Attainment test of a medley of syllables

- look at the word
- highlight the suffix
- code the vowel
- divide the word with a syllable-division line
- place the index fingers of both hands and a middle finger under each vowel
- read the word

locomotive	epidemic	indignant
congratulate	sarcastic	sextuplet
cosmetic	indignant	expectant
begonia	ambulance	exhibition
employee	peninsula	inhabit
bacteria	annul	cosmetic
alcoholic	accommodate	instrument
laboratory	propeller	competent
correspondent	governor	arrogant
enigma	refrigerator	interrupt

ACTIVITY

How much have you remembered?

Attainment test of a medley of syllables

- look at the word
- highlight the suffix/prefix
- code the vowel
- divide the word with a syllable-division line
- place the index fingers of both hands and a middle finger under each vowel
- read the word

pelmet	terrapin	misdirected
lady	kennel	rifle
copper	curriculum	moody
symbol	data	trainer
oxygen	appendix	confusion
emperor	supermarket	octopus
opportunity	promotion	interesting
zigzag	screwdriver	inhabited
thimble	interrupted	canvas
animal	stringing	remember
kindergarten	demarcation	kilogram

CONTINUED

microcomputer   freeholder   ineradicable

philosopher   romantic   momentary

reluctant   situation   parapet

superintendent   protagonist   circumference

trapezium   residual   combustion

artichoke   settlement

There are 2 marks for each correct answer

The optimum score is 100

Score

100	Excellent
99–80	Very Good
79–70	Good
69–60	Not Bad
59 or Less	Keep Trying

ACTIVITY

The Super Sleuth's Syllable Challenge

- highlight the vowels
- mark the blends, digraphs, diphthongs, suffixes and prefixes
- code the vowels
- read the word

There are 12 syllables in this word:

a n t i d i s e s t a b l i s h m e n t a r i a n i s m

Personal Score

There are 14 syllables in this word:

s u p e r c a l i f r a g i l i s t i c e x p i a l i d o c i o u s

Personal Score

Quiz answers

Quiz No. 1

1. Channel
2. shipment
3. prophet
4. ethnic
5. anthem
6. Orchid
7. shamrock
8. hatchet
9. Marshal
10. pamphlet

Quiz No. 2

1. inhabit
2. Atlantic
3. gymnastics
4. September
5. consultant
6. immortal
7. Forgotten
8. mistress
9. sarcastic
10. commandant

Quiz No. 3

1. parasol
2. polo
3. dodo
4. tango
5. veto
6. acrobat
7. arrogant
8. daffodil
9. extrovert
10. pendulum

Quiz No. 4

1. textile
2. capsize
3. capsule
4. retire
5. exile
6. baptise
7. empire
8. produce
9. escape
10. pancake

Quiz No. 5

1. daughters
2. childhood
3. straighten
4. complaint
5. thousand
6. laundry
7. fountain
8. loans
9. prowler
10. Spain

Quiz No. 6

1. scribble
2. poodle
3. castle
4. treacle
5. apple
6. bubble
7. maple
8. drizzle
9. candle
10. whistle

Quiz No. 7

1. tractor
2. equator
3. turkey
4. urgent
5. calendar
6. motorway
7. curler
8. orphan
9. burglar
10. mayor

Quiz No. 8

1. repaired
2. unafraid
3. contraflow
4. explosive
5. unisex
6. performance
7. forgetful
8. important
9. submarine
10. commandments

Quiz No. 9

1. chieftain
2. dumbfound
3. ashtray
4. anticlockwise
5. unbreakable
6. freedom
7. birthday
8. groundsman
9. Pretender
10. disentangle

3 How to Manage Plurals Painlessly

The aims of this chapter

They are to learn and understand the principles and processes involved when reading, writing and spelling plurals. To teach and learn plurals, it is important to be aware that individual spellers learn in different ways. Recall and retention of spellings can be established by using different strategies and a variety of tactics, depending on preferred learning style. Multi-sensory teaching of spelling has been found to be the most effective means of teaching spelling for all learners – including those with special educational needs – because all the senses are used simultaneously, thus utilising all the pathways to the brain as well as activating different areas. Target words have been provided with illustrations 'to establish a store of familiar words that are recognised immediately on sight and linked to their meanings' which the Rose Review points out as helpful for readers and spellers.

Plurals can be a challenge to learn as well as a persisting cause of difficulty and confusion for many spellers. They cause difficulties for those with poor visual memory, such as when having to remember how to spell the plural of try: is it trys, tries or tris?

The speller has to remember to use plural 's' and not confuse it with apostrophe 's'. Dyslexic spellers with sequencing problems and directionality difficulties often face a further challenge when trying to remember whether the apostrophe goes before the 's' or after the 's' when using a plural noun in the possessive form: is it the boys' classroom or the boy's classroom? Those with good visual memory can be encouraged to look at the picture on the page as well as the keyword associated with it. They can take a snapshot of these and retain them in their mind's eye. Attention needs to be drawn to the distinguishing feature, such as the change of a letter or letters: leaf/leaves. These can then be highlighted in colour. Knowing about the origin of words can be helpful as a memory device for some learners – for instance, gateau/gateaux is borrowed from French. The inclusion of a picture of musicians and musical instruments may help to memorise the rule that many words associated with music ending in 'o' add only 's' in the plural – piano/pianos – and it may act as a crutch for those who are good visualisers.

Those with good phonological and good auditory skills can utilise these skills by using the 'spelling pronunciation' of words such as kiss/kiss/es. It can be used to put emphasis on the tricky elements such as stress on the second syllable, which is helpful to differentiate between /s/ and the /z/ sound at the end of words. Silent letters or letters that elide can be 'pronounced' to emphasise their spelling woman/women. Those with good auditory skills will be helped to learn the rule and memorise it by saying it when applying it in sentences. Good visualisers and those with good auditory memory will find mnemonics useful, for example 'a goose is a goose but two are called geese, yet the plural of mouse is mice' – with, say, an illustration of a gaggle of geese and a nest of mice as a useful memory-jogger.

Differentiated activities

Section A

The learner:

- reads the sentence and the target words
- chooses the correct word
- completes the sentence

The objective is to learn, understand and discriminate visually between the spelling of the words and to choose the correct plural spelling by applying the rule. There is evidence that spellers' recall of words is improved when there is a meaningful connection between sentences and words.

Section B

The objective is to be able to use the plural words in context in sentences and when doing independent writing.

The learner:

- uses the target word in a sentence
- underlines or highlights the plural
- uses the proof-reading C-O-P-S

Section C

This utilises auditory sequential memory including short-term and working memory skills as well as visual memory for the spelling patterns.

Teacher and learner:

- read the passage through to practise seeing and hearing the plurals used in context

The learner:

- re-reads it sentence by sentence while copying out the passage
- underlines the plurals
- re-reads the passage using the proof-reading C-O-P-S
- uses the passage for dictation

Dictation can also be used by an individual without the help of a teacher/learning partner/parent, as follows.

The learner:

- reads the passage on to a cassette tape recorder or a minidisk recorder with a playback facility
- plays it back using headphones to listen to it sentence-by-sentence
- re-reads what he has written, using the proof-reading C-O-P-S and checking with the original passage.

These three sections use different learning strategies, a variety of tactics and different skills to teach, rehearse and reinforce plurals of nouns. They represent differentiated levels of difficulty to match different spelling abilities. Some individuals will be able to tackle all three activities during the 20 minutes of The Literacy Hour used 'for group or independent work'; others may work on just section A or B. The rule can be revised during the plenary session. Pupils can be asked to identify their 'best' strategy for remembering. Further examples can be noted during shared and guided text activities.

The sections can also be used for one-to-one learning and teaching. An individual may do one sentence each day from the three exercises, thus reinforcing the spelling of the plurals on a daily basis for five consecutive days to maximise learning. Constant repetition and repeated exposure – including the use of multi-sensory means – will help to develop mastery and automatic recall of the correct plural in independent writing.

How you can use these activities

Teach the following concepts and keywords; illustrate them with further examples generated in discussion. Pluralisation applies to nouns – cat/cats, dog/dogs – and pronouns – mine/ours, his/theirs. It also applies to verbs – She opens the door, They open the door. The text deals with plurals of nouns.

1. Singular means: a cat, the dog.
2. Plural means two or more: three cats, four dogs.
3. Establish that apostrophe 's' does not indicate a plural. Apostrophe 's' indicates ownership or possession – belonging:

   the horse's tail
   the horses' tails

4. Revise keywords such as vowel and consonant
5. Always teach and learn the regular rule first.
6. Tackle the Rather Rude Rule-Breakers separately.
7. Teach the rules in a cumulative and structured way, one at a time, step-by-step, week-by-week, and then use them in context during written activities.
8. Revise and rehearse the rules regularly, noting examples during the 'shared reading' activities during the Literacy Hour.
9. File these new examples in a personal 'Spellofax'.

The simultaneous use of seeing, saying, listening and writing applies multi-sensory learning strategies. This is the most effective method for learning and remembering spelling. Words are best learned and remembered when used in context, which is why sentence work is so important – rather than trying to learn spellings solely by memorising lists of words. Critics of multi-sensory teaching methods frequently derided the 'drill and skill' methods used and accused teachers of inducing 'death by workbook'. The criticism was valid when learners were given worksheets and were just asked to fill in or copy out missing words on the page. The current text includes explanation and multi-sensory strategies for learning.

The following are guidelines for learners when using a multi-sensory approach to learn a spelling rule.

- look at the rule and read it – take a 'snapshot' of the illustrations and keyword examples
- say the rule while looking at the words
- cover it and try to memorise the words – try to visualise the illustration in your 'mind's eye'

The odd squad of plurals

The following poem can be read aloud and discussed. Computer printouts can be given, to be retained in a personal Spellofax for easy reference and for a light-hearted revision of the pitfalls associated with plurals. A coloured pen can be used to highlight the plurals. It can also be used to signpost the ten major categories of plural nouns.

The odd squad of plurals

We'll begin with a box, and the plural is **boxes**.

But the plural of ox should be **oxen**, not *oxes*.

Then one fowl is a goose, but two are called **geese**.

Yet the plural of moose should never be *meese*.

You may find a lone mouse or a nest full of **mice**.

Yet the plural of house is **houses** not *hice*.

If the plural of man is always called **men**,

Why shouldn't the plural of pan be called *pen*?

If I spoke of my foot and show you my **feet**,

And I give you a boot, would a pair be called *beet*?

If one is a tooth and a whole set are **teeth**,

Why shouldn't the plural of booth be *beeth*?

Then one may be that, and three would be **those**,

Yet hat in the plural would never be *hose*.

And the plural of cat is **cats**, not *cose*.

We speak of a brother and also **brethren**.

But though we may say mother, we never say *methren*.

Then the masculine pronouns are, he, his and him.

But imagine the feminine, she, *shis* and *shim*.

So English, I fancy you will agree,

Is the craziest language you ever did see.

Rule One for plurals of nouns

The most common way to make a noun plural is to *add* 's'

- look at the rule
- look at the pictures, then read the words aloud
- say the rule, cover it, say it again
- read the target words

| friends | teachers | pens |

's'

pen	pens	friend	friends
car	cars	teacher	teachers
girl	girls	school	schools
paw	paws	egg	eggs
bell	bells	mug	mugs

Section A

- read the sentence
- choose the correct word
- complete the sentence

1. We needed black, red and blue	pencill/pencils
2. Most . . . . need food and water.	pets/petts
3. . . . . make nests in spring.	birdz/birds
4. Fish and . . . . go well together.	chipps/chips
5. The Harry Potter . . . . are a good read.	books/boks
6. My friend has two black	cat's/cats
7. Bacon and . . . . were on the menu.	eggs/egss
8. The pub had lots of . . . . of flowers.	tubes/tubs
9. Golf . . . . get lost in long grass.	balls/bals
10. Cakes and . . . . always sell well at the school fete.	bunz/buns

Section B

- use each word in a sentence
- highlight the plural
- use the proof-reading C-O-P-S

1. televisions_____

2. toys _____

3. months_____

4. computers _____

5. programmes_____

6. games_____

7. films _____

8. plays_____

9. ovens _____

10. kettles_____

Section C

- read the passage
- copy it out
- underline the plurals
- write the passage to dictation

Shopping for a camping holiday

Hateful Henry and Horrible Harry made a long list of what they needed to pack in their rucksacks to take camping. Hateful Henry said, 'I will get the food, including beans, teabags, eggs, drinks, bacon, tins of fruit and lots of biscuits and crisps'. Horrible Harry went to the chemist and bought films, aspirins and sticking plasters.

They checked what they had bought when they got home. Horrible Harry went into a sulk when he found that the cheese and onion crisps were missing. Hateful Henry moaned when he saw that the films were black and white, and not colour.

Rule Two for plurals of nouns

Nouns ending in 's', 'x', 'z', 'ch' or 'sh' *add* 'es' in the plural

- look at the rule
- look at the pictures, then read the words aloud
- say the rule, cover it, say it again
- read the target words

| **boxes** | **quizzes** | **buses** |

| **coaches** | **crashes** |

's'		**'x'**		**'z'**	
bus	buses	box	boxes	topaz	topazes
glass	glasses	fox	foxes	waltz	waltzes
kiss	kisses	mix	mixes	buzz	buzzes
plus	pluses	index	indexes	fez	fezzes
gas	gases	tax	taxes	quiz	quizzes

- Notice that 'fez' and 'quiz' have double-z in the plural, but 'topaz' does not

'ch'		**'sh'**	
branch	branches	bush	bushes
coach	coaches	crash	crashes
church	churches	dish	dishes
stitch	stitches	wish	wishes
witch	witches	thrush	thrushes

Rule Breaker

If the noun ends in 'ch' but says /k/, just add 's':

> **monarch   monarchs   stomach   stomachs**

Section A

- read the sentence
- choose the correct word
- complete the sentence

1. The teacher/learning partner bought two . . . . , one for the classroom, one for the library.   atlasses/atlases

2. The children got on the . . . . after the rugby match.   coachs/coaches

3. Tom was given two . . . . for his homework today.   pluses/plus's

4. The . . . . have tall spires.   churches/church

5. Get me a box of . . . .   matchs/matches

6. There is a parable about loaves and . . . . in the gospel.   fish/fishes

7. The cross-country riders jumped . . . . and hedges.   ditchs/ditches

8. The player had to have ten . . . . in his leg.   stitchse/stitches

9. The . . . . in the rowing boat are usually very light in weight.   coxs/coxes

10. Pub . . . . have become very popular.   quizzs/quizzes

Section B

- use each word in a sentence
- highlight the plural
- use the proof-reading C-O-P-S

1. coaches _____

2. rhinoceroses_____

3. arches_____

4. kisses _____

5. stitches_____

6. bushes _____

7. mixes _____

8. indexes_____

9. dashes _____

10. crashes_____

Section C

- read the passage
- copy it out
- underline the plurals
- write the passage to dictation

The football match

Hateful Henry is a Manchester United fan and Horrible Harry supports Arsenal. All season they had gone to the away matches on coaches and local buses, even taking a day's holiday. On the way to the Cup Final at Cardiff two of the Manchester United coaches were involved in crashes in fog on the motorway. Supporters stopped and gave the injured glasses of water and lifts to the match.

   Some fans were not so lucky and had to be taken to hospital to have stitches for their cuts and bruises. 'All my wishes of seeing my team win have been dashed by this mess,' cried Hateful Henry as he watched the match from his hospital bed. He felt more ill when he saw Horrible Harry grinning from one of the sponsors' boxes, which was lent to injured fans.

Rule Three for plurals of nouns

Nouns ending in 'f' *change* **'f' to 'v' and** *add* **'es' in the plural**

Nouns ending in 'fe' *change* **'f' to 'v' and** *add* **'s' in the plural**

- look at the rule
- look at the pictures, then read the words aloud
- say the rule, cover it, say it again
- read the target words

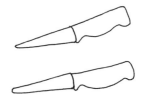

loaves　　　　　　**halves**　　　　　　**knives**

'f'		**'fe'**	
elf	elves	knife	knives
half	halves	life	lives
loaf	loaves	wife	wives
shelf	shelves		
thief	thieves		

Section A

- read the sentence
- choose the correct word
- complete the sentence

1. Cut the cake into two . . . .   halves/halfes

2. Jim must put the library books back on the . . . .   shelfs/shelves

3. The farmer had lots of . . . . and lambs in the fields in spring.   calfs/calves

4. Rich men's . . . . have time for long lunches.   wives/wifes

5. All good cooks need a set of sharp . . . . in the kitchen.   knifes/knives

6. 'The . . . . and the shoemaker' is a popular fairy tale.   elfs/elves

7. There are so many of us that we will need two . . . . of bread.   loafs/loaves

8. They say a cat has nine . . . .   lifes/lives

9. The top . . . . in the cupboard are too high to reach.   shelfs/shelves

10. Those . . . . have taken my purse.   thievs/thieves

Section B

Use each word in a sentence

1. loaves _____

2. halves _____

3. stoves _____

4. leaves _____

5. thieves _____

6. groves _____

7. wolves _____

8. elves _____

9. lives _____

10. sheaves _____

The Rather Rude Rule-Breakers

Some nouns ending in '**f**' just *add* '**s**' in the plural

- look at the rule
- look at the pictures, then read the words aloud
- say the rule, cover it, say it again
- read the target words

chefs   **cliffs**

cuffs   **roofs**

belief	beliefs	handkerchief	handkerchiefs
chef	chefs	proof	proofs
chief	chiefs	puff	puffs
cliff	cliffs	relief	reliefs
cuff	cuffs	reef	reefs
gulf	gulfs	roof	roofs

Section A

- read the sentence
- choose the correct word
- complete the sentence

1. The White . . . . of Dover are famous.   cliffes/cliffs

2. He spilled wine on the . . . . of his shirt.   cuffes/cuffs

3. The army and navy . . . . of staff had a meeting.   chiefs/chieves

4. The tiles fell off the . . . . in the gale.   roofs/rooves

5. . . . . must always wash their hands before they cook.   cheves/chefs

6. I went to collect the . . . . of the wedding invitations.   proves/proofs

7. The ships with cargoes of timber were tied up at the . . . .   wharfes/wharfs

8. Some followers are prepared to suffer for their . . . .   believes/beliefs

9. Master . . . . such as Jamie Oliver often write recipe books.   cheves/chefs

10. The horses' . . . . left prints all over the lawn.   hoofse/hooves

Section B

Use each word in a sentence

1. beliefs_____

2. chiefs _____

3. cuffs _____

4. puffs_____

5. roofs _____

6. proofs _____

7. cliffs _____

8. handkerchiefs_____

9. chefs _____

10. reefs_____

The Impossibly Rude Rule-Breakers

Some nouns ending in 'f' cannot make their minds up. Sometimes they change 'f' to 'v' and add 'es' but other times they just add 's' in the plural

	've'	's'
dwarf	dwarves	dwarfs
hoof	hooves	hoofs
scarf	scarves	scarfs
wharf	wharves	wharfs

- Write out each sentence, with the word in brackets in the plural

1. The Indian (chief) had a pow-wow.
2. The robbers ran across the (roof) of the houses.
3. Snow White met seven (dwarf) who became her friends.
4. There are very high (cliff) in Cornwall.
5. The restaurant has two excellent (chef).
6. The horse kicked me with its (hoof).
7. The little girl lost her (handkerchief).
8. The boat sailed close to the coral (reef).
9. Sophie has a lot of silk (scarf).
10. The leaking oil tanker polluted the sea around the (wharf).

_____
_____
_____
_____
_____
_____
_____
_____
_____
_____
_____
_____
_____
_____
_____
_____
_____
_____
_____
_____

Section C

- read the passage
- copy it out
- underline the plurals
- write the passage to dictation

Holiday nightmare

Hateful Henry and Horrible Harry had dreamed all their lives about a trip to the Canadian Rockies. When they arrived there, they went tracking in the woods. They parked their camper van on top of the cliffs overlooking a gorge with lots of dense leaves and branches. They had a picnic in the shade and fell asleep after lunch. Horrible Harry woke with a start when he heard strange noises. Two brown bears were eating the remains of both halves of their half-eaten chicken sandwiches.

They grabbed their hunting knives and ran for their lives to their camper van. They were in deep shock when they discovered that thieves had stolen their cash and mobile phone. 'It's all your fault,' wailed Horrible Harry, 'roofs on camper vans should be locked'. They both fell asleep. Hateful Henry woke up in the middle of the night yelling, 'We are being chased by a pack of wolves'. He looked out of the window and saw the brown bears in the moonlight. 'What a nightmare trip,' they sighed.

_____
_____
_____
_____
_____
_____
_____
_____
_____
_____
_____
_____
_____
_____
_____
_____
_____
_____
_____
_____

Rule Four of plurals of nouns

Nouns ending in 'y' *change* 'y' to 'i' and *add* 'es' in the plural

- look at the rule
- look at the pictures, then read the words aloud
- say the rule, cover it, say it again
- read the target words

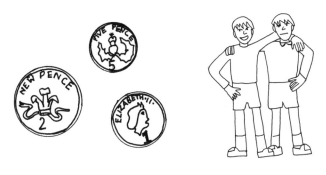

pennies	**allies**

'y'

ally	allies	diary	diaries
baby	babies	fly	flies
city	cities	penny	pennies
copy	copies	story	stories
daisy	daisies	try	tries

Section A

- read the sentence
- choose the correct word
- complete the sentence

1. The little girl picked lots of . . . . in the meadow.   daisys/daisies

2. He painted watercolour pictures of . . . . , birds and bees.   butterflies/butterflys

3. Ian made six . . . . of the form, in case he made a mistake.   copys/copies

4. Do you believe in . . . . and ghosts?   fairys/fairies

5. Our dog had a litter of six . . . . – four dogs and two bitches.   puppes/puppies

6. My granny used to say "Look after the . . . . and the pounds will look after themselves".   pennys/pennies

7. Alan Clarke's . . . . were a record of the Thatcher government.   diaries/daires

8. I love reading . . . . about real-life adventures.   storyes/stories

9. Towns that have a cathedral are called . . . .   citys/cities

10. Jonny Wilkinson scored many goals and . . . . for England's rugby team.   trys/tries

Section B

- use each of the following words in sentences
- highlight the plural
- use the proof-reading C-O-P-S

1. stories _____

2. hobbies _____

3. strawberries _____

4. tries _____

5. diaries _____

6. armies _____

7. fairies _____

8. bodies _____

9. cities _____

10. parties _____

The Rather Rude Rule-Breakers

If there is a vowel before the 'y' just *add* 's'

- look at the rule
- look at the pictures, then read the words aloud
- say the rule, cover it, say it again
- read the target words

boys   **donkeys**

abbey	abbeys	holiday	holidays
boy	boys	jersey	jerseys
chimney	chimneys	trolley	trolleys
donkey	donkeys	turkey	turkeys
guy	guys	valley	valleys

Section A

- read the sentence
- choose the correct word
- complete the sentence

1. We filled up our . . . . at the supermarket   trolleys/trollies
2. In the Welsh . . . . they have many male voice choirs.   vallies/valleys
3. Hampton Court Palace has many . . . .   chimneys/chimnies
4. The . . . . parked their caravans in the lay-by.   gypsies/gypseys
5. The leading race . . . . are Frankie Dettori on the flat and Tony
   McCoy over jumps.   jockies/jockeys
6. The coast guards put down . . . . for the swimmers' safety.   buoys/buoyies
7. There are no . . . . on Monkey Island on the Thames.   monkeys/monkies
8. . . . . *and Dolls* was a very popular musical.   *Guies/Guys*
9. . . . . are also called playthings.   Toys/Toyes
10. 'Georgie Porgie, pudding and pie, kissed the girls and made them cry.
    All the . . . . ran off to play'.   boyes/boys

Section B

- use each of the following words in sentences
- highlight the plural
- use the proof-reading C-O-P-S

1. keys _____

2. holidays _____

3. guys _____

4. turkeys _____

5. jerseys _____

6. trolleys _____

7. toys _____

8. donkeys _____

9. boys _____

10. chimneys _____

Section C

- read the passage
- copy it out
- underline the plurals
- write the passage to dictation.

Christmas holidays

Hateful Henry and Horrible Harry were invited to their cousins' farm in Yorkshire for the Christmas holidays. They both preferred the country to cities at this time of the year. They took some extra days off and helped with the preparations. They went out to look for holly with lots of red berries. They helped decorate the tree. At lunchtime they had a couple of bottles of red wine.

    Later on, a row broke out when their cousin Guy found out that someone had left the farm gates open. Two donkeys and three ponies had escaped on to the main road. The police came round with copies of the summons. Hateful Henry said, 'You country boys think we city boys are to blame'. 'You are all wrong,' said Horrible Harry, 'Look what I have just found'. He pulled out a black balaclava that he had just found. 'The owner must have come to steal the turkeys in the barn. Let's all be happy and sing 'I'm dreaming of a white Christmas'.

Rule Five for plurals of nouns ending in 'o'

Nouns ending in 'o' some *add* 's' in the plural, others *add* 'es'

HANDY HINT

Many words associated with music just add 's' in the plural

- look at the rule
- look at the pictures, then read the words aloud
- say the rule, cover it, say it again
- read the target words

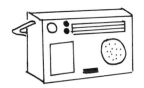

photos   **radios**

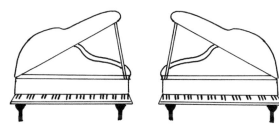

pianos

's'

cello	cellos	radio	radios
disco	discos	solo	solos
kilo	kilos	soprano	sopranos
patio	patios	stereo	stereos
photo	photos	stiletto	stilettos
piano	pianos	zoo	zoos

Section A

- read the sentence
- choose the correct word
- complete the sentence

1. I have lots of . . . . in my album to remind me of my holidays. photoes/photos

2. The choir has many excellent . . . . with wonderful voices. sopranoes/sopranos

3. . . . . have heels that damage polished floors. stilettos/stilettoes

4. Many children now have their own . . . . radios/radioes

5. I need two . . . . of fresh mixed vegetables for the soup. kiloes/kilos

6. Some . . . . help to preserve endangered animals with their breeding programmes. zoos/zosz

7. . . . . provide great entertainment and are popular with young people. diskos/discos

8. Last Christmas personal . . . . were top of many teenagers' list of presents. steros/stereos

9. Some . . . . live in igloos, which are built from blocks of ice. Escimos/Eskimos

10. Salads taste delicious when chopped . . . . are added. avocodoes/avocados

Section B

- use each of the following words in sentences
- highlight the plural
- use the proof-reading C-O-P-S

1. kilos _____

2. radios _____

3. stereos _____

4. solos _____

5. zoos _____

6. oboes _____

7. discos _____

8. altos _____

9. avocados _____

10. sopranos _____

The Rather Rude Rule-Breakers

Nouns ending in 'o' which *add* 'es' in the plural

- look at the rule
- look at the pictures, then read the words aloud
- say the rule, cover it, say it again
- read the target words

tomatoes

potatoes

'es'

buffalo	buffaloes
cargo	cargoes
dingo	dingoes
domino	dominoes
echo	echoes
hero	heroes
mango	mangoes
potato	potatoes
tomato	tomatoes
volcano	volcanoes

Section A

- read the sentence
- choose the correct word
- complete the sentence

1. There were loud . . . . in the caves.   echos/echoes
2. . . . . are given medals for bravery.   heroes/heros
3. Jacket . . . . are delicious with melted butter.   potatos/potatoes
4. Native Americans hunted . . . .   buffaloes/buffalos
5. . . . . are wild dogs from Australia.   dingos/dingoes
6. Mount Etna and Mount Vesuvius are both active . . . .   volcanoses/volcanoes
7. Mozzarella is a soft Italian cheese once made from the milk
   of . . . .   bufalos/buffaloes
8. 'Tom Thumb' is an easy-to-grow variety of . . . .   tometoes/tomatoes
9. Many people play . . . . in English pubs.   dominoes/domenos
10. . . . . are wild dogs found in Australia.   dingoes/dings

Section B

- use each word in a sentence
- highlight the plural
- use the proof-reading C-O-P-S

1. echoes _____

2. heroes _____

3. volcanoes _____

4. dingoes _____

5. potatoes_____

6. cargoes _____

7. buffaloes_____

8. dominoes_____

9. tomatoes _____

10. torpedoes _____

Section C

- read the passage
- copy it out
- underline the plurals
- write the passage to dictation

Bargains on the Internet

Hateful Henry was browsing on the Internet looking at stereos. Then his eye caught a page with oboes, cellos and pianos. He decided to buy two pianos, one for himself and the other for his brother. He didn't want to play solos.

Meanwhile Horrible Harry was listening to his radio. He heard that there was a farmers' market in town selling kilos of potatoes and tomatoes at half price. Horrible Harry burst into Hateful Henry's room yelling, 'I'm going into town! Come on! Put on your coat!' Hateful Henry replied, 'I can't. I'm half way through buying two pianos'. He wanted them both to play at discos. Then they would become pop stars and have photos taken of themselves. They would be the heroes of the world.

'If I were you I'd stick to buying stereos which even a fool like you can play,' said Horrible Harry as he dashed out of the door, like a herd of hungry buffaloes, dropping two yo-yos as he ran. Hateful Henry could still hear the echoes five minutes later.

The Impossibly Rude Rule-Breakers

Some nouns ending in 'o' cannot make their minds up. Sometimes they *add* 's' other times they *add* 'es'

- look at the rule
- look at the pictures, then read the words aloud
- say the rule, cover it, say it again
- read the target words

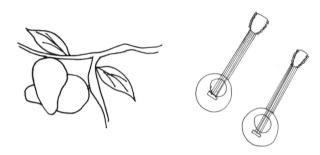

mangos/mangoes   **banjos/banjoes**

's'   'es'

banjo	banjos	banjoes
buffalo	buffalos	buffaloes
commando	commandos	commandoes
halo	halos	haloes
mango	mangos	mangoes
manifesto	manifestos	manifestoes
memento	mementos	mementoes
mosquito	mosquitos	mosquitoes
motto	mottos	mottoes
innuendo	innuendos	innuendoes
tornado	tornados	tornadoes
torpedo	torpedos	torpedoes
zero	zeros	zeroes

Section B

- use each word in a sentence
- highlight the plural
- use the proof-reading C-O-P-S

1. banjos_____

2. pianos_____

3. mementos _____

4. sopranos _____

5. innuendos_____

6. haloes_____

7. mangoes_____

8. mosquitos_____

9. buffaloes_____

10. zeroes_____

How much have you remembered?

- Write out these sentences, with the words in brackets in the plural

1. The ships had (cargo) of (tomato) and new (potato).
2. The (dingo) bit the baby, but we have (photo).
3. The (echo) from the organ rang out as the choir sang extracts from popular operas.
4. Greek (hero) often fell in love with beautiful goddesses wearing (halo).
5. I have photos as (memento) of the extinct (volcano) we visited in Mexico.
6. I took lots of (photo) at the wedding and have a recording of the (soprano) singing Ave Maria.
7. Many musicians have their own (studio) and can use (stereo) for their recordings.
8. The (tornado) caused terrible damage including flooding and a plague of (mosquito).
9. Elton John sings (solo), and many (radio) and (disco) play his music.
10. Some (zoo) have (kangaroo) and (koala), which were born in Australia.

Proof-read with the C-O-P-S

Section C

- read the passage
- copy it out
- underline the plurals
- write the passage to dictation

The Spanish fiesta on holiday

Hateful Henry and Horrible Harry were on holiday on the Costa del Sol. One day they went to a fiesta and took lots of photos of the people. There was music everywhere. Radios were blaring and music was coming from personal stereos. People were sitting on their patios, as well as drinking beer and eating tapas at the local bars.

Later they went to the market and bought two kilos of tomatoes, potatoes and eggs to make a Spanish omelette, and some mangoes for pudding, to eat in their apartment. 'Let's have an early night before our trip to Marbella tomorrow; those mosquitoes kept me awake half the night,' said Hateful Henry, yawning. 'No way!' said Horrible Harry. 'I'm off to try the bars and discos and to meet the locals; you are such a wimp.'

_____
_____
_____
_____
_____
_____
_____
_____
_____
_____
_____
_____
_____
_____
_____
_____
_____
_____
_____
_____
_____
_____
_____
_____
_____

Rule Six for plural nouns

Some nouns are *always plural*

* look at the rule
* look at the pictures, then read the words aloud
* say the rule, cover it, say it again
* read the target words

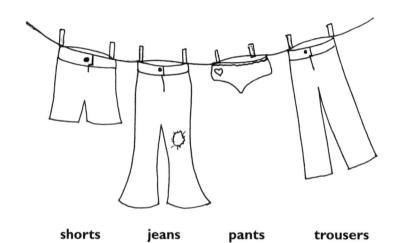

| shorts | jeans | pants | trousers |

arms (weapons)	crossroads	pants	suds
barracks	gallows	pincers	thanks
bellows	headquarters	remains	tongs
binoculars	jeans	scissors	trousers
braces	knickers	series	tweezers
clippers	means	shears	
corps	measles	shorts	

Section A

- read the sentence and the target words on page 204
- choose the correct word from those on page 204
- complete the sentence

1. I wear long . . . . in winter and shorts in summer.
2. Nail . . . . are very useful for cutting toenails.
3. The hairdresser always has sharp . . . .
4. . . . . is an old-fashioned word; most women now call them pants.
5. The farmer uses electric . . . . to shear his sheep.
6. The United Nations . . . . is in New York.
7. Jane has to wear . . . . on her teeth for twelve months.
8. Little Georgina cried when the soap . . . . got in her eyes.
9. . . . . can give you a bad rash and can harm your eyesight.
10. The bomb-blast victims' . . . . were put in coffins for burial.

Section B

- use each word in a sentence
- highlight the plural
- use the proof-reading C-O-P-S

1. barracks _____

2. tongs _____

3. gallows _____

4. crossroads _____

5. pants _____

6. arms _____

7. trousers _____

8. knickers _____

9. headquarters _____

10. shorts _____

Section C

- read the passage
- copy it out
- underline the plurals
- write the passage to dictation

The army camp experience

Hateful Henry and Horrible Harry had to go on a series of training weekends. They left their car at the army headquarters where the course was held. They had to sleep in an old barracks.

They had each packed shorts, but no long trousers as it was summertime. Everyone else was wearing jeans. They got stung by nettles and thistles as they tramped across the moor with their heavy rucksacks. 'I wish I had some shears with me,' whispered Horrible Harry as he trudged through briars and bushes. 'My hands are full of spots where I have been stung. I look as if I have measles,' wailed Hateful Henry. The team leader was watching through his binoculars. 'Hurry along, you lazy louts!' he bellowed.

Rule Seven for plural nouns

Some nouns are the *same* in the *singular* and *plural*

- look at the rule
- look at the pictures, then read the words aloud
- say the rule, cover it, say it again
- read the target words

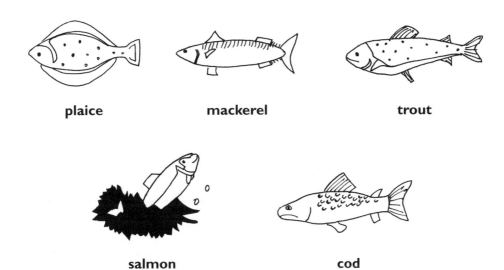

plaice   **mackerel**   **trout**

salmon   **cod**

HANDY HINT

Many words associated with fish are the same in singular and plural

aircraft	cod	plaice	swine
bison	deer	police	trout
cattle	grouse	salmon	vermin
cannon	hovercraft	sheep	whiting
chickenpox	mackerel	spacecraft	

Section A

- read the sentence and the target words on page 207
- choose the correct word from those on page 207
- complete the sentence

1. There is a big herd of . . . . in Richmond Park.

2. The navy sent a huge . . . . carrier to the Gulf.

3. Chip shops sell lots of battered . . . . and chips.

4. The Russian . . . . landed on the moon.

5. Michael loves smoked . . . . sandwiches and a glass of white wine for supper.

6. Baa, baa, black . . . . , have you any wool?

7. When we went to Calais by . . . . , I was sick all the way.

8. My favourite fish is a fillet of . . . . cooked in white wine.

9. Salmon . . . . belong to the salmon family.

10. . . . . is often used to make fish fingers.

Section B

- use each word in a sentence
- use the proof-reading C-O-P-S

1. hovercraft_____

2. swine _____

3. salmon _____

4. grouse _____

5. aircraft _____

6. smallpox_____

7. chickenpox_____

8. spacecraft_____

9. sheep _____

10. mackerel_____

Section C

- read the passage
- copy it out
- underline the plurals
- write the passage to dictation.

A holiday in the highlands of Scotland

Hateful Henry and Horrible Harry decided to go fishing in Scotland. Lots of people told them to stay at youth hostels. They both love Highland cattle and were delighted to see a herd on their first day. Deer and sheep roamed in the wild. Grouse and pheasant were on sale in the local butcher's shop.

They went fishing on the River Spey and caught two salmon and three brown trout. 'This is the life for me,' whistled Hateful Henry. When the local police patrol car went past he waved at the policeman who stopped and wound down the window and said, 'Have you got a fishing permit?' 'No! We don't,' they both said. 'I'll let you off this time,' said the policeman with a wink. 'Tomorrow go and fish in the bay and you will get mackerel, plaice and whiting.'

'Phew, that was a narrow escape.' 'It's all your fault,' muttered Horrible Harry, 'You should have read the leaflets the tourist board sent us; we were lucky to escape a fine.'

_____
_____
_____
_____
_____
_____
_____
_____
_____
_____
_____
_____
_____
_____
_____
_____
_____
_____
_____
_____
_____

Rule Eight for plurals of compound nouns

Some *compound nouns* (two or more words joined together to make one noun) add 's' to the *first word* in the plural; others add 's' to the *second word* in the plural

- look at the rule
- look at the pictures, then read the words aloud
- say the rule, cover it, say it again
- read the target words

passers-by

lookers-on

's' added to the **first** word

brother-in-law	brothers-in-law
chief-of-staff	chiefs-of-staff
commander-in-chief	commanders-in-chief
court-martial	courts-martial
father-in-law	fathers-in-law
hanger-on	hangers-on
looker-on	lookers-on
maid-of-honour	maids-of-honour
mother-in-law	mothers-in-law
passer-by	passers-by
sister-in-law	sisters-in-law

Section A

- read the sentence
- choose the correct word
- complete the sentence

1. It is a . . . . offence to be absent without leave in the army.

   court-martial/court-martials

2. The . . . . were terrified as the gunman escaped down the street.

   passers-by/passer-bys

3. The Queen had eight . . . . at her Coronation to carry her train.

   maids-of-honours/ maids of honour

4. Princess Anne once had two . . . . , Princess Diana and the Duchess of York.

   sisters-in-law/sister-in-laws

5. The politician was surrounded by many . . . . when he was campaigning.

   hangers-on/hanger-ons

6. The . . . . of the British Armed Forces can be from the navy, army or air force.

   commander-in-chiefs/ commanders-in-chief

7. . . . . can tell embarrassing tales about your husband when he was little.

   father-in-laws/ fathers-in-law

8. The police moved the . . . . from the scene of the accident.

   lookers-on/looker-ons

9. My . . . . were a great support when my husband was in hospital.

   brother-in-laws/ brothers-in-law

10. . . . . have a bad reputation for interfering in their families' lives.

    mothers-in-law/ mother-in-laws

Section B

- use each word in a sentence
- highlight the plural
- use the proof-reading C-O-P-S

1. passers-by _____

2. chiefs-of-staff _____

3. brothers-in-law_____

4. runners-up _____

5. mothers-in-law_____

6. courts-martial_____

Some compound nouns add 's' to the second word in the plural

- look at the rule
- look at the pictures, then read the words aloud
- say the rule, cover it, say it again
- read the target words

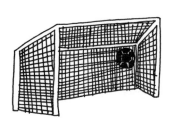

play-offs

's'

by-way	by-ways
by-law	by-laws
drive-in	drive-ins
lay-by	lay-bys
lord-lieutenant	lord-lieutenants
man-hour	man-hours
part-timer	part-timers
play-off	play-offs
spin-off	spin-offs
take-off	take-offs
tie-up	tie-ups
tip-off	tip-offs

Section A

- Read the sentence and the target words on page 212
- choose the correct word
- complete the sentence

1. The . . . . for the medals in the World Cup took place on Saturday   play-off/play-offs

2. The . . . . represent the Queen at civic events.   lord-lieutenants/ lords-lieutenant

3. The travellers knew all the highways and . . . . from their wanderings.   bye-ways/by-ways

4. In America many cinemas are . . . .   drive-inns/drive-ins

5. Chip vans often park in . . . .   lay-bys/lay-byes

6. Councils have . . . . to protect the public from nuisances and disorder.   bys-laws/by-laws

7. . . . . are playing an increasingly important role in many hospitals.   party-timers/ part-timers

8. This piece of art took a huge number of . . . . to sculpt.   mans-hours/man-hours

9. The prisoners staged many . . . . to protest at their overcrowded cells.   sit-ins/sitts-in

10. Tim Henman's sponsorship deal had many . . . . for him.   spins-off/spin-offs

Section B

- use each word in a sentence
- highlight the plural
- use the proof-reading C-O-P-S

1. drive-ins _____

2. lay-bys _____

3. man-hours _____

4. play-offs _____

5. tie-ups _____

6. spin-offs _____

7. sit-ins _____

8. part-timers _____

Section C

- read the passage
- copy it out
- underline the plurals
- write the passage to dictation

Spring Bank Holiday in Devon

Hateful Henry and Horrible Harry were invited by their brothers-in-law to spend the weekend in Devon. On Saturday the village show took place. Part-timers and a full-time secretary had organised it. There had been many man-hours of preparation for the big event. NATO chiefs-of-staff were meeting at a naval base in nearby Plymouth and came to see the show. Two of them even took part in the play-offs of the tug-o-war competition. Another refereed the play-offs of the six-a-side football competition.

Later, Hateful Henry whispered to Horrible Harry, 'I think the organiser, Major Smith, should be nominated for the Nobel Peace Prize for getting all these chaps to work together'. 'Don't be so silly: they all fight on the same side,' muttered his parents-in-law under their breath. Horrible Harry burst out laughing, watched by passers-by who were busy clearing up.

_____

_____

_____

_____

_____

_____

_____

_____

_____

_____

_____

_____

_____

_____

_____

_____

_____

_____

_____

_____

_____

Rule Nine for plurals of nouns

Old English words are words that have survived from Anglo-Saxon. They follow their _own rules._

- look at the rule
- look at the pictures, then read the words aloud
- say the rule, cover it, say it again
- read the target words

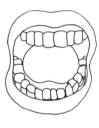

teeth

mice

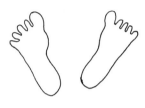

feet

child	children	man	men
die	dice	mouse	mice
foot	feet	ox	oxen
goose	geese	tooth	teeth
louse	lice	woman	women

Section A

- read the sentence and the target words on page 215
- choose the correct word
- complete the sentence

1. The . . . . lost their pencil cases.	childs/children
2. Dentists spend most of their time filling	tooths/teeth
3. Each term the school nurse checks the learners' hair for	lices/lice
4. Some people say that . . . . are as good as guard dogs.	geese/gooses
5. The . . . . all went to play bingo last night.	woman/women
6. . . . . and women's clothes are in different departments.	men's/men
7. Field . . . . often make nests in my garage.	mouses/mice
8. . . . . are used to plough the fields in some countries.	oxs/oxen
9. He had three . . . . in his pocket.	dise/dice
10. She put her . . . . up and had a good rest.	feet/foots

Section B

- use each word in a sentence
- highlight the plural
- use the proof-reading C-O-P-S

1. feet_____

2. women_____

3. children _____

4. teeth _____

5. mice_____

6. lice _____

7. oxen_____

8. dice _____

9. men _____

10. geese _____

The Rather Rude Rule-Breakers

Some Old English words can't make their minds up how they are spelt. They can be spelt *either way* in the plural.

- look at the rule
- look at the pictures, then read the words aloud
- say the rule, cover it, say it again
- read the target words

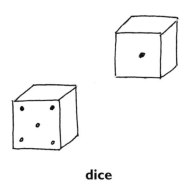

dice

brother	brothers	brethren
cloth	cloths	clothes
die	dies	dice
pea	peas	pease
penny	pennies	pence

Section A

- read the sentence
- choose the correct word
- complete the sentence

1. The Plymouth . . . . are a religious sect.   brothren/brethren

2. . . . . are very useful for mopping up spills.   clothse/cloths

3. Mushy . . . . and mash is a traditional English dish.   peaces/peas

4. There used to be twelve . . . . in a shilling and twenty shillings
   in a pound.   pennies/pennys

5. The . . . . have been thrown and will decide my fate.   dies/dice

Section B

- use each word in a sentence
- highlight the plural
- use the proof-reading C-O-P-S

1. pence _____

2. peas _____

3. brethren _____

4. pennies _____

5. brothers _____

Section C

- read the passage
- copy it out
- underline the plurals
- write the passage to dictation

Foreign holiday health hazards

Hateful Henry and Horrible Harry decided to take their cousins and their children on a holiday to Paris. They sent out an e-mail saying that men, women and children coming should bring warm clothes and sensible shoes for their feet. They went on the EuroStar train to Paris. The children played snakes and ladders on the journey. They had two boards and two dice to keep the children quiet.

At the hotel in the middle of the night, one of the children woke up screaming that there were mice in the room. Another little girl cried that there were lice on her pillow. Tariq woke up and was sick because he had eaten too many mussels and chips. The youngest boy kept yelling that his teeth were paining him because of his new brace.

Next morning Horrible Henry muttered behind his hand to Hateful Henry, 'What a bunch of moaning minnies!'

_____

_____

_____

_____

_____

_____

_____

_____

_____

_____

_____

_____

_____

_____

_____

_____

_____

_____

_____

_____

_____

_____

Rule Ten for plurals of words from other languages

Words borrowed from other languages usually form their plurals according to the rules of their own language; some, however, just add 's' or 'es'

Words derived from Latin

alga	algae	
alumnus	alumni	
antenna	antennae	antennas
appendix	appendices	appendixes
bacterium	bacteria	
cactus	cacti	cactuses
crocus	crocuses	
curriculum	curricula	
datum	data	
fungus	fungi	
gladiolus	gladioli	
gymnasium	gymnasia	
larva	larvae	
medium	media	
nebula	nebulae	
radius	radii	
referendum	referenda	referendums
stadium	stadia	stadiums
stoma	stomata	
stratum	strata	
terminus	termini	terminuses

(See also checklist of useful Latin root words on p. 347.)

Words derived from Greek

analysis	analyses
crisis	crises
criterion	criteria
hypothesis	hypotheses
oasis	oases
parenthesis	parentheses
phenomenon	phenomena
schema	schemata
synopsis	synopses
thesis	theses

(See also checklist of useful Greek root words on p. 348.)

Words borrowed from the French

However, plurals of many of these words in English are now often made by adding 's'

beau	beaux	beaus
bureau	bureaux	bureaus
chateau	chateaux	chateaus
gateau	gateaux	gateaus
plateau	plateaux	plateaus

Section A

- read the sentence
- choose the correct word
- complete the sentence

1. The antique . . . . were made from walnut.   bureaus/bureaux

2. We had to read . . . . of Shakespeare's plays – *Macbeth*, *Romeo and Juliet* and *Hamlet* – before seeing them on stage.   synopses/synopsis

3. We saw many giant . . . . in the desert in Arizona.   cactusses/cacti

4. The university . . . . had a silver jubilee reunion.   alumni/alumniuses

5. The . . . . at the end of the book had useful information about where to buy things.   appendices/appendixs

6. Gathering . . . . to use in cooking is a great pastime in the autumn in some European countries.   funguses/fungi

7. An eclipse of the sun is one of nature's great . . . .   phenomenon/phenomena

8. There were different types of . . . . to choose from at the party.   gatos/gateaux

9. My grandfather had a collection of over fifty different . . . .   cactus/cacti

10. This . . . . can give you a very nasty illness.   bacteria/bacterium

Section B

- use each word in a sentence
- highlight the plural
- use the proof-reading C-O-P-S

1. radii _____

2. terminals_____

3. cacti _____

4. curricula _____

5. theses_____

6. plateaux _____

7. bacteria _____

8. oases _____

9. stadiums _____

Section C

- read the passage
- copy it out
- underline the plurals
- write the passage to dictation

Pride before a fall

Hateful Henry and Horrible Harry went on a holiday on a cruise ship. There were lots of different entertainments. Their favourite was the quiz competition. They both made it to the semi-finals. Horrible Harry got to the final. 'I think I'm going to win the cruise's first prize tonight – I got an 'A' in French and was always top of my class in Latin,' he boasted.

He answered the following questions correctly:

1. Where do bacteria occur?
2. What dye and food seasoning is made from dried crocuses?
3. Can you name three fungi?
4. Can you name the two airport terminals for Paris?
5. Can you name three chateaux in the Loire valley in France?
6. Can you name three edible items found in oases?

The final question was 'What is the plural of medium?' Horrible Harry gave the wrong answer and lost the prize. He stormed off in a rage. 'What a fool you are! Everybody knows it's 'media', smirked Hateful Henry.

_____
_____
_____
_____
_____
_____
_____
_____
_____
_____
_____
_____
_____
_____
_____
_____
_____

Rather Rude Rule-Breakers

Some foreign words can't make their minds up and can be spelt *either way* in the plural

- look at the rule
- look at the pictures, then read the words aloud
- say the rule, cover it, say it again
- read the target words

fungi   **cacti**

appendix	appendices	appendixes
cactus	cacti	cactuses
fungus	fungi	funguses
formula	formulae	formulas
memorandum	memoranda	memorandums
syllabus	syllabi	syllabuses
terminus	termini	terminals

REVISION TESTS

Revision of Rules One and Two of plurals

- Copy out the sentences in the plural
- Use them for dictation

(If necessary change other words to make sense)

1. The (church) had a tall (spire) and a wonderful peal of (bell).

_____

_____

2. The (coach) collect some children from (school); others use (taxi).

_____

_____

3. The (bus) is always late because of traffic (jam).

_____

_____

4. The (box) of matches are empty, so run to the (shop) before they close.

_____

_____

5. The Beckhams have matching wrist (watch) and diamond (earring).

_____

_____

6. Fantastic Mr Fox and all the little (fox) chased the (hen).

_____

_____

7. The (car) had piles of (leaf) stuck to the windscreen.

_____

_____

8. I like to read a good (book) curled up under the (bush) in the garden.

_____

_____

9. The poisonous (gas) escaped and caused pollution for several days.

_____

_____

10. The (pen) is very messy: it has a crack in the barrel.

_____

_____

How well did you do?

There are 2 marks for each correct answer. The optimum score is 40.

Your score ☐

Excellent	40
Very Good	39–35
Not Bad	34–30
Keep Trying	29 or less

Revision of Rules Three and Four of plurals

There are 2 marks for each correct answer. The optimum score is 40.

- Copy out the sentences in the plural
- Use them for dictation

(If necessary change other words to make sense)

1. The (farmer) had a (donkey) for the children's rides.

_____

_____

2. The (jockey) often used to ride a (pony).

_____

_____

3. The (shelf) in the shop was full of new (toy) and computer games.

_____

_____

4. The (boy) helped push the supermarket (trolley) and load the car.

_____

_____

5. Hans Andersen's (story) about (fairy) do not always end happily.

_____

_____

6. The (lady) had a red (jersey) and a navy Guernsey sweater.

_____

_____

7. The (girl) lost the (key) to the flat and had to call the locksmith.

_____

_____

8. The (lady) had knitted cardigans with matching (cuff) and collars.

_____

_____

9. The (lorry) drove down the (valley) to collect the fruit harvest.

_____

_____

10. The (factory) had tall (chimney), which was a well known local landmark.

_____

_____

Your score ▢

Excellent	40
Very Good	39–35
Not Bad	34–30
Keep Trying	29 or less

Revision of Rule Five of plurals

There are 2 marks for each correct answer. The optimum score is 40.

- Copy out the sentences in the plural
- Use them for dictation

(If necessary change other words to make sense)

1. When we took (photo) of the bats in the caves, I could hear (echo).

    _____

    _____

2. The (soprano) all sang (solo) in the concert at the Royal Albert Hall.

    _____

    _____

3. Many (zoo) do not have (buffalo) or kangaroos.

    _____

    _____

4. (Eskimo) have (stereo) and television, and can receive the news in their Inuit language.

    _____

    _____

5. There were signs saying no admission to the (disco) for people wearing (stiletto).

    _____

    _____

6. Many (negro) became famous for their playing of banjoes, (piano) and cellos.

    _____

    _____

7. We used lots of (avocado) and (tomato) for the salad.

_____

_____

8. The ship's (cargo) had 50 (kilo) of illegal drugs hidden by smugglers.

_____

_____

9. We took lots of (photo) of the smouldering (volcano) in Alaska.

_____

_____

10. They kept (banjo) as (memento) of their visit to the jazz festival in New Orleans.

_____

_____

Your score ⬜

Excellent	40
Very Good	39–35
Not Bad	34–30
Keep Trying	29 or less

Revision of Rules Six and Seven of plurals

There are 2 marks for each correct answer. The optimum score is 40.

- Copy out and choose the correct word
- Use them for dictation

(If necessary change other words to make sense)

1. There was a bad outbreak in the (barrack/barracks) of (measle/measles) and (chickenpocks/chickenpox).

_____

_____

2. There were four (hovercrafts/hovercraft) tied up in harbour, which the coast guard could see with his (binoculars/binocular) from the (headquarter/headquarters).

_____

_____

_____

3. Armies had lots of (cannon/cannons) in the last century.

_____

_____

4. The mechanic had (pincer/pincers) as well as a spanner in his (trousers/trouser) pocket.

_____

_____

5. The old (barracks/barrack) had an ancient (gallow/gallows).

_____

_____

6. The nail (scissor/scissors) are in the bathroom beside that pile of (clothe/clothes) for washing.

_____

_____

7. The farmer's (swines/swine) had swine fever and his (cattle/cattles) had foot-and-mouth disease.

_____

_____

8. They had (grouses/grouse) on the menu as well as (trouts/trout) caught in the loch that morning.

_____

_____

9. NATO (aircrafts/aircraft) were on stand-by.

_____

_____

10. The children packed (short/shorts) and long (trouser/trousers) when they went climbing.

_____

_____

Your score ☐

Excellent	40
Very Good	39–35
Not Bad	34–30
Keep Trying	29 or less

Revision of Rules Eight and Nine of plurals

There are 2 marks for each correct answer. The optimum score is 40.

- Copy out and choose the correct word
- Use them for dictation

(If necessary change other words to make sense)

1. The two (brother-in-laws/brothers-in-law) went to one of the many (drive-in/drive-ins) cinemas in Boston when they were in America.

_____

_____

2. (Louse/lice) like nice clean hair, particularly (woman/women's) long hair.

_____

_____

3. A dead heat by the (runner-up/runners-up) caused the (childs/children's) egg-and-spoon race to be run again.

_____

_____

4. The pilots had to wait for (take-off/take-offs) on the runway because a flock of (geese/goose) had landed there.

_____

_____

5. Many (men-hour/man-hours) are spent cleaning our streets because (passers-by/passer-by) keep dropping litter.

_____

_____

6. The police were given a few (tip-off/tip-offs) about two gangs selling smuggled cigarettes in a (lay-by/lay-bys).

_____

_____

7. It was once fashionable to have gold fillings in (tooths/teeth).

_____

_____

8. The two (sisters-in-law/sister-in-laws) work as (part-time/part-timers).

_____

_____

9. Many games can be played with (dies/dice) by (men/mans) and (woman/women) of all ages.

_____

_____

10. Mothers say their (childs/children) should be seen but not heard when they visit their (fathers-in-law/father-in-laws).

_____

_____

Your score ☐

Excellent   40
Very Good   39–35
Not Bad   34–30
Keep Trying   29 or less

Revision of Rule Ten of plurals

There are 2 marks for each correct answer. The optimum score is 40.

- Copy out these sentences in the plural
- Use them for dictation

(If necessary change other words to make sense)

1. His (mother-in-law) has two step-(child).

    _____

    _____

2. They caught a (cod), using fishing nets.

    _____

    _____

3. The ship's (cargo) had (tomato) and (lettuce).

    _____

    _____

4. The (dwarf) left his (handkerchief) in the supermarket (trolley).

    _____

    _____

5. The farmer had an (ox) and a (man-servant).

    _____

    _____

6. The fox climbed on to the (roof) of the (house).

_____

_____

7. The car drove along the (cliff) and down into the (valley).

_____

_____

8. The fisherman on the trawler caught (plaice) and (whiting).

_____

_____

9. The boy went by bus to visit the (church) and (abbey) on the moor.

_____

_____

10. We had a dish of crisps and a (glass) of red wine.

_____

_____

Your score [   ]

Excellent   40
Very Good   39–35
Not Bad   34–30
Keep Trying   29 or less

Revision of all Ten Rules of plurals

There are 4 marks for each correct answer.

The optimum score is 100.

1. The (chef) made six Black Forest (gateau) and ten apple (pie) using his own (recipe).

_____

_____

2. NATO sends out many (memorandum) to different countries to deal with (crisis).

_____

_____

3. What are the (criterion) used to show that (hippopotamus) kill more people in Africa than lions or (rhinoceros) do?

_____

_____

4. There are four (terminal) at Heathrow Airport, each ready to deal with any terrorist (attack).

_____

_____

5. My aunt has several (cactus) in her kitchen beside pots of dried (crocus) petals.

_____

_____

6. We had to measure the (radius) of the circles with (compass) in many of the examination (syllabus).

_____

_____

7. Scientists use many (formula) in their work. All their (datum) are checked. Then they think of (hypothesis) to explain their results.

_____

_____

8. The gardener grew lots of (gladiolus) as well as (narcissus).

_____

_____

9. In one of the (appendix) of the travel book it gave the names of (oasis) where hotels overlook palm tree groves.

_____

_____

10. The students had to make lots of (synopsis) of their notes for revision, as well as (copy) of diagrams.

_____

_____

Excellent	100
Very Good	99–90
Not Bad	89–80
Keep Trying – you are doing well	79–70
If at first you don't succeed, try again!	69 or less

Total Score ☐

Dictation tests for all ten rules of plurals

The Ten Commandments of plurals – revision test

(by teacher/learning partner or self-recorded on tape)

A

The boys and girls come out to play. They like picnics and playing in the sun. Some play with toys and footballs; others sit and make chains with daisies. Often they bring bicycles and ride them on the footpaths through villages, down valleys and up the local hills.

B

The supermarket shelves were bulging with bargains according to the local newspapers. People rushed out to find these, which included cans of tomatoes and packets of cornflakes at half price. They also had special offers on boxes of matches and batteries for kitchen radios and bathroom scales. The batteries were fifty pence more than at the market. What tricks advertisers play! Don't believe all you read in the media.

C

The weekend sailors' boats sank in the storms. The coastguards called the local army barracks for help. Luckily the soldiers' families were also keen sailors. They had six helicopters on stand-by. The pilots searched for survivors. They found two families including two sisters with their brothers-in-law and twin boys with no lifejackets. They were lucky to survive in icy water.

D

The singers belong to different choirs. They have sopranos and altos. Some members also belong to various orchestras and play instruments such as guitars and pianos. There are even a few who play violins and cellos. The conductors organise many concerts and recitals. They have made many recordings, live as well as in recording studios.

Test, then rest on your laurels when you can manage plurals painlessly

The optimum score is 100. Deduct 2 marks for each error.

Dictation

1. The houses had flat roofs which the thieves used to escape across.
2. The team scored goals and lots of tries in the rugby final.
3. The miners' wives worried when the collieries were flooded.
4. The commandos wore black jerseys and masks during the raid.
5. The chiefs-of-staff met their allies' generals.
6. My mother's brother-in-law had a row with her over the beer stains on the carpet.
7. Our horses live in stables, the pigs live in sties, the donkeys in the fields, but the dog sleeps on our bed.
8. The chefs cooked salmon and trout for the wedding reception.
9. When the Queen opened the new factory, she had two ladies-in-waiting with her.
10. The bosses went on strike over their salaries.
11. We picked a kilo of raspberries and five kilos of potatoes.
12. There were two crashes at the crossroads last weekend.
13. Some charities give clockwork radios to African families.
14. Poppies are sold to raise money for those who died in wartime.
15. Egyptian mummies were buried in tombs with food and luxuries.
16. Missionaries often have to deal with diseases carried by mosquitoes.
17. The mongooses chased after the snakes while the lookers-on stood and shivered.
18. The passers-by helped the car accident victim.
19. For centuries convoys of ships carried slaves on their deck.
20. The cargo of wheat was infested with cockroaches.

How well did you do?

SCORE: GOLD 100–95
SILVER 94–80
BRONZE 79–70

4 How to Manage Homophones Happily

The aims of this chapter

They are to learn to read, write and spell homophones, which are words that sound the same but have a different meaning and a different spelling – such as to/two/too. Homophones can be a challenge to learn as well as a persisting cause of confusion for many spellers. They cause difficulties such as their/there/they're for those with poor visual memory. The speller has to remember the meaning of the word and then remember which spelling is which. Dyslexic spellers with sequencing problems often face a further difficulty when trying to remember the order of the letters – such as whether to use 'thier' or 'their'?

To teach and learn homophones it is also important to be aware that individual spellers learn in different ways. Successful memorisation and recall can be established by using different strategies and a variety of tactics, depending on preferred learning style.

The teacher/learning partner and learner look at the pictures on the page, or the teacher can put these on an overhead transparency (OHT) or an interactive white board. The meaning of the word and the examples of its use in sentences are discussed. Attention is drawn to distinguishing features such as a letter pattern for spelling or a word written within a word such as 'ear' in heard (but not herd). These can then be highlighted. This activity can be undertaken during whole-class teaching. The activity sheets A, B, C, can then be used for group or independent work.

There are various ways of remembering which homophone is which; they include grammatical, semantic and phonological cues. The NLS (1999) Spelling Bank suggests that 'many homophone choices are best taught as a grammatical issue', such as verbs using the past tense adding 'ed': fined/find. Others can be memorised when linked to the simple present tense of verbs: knows/nose. Other pairs of homophones can be remembered when attention is drawn and linked to the function of the word, such as the noun 'practice' and the verb 'practise'. Its/it's is best remembered when attention is drawn to the contraction it's for 'it is'. Discussion and working from the long form helps to make sense of examples such as 'the horse lost its (not 'it is') shoe'.

Knowing about the meanings of words such as ark/arc can be helpful as a memory device for some learners. The inclusion of a picture of Noah's ark and the arc of a rainbow will help to memorise the words and act as a crutch for those who are good visualisers.

Those with good phonological and good auditory skills can make use of the 'spelling pronunciation' of words such as des/ert and de/ssert, which are visually easily confusable. It can be used to put emphasis on the tricky elements such as the stress on the long vowel which is helpful to differentiate between v<u>a</u>cation/v<u>o</u>cation. Silent letters can be 'pronounced' to emphasis their spelling: <u>k</u> night/night. Good visualisers and those with good auditory memory will find mnemonics useful: for example, 'I will eat a p<u>ie</u>ce of p<u>ie</u>' with an illustration, to differentiate between piece/peace.

Differentiated activities

Section A

Words are best learned and remembered when used in context, which is why sentence work is so important.

The objective is to use a multi-sensory approach to:

- look at the word and take a mental snapshot of it
- say the word while looking at it and to listen to the sounds as it is spelt aloud
- cover the word and look at it in the mind's eye
- write the word using cursive writing
- check the spelling by comparing it with the original spelling

Section B

The objective is to be able to understand the words in context when reading sentences and when doing independent writing – and also dictation, when the learner:

- reads the passage through to practise seeing and hearing the homophones in context
- re-reads sentence by sentence (longer sentences may need to be broken into shorter, meaningful phrases)
- write the passage to dictation
- re-read using the proof-reading C-O-P-S to check:

  <u>C</u>apital Letters
  <u>O</u>missions
  <u>P</u>unctuation
  <u>S</u>pelling

Dictation can also be used by an individual without the help of a teacher/learning partner/parent. The learner:

- reads the passage onto a cassette tape recorder or a minidisk recorder with playback facility
- plays it back, using headphones to listen to it sentence by sentence and then writes it down
- proof-reads what has been written by checking with the original passage and using the proof-reading C-O-P-S

Section C

The crossword puzzle activity is more challenging and can be used for older learners and good spellers to enhance language skills, including idioms and general knowledge.

Dictionary work will provide examples of the words used in phrases and sentences as clues.

These three sections use different learning strategies, a variety of tactics and different skills to teach, rehearse and reinforce homophones. They represent differentiated levels of difficulty to match different spelling abilities. Some individuals will be able to tackle all three activities during the 20 minutes of The Literacy Hour used 'for group or independent work'; others may work just on section A or B. The rule can be revised during the plenary session. Children can be asked to identify their 'best' strategy for remembering. Further examples can be noted during shared and guided text activities and included in a personal 'spellofax'.

The three sections can also be used for one-to-one learning and teaching. An individual may do one sentence each day from the three exercises, thus reinforcing the spelling of homophones on a daily basis for five consecutive days to maximise learning. Constant repetition and repeated exposure – including the use of multi-sensory means – will help to develop mastery and automatic recall of the correct homophone in independent writing.

How you can use these activities

The learner looks at the picture and reads the keywords. This helps those who are strong visualisers to associate the word with the picture, as well as noting the different spelling. There is evidence that spellers' recall of words is improved when there is a meaningful connection between the sentences and words. They can take a 'snapshot' of the spelling pattern and match it to the picture in their mind's eye. Using colour to highlight distinguishing features is helpful. Those who are stronger auditorially will learn by remembering the words when they say them and this will help them to discriminate between the words when they say and copy out the sentence.

The simultaneous use of seeing, saying, listening and writing applies multi-sensory learning, which is most effective for learning and remembering spelling. There are three main activities – differentiated to match individual development and skills – as well as the extension level, using the crossword puzzle.

Multi-sensory teaching of spelling has been found to be the most effective means of teaching spelling for all learners – including those with special educational needs – because all the senses are used simultaneously, thus utilising all the pathways to the brain. This includes using the eyes to look at the word, the lips to say the word, the ears to hear the word, and the hand to use motor muscle/kinesthetic memory when writing it.

Critics of multi-sensory teaching methods frequently derided the 'drill and skill' methods used and accused teachers of inducing 'death by workbook'. The criticism was valid when learners were given worksheets and were just asked to fill in or copy out missing words on the page. The current text includes explanation and multi-sensory strategies for learning.

allowed / aloud

(a) allowed  (b) aloud

No smoking **allowed** He is reading **aloud**

- <u>look</u> at the pictures; read each sentence aloud
- <u>say</u> homophone (a) and spell it out, aloud
- <u>cover</u> it
- <u>write</u> the word in the box below, while saying the letter names
- <u>check</u> the spelling; re-read the sentence
- <u>repeat</u> for homophone (b)

Section A

allowed   aloud

- read the sentence
- fill in the missing homophone and highlight it

1. We are not _____ to walk on the grass.
2. Tom is _____ to walk home from the shops on his own.
3. I do not like reading _____ in public.
4. We were _____ to wear home clothes at school on Comic Relief Day.
5. We said prayers _____ today for those killed in the Second World War.
6. Airline passengers are not _____ to use mobile phones on planes.
7. We were not _____ to smoke in the restaurant.
8. The National Anthem is sung _____ before rugby international matches.
9. *I'm a celebrity, get me out of here* contestants were not _____ to contact their friends.
10. Airline passengers are not _____ to have scissors in their hand luggage.

Section B

allowed   aloud

- • read the passage
- • copy it out below
- • highlight the homophones
- • write the passage to dictation

Horrible Harry never allowed his twin to sing aloud. He said he did not like the sound of it. Hateful Henry got into a sulk and said Harry could not stop him from singing: 'I am allowed to do what I like; it's a free country'. He began to sing 'I did it my way' as he sat in the bus. The bus driver slammed on the brakes and said that singing aloud was not allowed on buses because it distracts the driver.

_____
_____
_____
_____
_____
_____
_____
_____
_____
_____
_____
_____
_____
_____
_____
_____
_____
_____
_____
_____
_____
_____
_____
_____
_____
_____
_____
_____

Section C

Crossword Puzzle No. 14

Clues

1. Hunting is banned and is not . . . . on National Trust land.

2. Calculators are . . . . in some mathematics examinations.

3. Football fans have sing-songs on the way to matches; the fans sing . . . . . .

4. Children often learn times tables by chanting them . . . . . .

5. Running in school corridors is forbidden; it is not . . . .

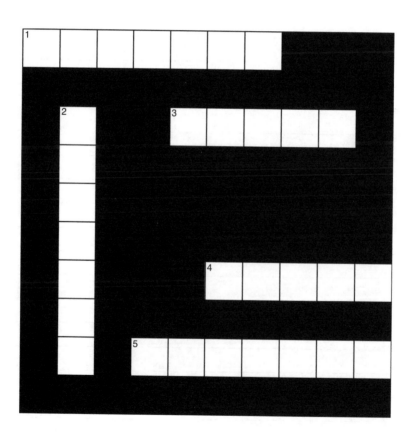

ate / eight

(a) ate

I **ate** an apple

(b) eight

He caught **eight** fish

- <u>look</u> at the pictures; read each sentence aloud
- <u>say</u> homophone (a) and spell it out, aloud
- <u>cover</u> it
- <u>write</u> the word in the box below, while saying the letter names
- <u>check</u> the spelling; re-read the sentence
- <u>repeat</u> for homophone (b)

Section A

ate   eight

- Read the sentence
- Fill in the missing homophone and highlight it

1. There is an _____ -sided shopping centre called The Octagon in High Wycombe.
2. They _____ all the birthday cake.
3. He had food poisoning; it must have been caused by something he _____ .
4. I _____ a lot of fresh fish when we were on holiday in Cornwall.
5. We had a dinner party for _____ people.
6. Jack Sprat _____ no fat and his wife would eat no lean.
7. There were _____ little dickie birds sitting on a wall, four named Peter, the other four Paul.
8. Tim invited _____ friends to his stag night.
9. We _____ at seven o'clock yesterday.
10. May I have _____ slices of ham?

Section B

ate   eight

- read the passage
- copy it out below
- highlight the homophones
- write the passage to dictation

Hateful Henry has a small collection of toy cars. He began to collect them when he was eight years old. He kept them in their eight original boxes in the attic. One day a mouse ate the cardboard boxes. Henry was distraught. He wailed, 'It is all your fault, Harry: you often ate a bag of crisps up in the attic and left crumbs, so then the mice came and ate my boxes'.

_____

_____

_____

_____

_____

_____

_____

_____

_____

_____

_____

_____

_____

_____

_____

_____

_____

_____

_____

_____

_____

_____

_____

Section C

Crossword Puzzle No. 15

Clues

1. A British crew of . . . . . won a gold medal for rowing in the Olympic Games.

2. We have . . . . . fingers and two thumbs.

3. They . . . wholemeal bread for breakfast.

4. She is on a diet so she . . . no nuts or crisps.

5. There were . . . . . children in the school mini-bus.

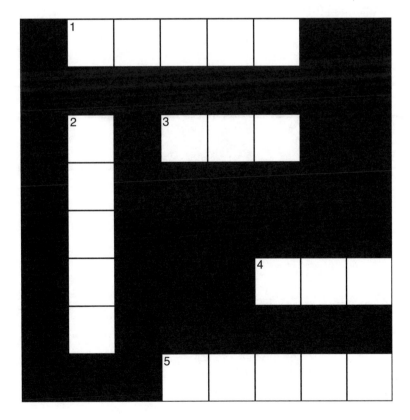

bean/been

(a) bean(s)   (b) been

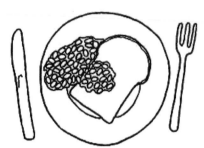

You can't beat **beans** on toast   I have **been** and seen the queen

- <u>look</u> at the pictures; read each sentence aloud
- <u>say</u> homophone (a) and spell it out, aloud
- <u>cover</u> it
- <u>write</u> the word in the box below, while saying the letter names
- <u>check</u> the spelling; re-read the sentence
- <u>repeat</u> for homophone (b)

Section A

bean(s)   been

- Read the sentence
- Fill in the missing homophone and highlight it

1. Green _____ go well with meat and vegetables.
2. Have you _____ to see the film *Titanic*?
3. We have _____ waiting for the bus for ages.
4. Can you get a tin of baked _____ please?
5. Uncle Sid grows runner _____ in his garden.
6. The milkman has _____ and gone already this morning.
7. The pantomime was *Jack and the _____ Stalk.*
8. Have you _____ hiding the cash under the bed?
9. The greengrocer sold broad, haricot and runner _____.
10. It is very mean to spill the _____ on your friends.

Section B

bean(s)   been

- read the passage
- copy it out below
- highlight the homophones
- write the passage to dictation

Hateful Henry can't stand green beans. He made such a fuss at lunch when the waiter put a plate with beans in front of him. He said he had not asked for beans. He got his plate and chucked the beans on the floor. Horrible Harry went red with rage and said, 'I've never been so cross in my life. I have been made to feel a fool over your silly beans'.

_____

_____

_____

_____

_____

_____

_____

_____

_____

_____

_____

_____

_____

_____

_____

_____

_____

_____

_____

_____

_____

_____

_____

_____

_____

_____

_____

_____

_____

_____

Section C

Crossword Puzzle No. 16

Clues

1. What does the slogan 'Beanz Meanz Heinz' refer to?

2. David Beckham has . . . . the captain of England's football team.

3. Tea is made from leaves; coffee is made from . . . . . .

4. Our dog sleeps on a . . . . bag.

5. Complete the nursery rhyme 'Pussy cat, pussy cat, where have you . . . . ?'

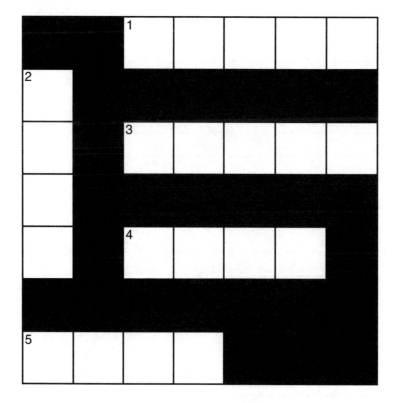

blew/blue

(a) blew

The wind **blew** the umbrella inside out

(b) blue

Boxers are sometimes black and **blue**

- <u>look</u> at the pictures; read each sentence aloud
- <u>say</u> homophone (a) and spell it out, aloud
- <u>cover</u> it
- <u>write</u> the word in the box below, while saying the letter names
- <u>check</u> the spelling; re-read the sentence
- <u>repeat</u> for homophone (b)

Section A

blew   blue

- Read the sentence
- Fill in the missing homophone and highlight it

1. The artist Picasso used _____ paint in many of his pictures.
2. My hands looked _____ with the cold.
3. The _____ whale is a large mammal.
4. When fat is really hot, there is _____ smoke.
5. The hurricane _____ the ship off course.
6. The landmine _____ up and exploded when it was touched.
7. Once in a _____ moon there are no traffic jams on the M25 motorway.
8. The balloon burst when he _____ it up.
9. They say _____ and green should never be seen.
10. The twin towers in New York _____ up on the 11th of September.

Section A

blew   blue

- read the passage
- copy it out below
- highlight the homophones
- write the passage to dictation

Horrible Harry and Hateful Henry yelled at each other until they were blue in the face. They both wanted to use the blue pen to fill in the form. The row blew into a fight. They hit each other and both ended up black and blue, just over a silly blue biro. The man next door banged on the door and said, 'What is all this blue murder about?'

_____

_____

_____

_____

_____

_____

_____

_____

_____

_____

_____

_____

_____

_____

_____

_____

_____

_____

_____

_____

_____

_____

_____

_____

Section C

Crossword Puzzle No. 17

Clues

1. Sailors in the navy often wear . . . . uniforms.

2. Frank Sinatra was often called 'Old . . . . .-eyes'.

3. The wolf came and . . . . down the little pig's house built of straw.

4. Someone chosen to play for the university team at Oxford or Cambridge is known as a . . . . .

5. Stilton cheese has veins of mould running through it; it is called a . . . . cheese.

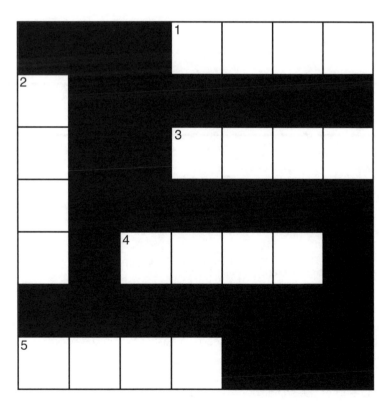

cent/scent/sent

(a) cent

(b) scent

(c) sent

Abraham Lincoln's head is on the back of a US **cent** coin

These flowers have a lovely **scent**

He **sent** a birthday card to his friend

*   <u>look</u> at the pictures; read each sentence aloud
*   <u>say</u> homophone (a) and spell it out, aloud
*   <u>cover</u> it
*   <u>write</u> the word in the box below, while saying the letter names
*   <u>check</u> the spelling; re-read the sentence
*   <u>repeat</u> for homophones (b) and (c)

Section A

cent   scent   sent

*   Read the sentence
*   Fill in the missing homophone and highlight it

1. How many _____s are there in a dollar?
2. Ben _____ a letter to complain to the manager about the food.
3. Pam wears horrid _____, which leaves a nasty smell in the room.
4. The postage stamp in Florida was twenty-five _____s.
5. Some people call perfume _____.
6. The police sometimes use sniffer dogs who can find the _____ of drugs.
7. The can of juice cost 45 _____s.
8. Hounds can follow the _____ of a fox.
9. The soldiers were _____ on a peace-keeping mission by the UN.
10. The detective was on the _____ of the burglar.

Section B

cent   sent   scent

- read the passage
- copy it out below
- highlight the homophones
- write the passage to dictation

Horrible Harry went to the bank to get cash for his trip to Las Vegas. He got lots of 10-cent coins for the slot machines. The bank ran out of cents. Next day the bank sent him a letter and told him not to do that again. He sent the manager a rude letter back and said, 'I won't come back to your bank'. The manager then sent him a bunch of flowers to say sorry. The flowers had a lovely scent.

Section C

Crossword Puzzle No. 18

Clues

1. Honeysuckle in a garden is unforgettable because of its . . . . . .

2. Someone is '. . . . to Coventry' if they are ignored.

3. Letters can be . . . . by first- or second-class post.

4. There are a hundred . . . . . in an American dollar.

5. A football player can be . . . . off the pitch for foul play.

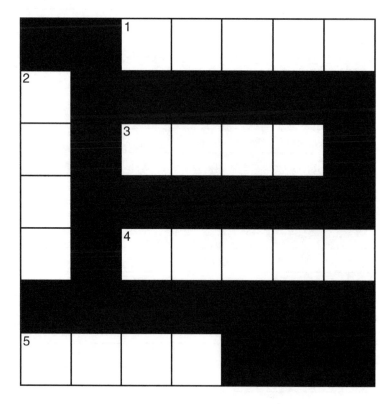

cereal/serial

(a) cereal

(b) serial

Breakfast **cereal** can keep you healthy

EastEnders is a popular **serial** on television

- <u>look</u> at the pictures; read each sentence aloud
- <u>say</u> homophone (a) and spell it out, aloud
- <u>cover</u> it
- <u>write</u> the word in the box below, while saying the letter names
- <u>check</u> the spelling; re-read the sentence
- <u>repeat</u> for homophone (b)

Section A

cereal   serial

- Read the sentence
- Fill in the missing homophone and highlight it

1. I had a bowl of _____ for breakfast.
2. You can buy bars of _____ biscuits.
3. Radio 4 often make books into a _____.
4. The _____ was shown on Channel 4.
5. Georgina likes eating _____ with her fingers.
6. The doctor said that a healthy diet should include _____.
7. The radio producer was asked to make a _____ about Harry Potter.
8. British farmers grow many _____ crops.
9. Kate Winslet had a leading role in that television _____.
10. *The Forsythe Saga* was a popular television _____.

Section B

cereal   serial

- read the passage
- copy it out below
- highlight the homophones
- write the passage to dictation

Horrible Harry was very mean when it came to choosing cereal. He would only eat one kind of cereal. He liked to sit in front of the television and munch a bowlful while he watched a video of his favourite serial. Hateful Henry ate the last packet of cornflakes and left the empty box on the shelf. Horrible Harry had a tantrum when he opened the empty cereal box.

_____

_____

_____

_____

_____

_____

_____

_____

_____

_____

_____

_____

_____

_____

_____

_____

_____

_____

_____

_____

_____

_____

_____

_____

Section C

Crossword Puzzle No. 19

Clues

1. Farmers grow . . . . . . to feed animals and humans.

2. The detectives hunted the . . . . . . killer who had terrorised Washington.

3. I love to listen to extracts from a favourite book made into a radio . . . .

4. Catherine Cookson's books are often used to make a . . . . . . on television.

5. The EU sometimes gives subsidies to farmers who grow . . . . . . crops.

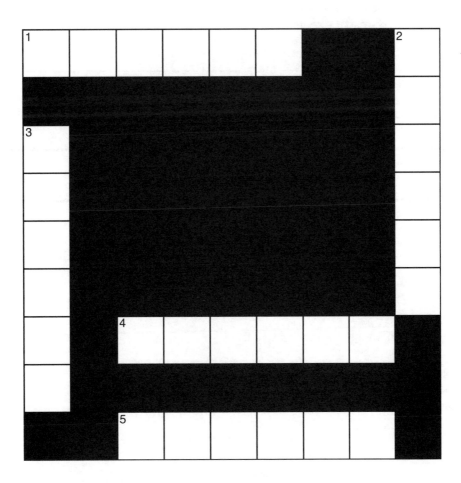

dear/deer

(a) dear

My granny is a real **dear**

(b) deer

Wild **deer** roam in the woods

- <u>look</u> at the pictures; read each sentence aloud
- <u>say</u> homophone (a) and spell it out, aloud
- <u>cover</u> it
- <u>write</u> the word in the box below, while saying the letter names
- <u>check</u> the spelling; re-read the sentence
- <u>repeat</u> for homophone (b)

Section A

dear   deer

- Read the sentence
- Fill in the missing homophone and highlight it

1. She began the letter by writing '_____ Tom'.
2. These shoes were very, very _____.
3. There are wild ponies and _____ in the New Forest in Hampshire.
4. The meat of _____ is called venison.
5. Can you be a _____ and help me with this?
6. _____ me! What a dreadful dress you are wearing!
7. In the highlands in Scotland there are many different types of _____.
8. Male _____ have antlers.
9. We sometimes see muntjac _____ in our gardens in Buckinghamshire.
10. Oh _____! What an awful mess you have made!

Section B

- read the passage
- copy it out below
- highlight the homophones
- write the passage to dictation

Hateful Henry got his gun and went out to shoot deer. A policeman saw him and told him not to shoot the muntjac deer in Burnham Beeches. Hateful Henry got into a rage and ranted, 'I'll do what I like'. The policeman arrested him for shooting deer on private land. He was fined £100. Horrible Harry said, 'That fun was a bit dear'. 'PC Black is not such a dear person after all,' said Hateful Henry.

_____
_____
_____
_____
_____
_____
_____
_____
_____
_____
_____
_____
_____
_____
_____
_____
_____
_____
_____
_____
_____
_____
_____
_____
_____
_____
_____

Section C

Crossword Puzzle No. 20

Clues

1. The antlers of . . . . are sometimes hung on walls as trophies.

2. Letters usually begin with the word '. . . .'.

3. That mistake will cost you . . . . .

4. My most loved possessions are very . . . . to me.

5. The old lady was not a . . . . . She was a contrary old woman.

flour/flower

(a) flour

(b) flower

Plain **flour** is used for bread

The **flower** likes a shower of rain

- <u>look</u> at the pictures; read each sentence aloud
- <u>say</u> homophone (a) and spell it out, aloud
- <u>cover</u> it
- <u>write</u> the word in the box below, while saying the letter names
- <u>check</u> the spelling; re-read the sentence
- <u>repeat</u> for homophone (b)

Section A

flour   flower

- Read the sentence
- Fill in the missing homophone and highlight it

1. The _____ in the gravy made it lumpy.
2. What is your favourite _____?
3. When will the tulips _____ in Holland?
4. The recipe said to use self-raising _____ in the cake.
5. Dip the fish in _____ before you fry it.
6. The shower had a curtain with _____s on it.
7. Chelsea _____ Show is world-famous.
8. _____ and milk are used to make batter.
9. My grandfather won first prize for his sweet peas at the _____ show.
10. It is necessary to sift the _____ when baking a cake.

Section B

flour   flower

- read the passage
- copy it out below
- highlight the homophones
- write the passage to dictation

Horrible Harry went to the supermarket to do the shopping. He slipped on a wet floor and a bag of flour fell on his head. He ranted and raved, and left his trolley full of fresh flowers. He dashed home to his power shower. As he got out of the shower, he slipped on the bath mat. A flowerpot fell from the shelf and hit his big toe. 'Serves you right!' smirked Hateful Henry as his brother limped up to bed.

Section C

Crossword Puzzle No. 21

Clues

1. Most florists will deliver fresh . . . . to the door.

2. When it is mixed with ground corn . . . . . ., it can be used to thicken soup or sauces.

3. He expressed his sympathy and sent a bunch of . . . .

4. Canadian farmers produce vast amounts of grain for . . . . . .

5. The slogan said 'Say it with . . . .'.

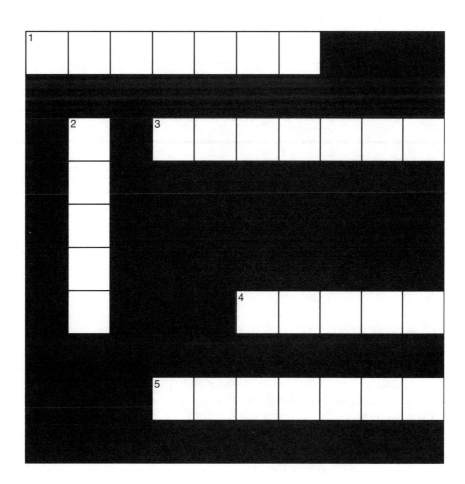

grate/great

(a) grate

(b) great

I **grate** the cheese for the pizza

It's **great** I passed my driving test

- <u>look</u> at the pictures; read each sentence aloud
- <u>say</u> homophone (a) and spell it out, aloud
- <u>cover</u> it
- <u>write</u> the word in the box below, while saying the letter names
- <u>check</u> the spelling; re-read the sentence
- <u>repeat</u> for homophone (b)

Section A

grate   great

- Read the sentence
- Fill in the missing homophone and highlight it

1. Timmy got some _____ news about a new job in the post today.
2. Ali got _____ grades in his GCSE French examination.
3. Can you _____ the bread for the sauce?
4. The Smiths got a new _____ for the fireplace.
5. The _____ War is another name for the First World War.
6. The _____ and good are commemorated at Westminster Abbey.
7. *The _____ escape* is one of the best war films.
8. Ireland suffered a _____ Famine which killed many of its people in 1845–7.
9. One of Cinderella's jobs was to clear the _____.
10. Charles Dickens wrote the book _____ *Expectations*.

Section C

grate   great

- read the passage
- copy it out below
- highlight the homophones
- write the passage to dictation

When Hateful Henry and Horrible Harry are in the kitchen, they rant and rave at each other a great deal of the time. Today they had a great row when Hateful Henry cut his finger, when he tried to grate the cheese. He threw the end bit of the cheese in the grate and yelled, 'It's all your fault, you greedy thing! You ate a great deal of this lump of cheese, so this bit of cheese is too small to grate'.

_____

_____

_____

_____

_____

_____

_____

_____

_____

_____

_____

_____

_____

_____

_____

_____

_____

_____

_____

_____

_____

_____

_____

_____

_____

_____

_____

_____

_____

_____

_____

Section C

Crossword Puzzle No. 22

Clues

1. You must . . . . . nutmeg before it is used in cooking.

2. Alexander the . . . . . was a well-known leader.

3. You need to . . . . . a piece of Parmesan cheese to use it on pizza.

4. The biggest train robbery in Britain became known as the . . . . . Train Robbery.

5. The blacksmith will make a . . . . . for the fireplace.

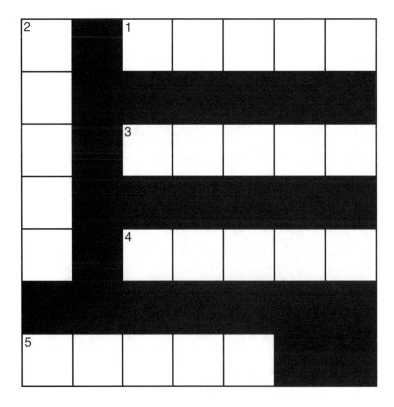

hair / hare

(a) hair

(b) hare

Can I have my **hair** cut?

There is a fable about a **hare** and a tortoise

- <u>look</u> at the pictures; read each sentence aloud
- <u>say</u> homophone (a) and spell it out, aloud
- <u>cover</u> it
- <u>write</u> the word in the box below, while saying the letter names
- <u>check</u> the spelling; re-read the sentence
- <u>repeat</u> for homophone (b)

| |
| |

Section A

hair   hare

- Read the sentence
- Fill in the missing homophone and highlight it

1. Viv has lovely, long, dark brown _____.
2. The hounds chased the _____.
3. Can you tell the difference between a _____ and a rabbit?
4. Patsy was having a 'bad _____' day.
5. I must go to the barber and have a number two _____ cut.
6. People who run with the _____ and hunt with hounds do not know which side to support.
7. My _____ stood on end when I saw a rat in my kitchen cupboard.
8. I passed a pub called the Old _____.
9. Vidal Sassoon is one of the world's best known _____ dressers.
10. Horse _____ was used to upholster chairs in the olden days.

Section B

hair   hare

- read the passage
- copy it out below
- highlight the homophones
- write the passage to dictation

Horrible Harry and Hateful Henry went for a walk. They had a punch-up about closing a gate and pulled each other's hair. It ended up with Hateful Henry dashing to the car and running down the path yelling. He came to a quick halt when a pack of hounds came round a bend chasing a hare. He soon forgot about his messy hair when he saw the hare and the hounds in full cry. To escape he ran into the barber's shop and had a haircut.

Section C

Crossword Puzzle No. 23

Clues

1. Aesop wrote a fable about a . . . . and a tortoise.

2. A sharp u-shaped bend on a mountainous road is called a . . . . pin bend because it bends like one.

3. They say that . . . . s go mad in March.

4. To split . . . . s is to argue over unimportant details.

5. Samson lost his strength when his . . . . was cut.

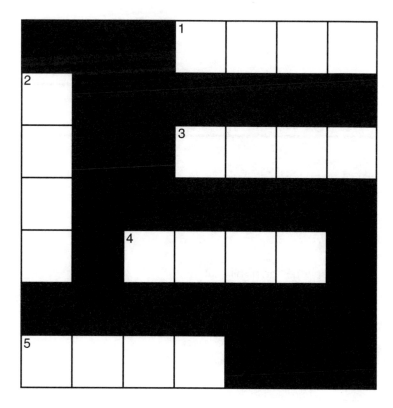

hear/here

(a) hear

(b) here

I can **hear** the church bells

Sign **here**, please

- <u>look</u> at the pictures; read each sentence aloud
- <u>say</u> homophone (a) and spell it out, aloud
- <u>cover</u> it
- <u>write</u> the word in the box below, while saying the letter names
- <u>check</u> the spelling; re-read the sentence
- <u>repeat</u> for homophone (b)

Section A

hear   here

- Read the sentence
- Fill in the missing homophone and highlight it

1. Did you _____ the joke about the big chimney and the little chimney?
2. When did you _____ about Princess Diana's death?
3. _____ is my essay that I have slaved over.
4. Don't leave it _____; put it in your file.
5. I _____ that you have a new computer.
6. I looked _____, there and everywhere for my lost diamond ring.
7. _____ goes! I am going to dive into the pool.
8. _____! _____! What a clever answer.
9. Did you _____ the rumour that he won the lottery?
10. Her boyfriend would not _____ of her paying for the drinks.

Section B

hear   here

- read the passage
- copy it out below
- highlight the homophones
- write the passage to dictation

Horrible Harry was showing off to his friends and he said, 'Listen here! Did you hear the one about what the big chimney said to the little chimney?' 'Oh! That's an old one,' interrupted Hateful Henry. 'Everyone knows the answer: "You're too young to smoke".' 'I hate you!' yelled Horrible Harry, 'You are such a spoilsport.'

_____

_____

_____

_____

_____

_____

_____

_____

_____

_____

_____

_____

_____

_____

_____

_____

_____

_____

_____

_____

_____

_____

_____

_____

_____

Section C

Crossword Puzzle No. 24

Clues

1. Deaf people cannot . . . . .

2. The form said 'sign . . . . on the dotted line'.

3. The parking attendant pointed and said, 'Leave the car . . . .'.

4. Catherine Zeta-Jones lived . . . . in Cardiff.

5. You can . . . . your neighbours if you live below a flat with bare floorboards.

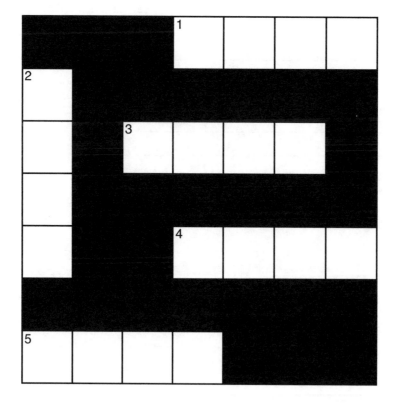

heard/herd

(a) heard

(b) herd

I **heard** the phone

The farmer has a **herd** of cattle

- <u>look</u> at the pictures; read each sentence aloud
- <u>say</u> homophone (a) and spell it out, aloud
- <u>cover</u> it
- <u>write</u> the word in the box below, while saying the letter names
- <u>check</u> the spelling; re-read the sentence
- <u>repeat</u> for homophone (b)

Section A

heard   herd

- Read the sentence
- Fill in the missing homophone and highlight it

1. I _____ the news on the radio.
2. I _____ that you are a brilliant golfer.
3. The _____ of elephants roamed in the jungle.
4. I _____ that you won a prize in an art competition.
5. Peter saw a _____ of cattle in the field.
6. Farmer Smith has a prize _____ of Aberdeen Angus cows.
7. Fatima _____ a rumour that she was to be promoted to a new job.
8. The explosion was _____ two miles away.
9. Ben jumped out of bed when he _____ the breaking glass.
10. It was not necessary to _____ the prisoners into a pen.

Section B

heard   herd

- read the passage
- copy it out
- highlight the homophones
- write the passage to dictation

Horrible Harry heard on the news that a herd of cows had escaped from a lorry on the M1 near his home. He ran down the road and left the garden gate open. As he did so, the mad herd of cows came rushing through his gate. Hateful Henry had a fit when he heard the herd in the garden making a mess. His heart sank when he heard the breaking glass in his greenhouse.

Section C

Crossword Puzzle No. 25

Clues

1. They say that the . . . . instinct is very strong in humans too.

2. My grandmother always told me not to believe everything I . . . . . .

3. In olden times children were expected to be seen but not . . . . . .

4. When on safari in South Africa we saw many . . . . of different animals.

5. Ned listened to 'Jingle Bells' on the radio. He kept it in his head because once he had . . . . . a tune he never forgot it.

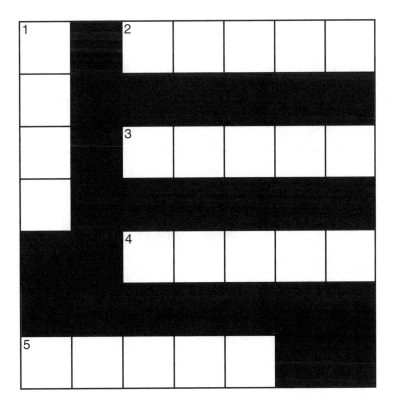

hole/whole

(a) hole

(b) whole

There's a **hole** in my bucket

The greedy boy ate the **whole** pizza

- <u>look</u> at the pictures; read each sentence aloud
- <u>say</u> homophone (a) and spell it out, aloud
- <u>cover</u> it
- <u>write</u> the word in the box below, while saying the letter names
- <u>check</u> the spelling; re-read the sentence
- <u>repeat</u> for homophone (b)

Section A

hole   whole

- Read the sentence
- Fill in the missing homophone and highlight it

1. Do you know the song, 'There's a _____ in my bucket, dear Liza'?
2. I had a bar of _____ nut chocolate.
3. The Smiths always have _____ meal bread.
4. Oil comes from a _____ in the ground called a well.
5. Adam had a _____ in his tooth and had to have a filling.
6. Piglet fell down a _____ in the ground as he rushed to meet Eeyore.
7. The child was born with a _____ in his heart, which has now been repaired.
8. Don't make judgements until you know the _____ story.
9. The _____ of the school building was damaged by fire.
10. His _____ world fell apart when he crashed his brand-new car.

Section B

hole   whole

- read the passage
- copy it out below
- highlight the homophones
- write the passage to dictation

Hateful Henry was out shopping when he tripped and fell into a hole in the High Street. He hit his head and broke the whole of one of his front teeth. He was yelling in agony. Mrs O'Sullivan the dentist ran out when she saw him on the ground. Just then Horrible Harry dashed up and said, 'You're such a fool to fall down a hole in broad daylight'. Mrs O'Sullivan said, 'Don't worry, I'll mend that hole where your front tooth was'.

Section C

Crossword Puzzle No. 26

Clues

1. You need to see a dentist when you have a . . . . in a tooth.

2. Golfers are usually given a prize when they hit a . . . . in one.

3. He spent all his savings. The . . . . . lot went on a shopping spree.

4. . . . . . numbers are not fractions.

5. The . . . . . sale price was 50 per cent less than the retail price.

made/maid

(a) made

The chef **made** a wedding cake

(b) maid

The **maid** came when I rang the bell

- <u>look</u> at the pictures; read each sentence aloud
- <u>say</u> homophone (a) and spell it out, aloud
- <u>cover</u> it
- <u>write</u> the word in the box below, while saying the letter names
- <u>check</u> the spelling; re-read the sentence
- <u>repeat</u> for homophone (b)

Section A

made   maid

- Read the sentence
- Fill in the missing homophone and highlight it

1. I _____ a lovely card for Mum for Mothering Sunday.
2. Where was this washing machine _____?
3. We _____ lovely presents for Christmas.
4. On holiday the _____ ironed my clothes.
5. Who _____ your hat? It looks like a Philip Tracey design.
6. The holiday villa in Portugal included _____ service.
7. Hand-_____ lace is highly prized and expensive.
8. Princess Diana had a private _____ to look after her clothes.
9. She had a _____-of-honour and two child bridesmaids at her wedding.
10. I threw a coin into the Trevi fountain in Rome and _____ a wish.

Section B

made   maid

- read the passage
- copy it out below
- highlight the homophones
- write the passage to dictation

Horrible Harry made Hateful Henry go with him on holiday to Spain. They made a fuss on the plane: they wanted lots of drinks and kept pushing the call button. The air stewardess got mad and said, 'I am not a maid'. 'We paid the full fare for this flight, so we can make a fuss when you made us wait so long for our drinks,' yelled Horrible Harry.

_____

_____

_____

_____

_____

_____

_____

_____

_____

_____

_____

_____

_____

_____

_____

_____

_____

_____

_____

_____

_____

_____

_____

_____

Section C

Crossword Puzzle No. 27

Clues

1. The . . . . had a lace cap and apron.

2. In Victorian times many rich people had a . . . . to clean and cook.

3. Always look on the label to check what processed foods are . . . . from.

4. Looking at pictures of the famine victims in Ethiopia . . . . me feel so sad.

5. Slaves were . . . . to work on cotton plantations in the southern states of America.

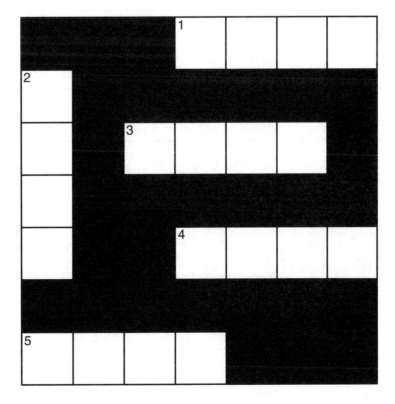

meat/meet

(a) meat

Can we eat **meat** on the bone?

(b) meet

Shake hands when we **meet**

- <u>look</u> at the pictures; read each sentence aloud
- <u>say</u> homophone (a) and spell it out, aloud
- <u>cover</u> it
- <u>write</u> the word in the box below, while saying the letter names
- <u>check</u> the spelling; re-read the sentence
- <u>repeat</u> for homophone (b)

Section A

meat   meet

- Read the sentence
- Fill in the missing homophone and highlight it

1. Can we _____ for lunch at the pub next week?
2. Where can we buy organic _____?
3. Some people do not eat _____ on Fridays.
4. Vegetarians do not eat _____ or fish.
5. He will _____ his friends at the cinema.
6. They say one man's _____ is another man's poison.
7. There are many different types of _____, including beef, lamb and pork.
8. Will you _____ the deadline for your coursework?
9. We had cold _____ and salad for supper.
10. One of the most popular songs sung by Vera Lynn during World War II was 'We'll _____ again'.

Section B

meat   meet

- read the passage
- copy it out below
- highlight the homophones
- write the passage to dictation

Horrible Harry argues a lot about the food they eat. He will not eat red meat. He says, 'I won't eat beef or pork meat'. They meet in town to do the weekend shopping. Hateful Henry goes shopping for meat and says to the butcher, 'I like nothing better than a nice rib of beef'. He comes home with a huge bit of meat and puts it in the fridge. Horrible Harry goes mad when he sees the raw meat dripping onto his veggie burgers in the fridge. He chucks the meat in the bin.

_____

_____

_____

_____

_____

_____

_____

_____

_____

_____

_____

_____

_____

_____

_____

_____

_____

_____

_____

_____

_____

_____

_____

_____

Section C

Crossword Puzzle No. 28

Clues

1. Do you like . . . . rare or well done?

2. The website Friends Reunited helps old friends to . . . . up again.

3. It often helps to solve a problem or misunderstanding if people can . . . . face to face.

4. Marinate the . . . . before you put it on the barbecue.

5. Cheap cuts of . . . . need long, slow cooking to make them tender.

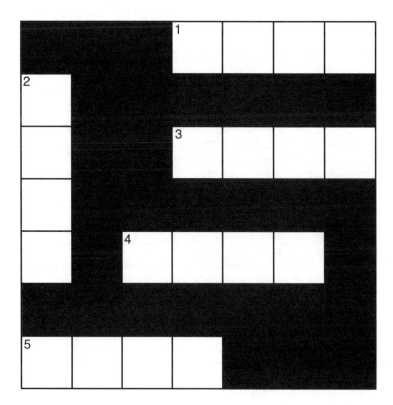

new/knew

(a) new

(b) knew

We have a **new** baby

He **knew** the rules but did not obey them

- <u>look</u> at the pictures; read each sentence aloud
- <u>say</u> homophone (a) and spell it out, aloud
- <u>cover</u> it
- <u>write</u> the word in the box below, while saying the letter names
- <u>check</u> the spelling; re-read the sentence
- <u>repeat</u> for homophone (b)

Section A

new   knew

- Read the sentence
- Fill in the missing homophone and highlight it

1. She bought a _____ black dress for the party.
2. She _____ my uncle and aunt who lived in Glasgow.
3. He _____ the word but could not spell it.
4. We have parked our _____ car outside our house.
5. They like this _____ book and will read it.
6. The _____ Harry Potter book was an instant best-seller.
7. Booking flights on the Internet is a _____ and cheaper way to buy tickets.
8. My granny always said that she _____ who her real friends were when she was in trouble.
9. _____ Age travellers often attend rock festivals such as Glastonbury.
10. Buying and selling nearly-_____ clothes has become quite fashionable.

Section B

new   knew

- read the passage
- copy it out
- highlight the homophones
- write the passage to dictation

Horrible Harry and Hateful Henry wanted to make a new fish stew. 'What about Gran's recipe for fish stew?' said Horrible Harry. Hateful Henry said that he knew what to do and did not need to look in a recipe book. He made the new stew for supper. 'Do you like it?' asked Hateful Henry. 'I knew you would not get it right,' said Horrible Harry, 'it has a horrid taste'. He gave his to the dog to eat.

_____

_____

_____

_____

_____

_____

_____

_____

_____

_____

_____

_____

_____

_____

_____

_____

_____

_____

_____

_____

_____

_____

_____

_____

Section C

Crossword Puzzle No. 29

Clues

1. They say that Jersey Royals are the best . . . potatoes.

2. They say children like to play with . . . toys.

3. The contestant on *Who Wants to be a Millionaire* said that he always . . . . the answers when he was watching television at home.

4. . . . . babies often cause their parents sleepless nights.

5. They carried on smoking even though they . . . . it damaged their health.

no/know

no

know

No smoking here, please!

Now I **know** how to spell

- <u>look</u> at the pictures; read each sentence aloud
- <u>say</u> homophone (a) and spell it out, aloud
- <u>cover</u> it
- <u>write</u> the word in the box below, while saying the letter names
- <u>check</u> the spelling; re-read the sentence
- <u>repeat</u> for homophone (b)

Section A

no   know

- Read the sentence
- Fill in the missing homophone and highlight it.

1. Do you _____ the answer to this sum?
2. _____ , you may not borrow my car: I need it for shopping.
3. I _____ the teacher hates messy writing.
4. The sign said '_____ smoking' in this part of the train.
5. I never say _____ to an invitation to a party.
6. That chap is such a bore and a _____-all.
7. Watch my lips: the answer is a firm _____.
8. Good cooks have skills and _____ how.
9. _____ good will come of this experience.
10. They say that in life you never _____ what is round the corner.

Section B

no   know

- read the passage
- copy it out below
- highlight the homophones
- write the passage to dictation

Horrible Harry did not see the 'No Entry!' sign on the door and rushed into the room in the middle of a meeting at work. 'I know you don't look where you are going, but you should know that it is good manners to knock on a door before you enter,' said his boss. 'There is no excuse; you should know better.' Horrible Harry slunk out of the door. As he did so, he saw Hateful Henry sniggering at his desk.

Section C

Crossword Puzzle No. 30

Clues

1. . . . is the opposite of yes.

2. Turkey imposed a . . -fly zone in its air space during the Gulf War.

3. This hotel provides . . room service.

4. There is an old saying that 'it is wise to . . . . which side your bread is buttered on'.

5. They say you can never . . . . it all even if you are an expert.

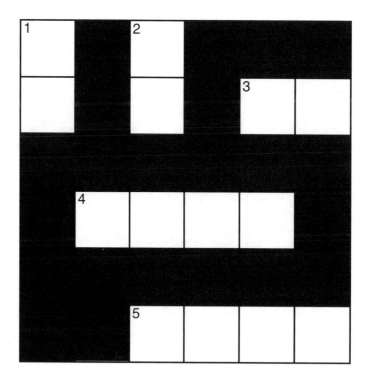

of / off

These two are not really homophones – 'of' says /ŏ/ /v/, whereas 'off' says /ŏ/ /f/ – but it is easy to get them wrong.

of

Is the table made **of** pine or oak wood?

off

You must always turn **off** the tap

- <u>look</u> at the pictures; read each sentence aloud
- <u>say</u> homophone (a) and spell it out, aloud
- <u>cover</u> it
- <u>write</u> the word in the box below, while saying the letter names
- <u>check</u> the spelling; re-read the sentence
- <u>repeat</u> for homophone (b)

Section A

of   off

- Read the sentence then
- Fill in the missing homophone and highlight it

1. The dress was made _____ pure wool.
2. He ran _____ to catch the last bus.
3. The cricket team was made up _____ eleven boys.
4. I will get _____ the train in Derby.
5. When do you go _____ on holiday?
6. The milk is _____; it was left out of the fridge last night.
7. This chair is made _____ solid mahogany wood.
8. He is one _____ of the most reliable people I know.
9. The cricket pitch is out _____ bounds while the grass is being re-seeded.
10. Smoked salmon is _____ the menu.

Section B

of off

- read the passage
- copy it out below
- highlight the homophones
- write the passage to dictation

Hateful Henry was in a bad mood.

'Would you like a glass of orange juice?' asked Horrible Harry.

'Yes, if it is made of fresh oranges,' replied Hateful Henry.

'Get off your bottom and get it yourself!' yelled Horrible Harry. 'I have not got the time for fuss pots like you. Why can't you drink it from a carton off the shelf like the rest of us?'

_____

_____

_____

_____

_____

_____

_____

_____

_____

_____

_____

_____

_____

_____

_____

_____

_____

_____

_____

_____

_____

_____

_____

Section C

Crossword Puzzle No. 31

Clues

1. Cilla Black said she was giving up doing television programmes, so *Blind Date* will be . . . our screens.

2. People who sing out of tune are said to be . . . key.

3. My granny says that the road to hell is full . . good intentions.

4. When people are rude they are sometimes . . . .-putting.

5. A penalty is given in a rugby match when a player is . . . side.

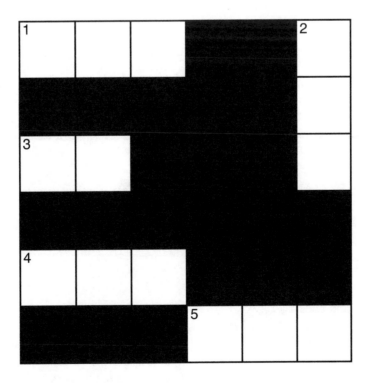

one/won

Not everyone says these the same way: some people say /w/ /ŏ/ /n/ for 'one'.

(a) one

He got a hole in **one**

(b) won

He **won** the race easily

- <u>look</u> at the pictures; read each sentence aloud
- <u>say</u> homophone (a) and spell it out, aloud
- <u>cover</u> it
- <u>write</u> the word in the box below, while saying the letter names
- <u>check</u> the spelling; re-read the sentence
- <u>repeat</u> for homophone (b)

Section A

one   won

- Read the sentence then
- Fill in the missing homophone and highlight it

1. _____ and one makes two.
2. Who _____ the Lotto this week?
3. Long John Silver had only _____ leg.
4. Michael Owen's goal _____ the match for England.
5. You have _____ more chance to see the film *Lord of the Rings*.
6. This is a _____-man-band operation.
7. Steve Redgrave _____ five gold medals in the Olympic Games.
8. Many supermarkets claim to provide _____-stop shopping.
9. The Duke of Wellington _____ the Battle of Waterloo.
10. The competition was very _____-sided.

Section B

one   won

- read the passage
- copy it out below
- highlight the homophones
- write the passage to dictation

Hateful Henry and his twin had one big row about which one of them was best at games.

'I won a cup for running when I was at school,' said Horrible Harry.

'I played football for the county,' boasted Hateful Henry. 'Look, I still have the medal I won, so I can show my sons,' he said.

'Your cup went back and we never saw it again,' sniggered Hateful Henry.

Section C

Crossword Puzzle No. 32

Clues

1. It is rare for a golfer to do a hole-in- . . . shot.

2. Someone . . . a million pounds on the programme *Who Wants to be a Millionaire*.

3. Bigamists have two wives. British law does not permit more than . . . .

4. Sir Jackie Stewart . . . the Formula One World Championship three times.

5. Sir Steven Redgrave has . . . more gold medals in the Olympic Games than any other sportsman.

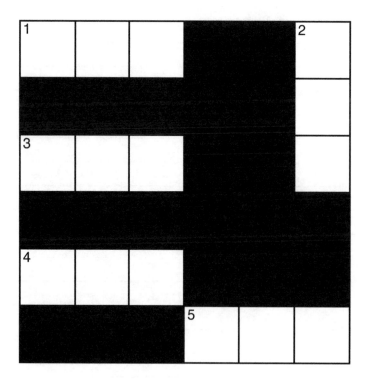

pair/pare/pear

(a) pair

This **pair** of boots was made for walking

(b) pare

You need a sharp knife to **pare** the skin of this apple

(c) pear

The partridge was in a **pear** tree

- <u>look</u> at the pictures; read each sentence aloud
- <u>say</u> homophone (a) and spell it out, aloud
- <u>cover</u> it
- <u>write</u> the word in the box below, while saying the letter names
- <u>check</u> the spelling; re-read the sentence
- <u>repeat</u> for homophones (b) and (c)

Section A

pair   pare   pear

- Read the sentence
- Fill in the missing homophone and highlight it

1. Andrew has a new _____ of walking boots.
2. We have a _____ of armchairs in front of the fire.
3. We had _____-flavoured ice-cream for pudding.
4. The twins are a terrible _____ of brothers.
5. A tasty _____ must be ripe and juicy.
6. Don't _____ the skin off the beetroot before you cook it.
7. There are some occasions when children are sent to work in _____s in the classroom.
8. _____ cooked in red wine make a delicious pudding.
9. Cinderella had to find the missing one of the _____ of glass slippers.
10. A _____ of Staffordshire china dogs is more valuable than two single dogs.

Section B

pair   pare   pear

- read the passage
- copy it out below
- highlight the homophones
- write the passage to dictation

Horrible Harry and Hateful Henry are a funny pair of twins. They love to argue and fight with each other. They can't ever agree about anything – even how to eat a pear or prepare vegetables. Hateful Henry always puts two pears on his plate but Horrible Harry only takes one at a time.

'I'm not greedy like you,' says Horrible Harry.

'Life is too short to mess around with one pear. You can eat two just as quickly, if you don't bother to pare the skins off,' smirked Hateful Henry.

Section C

Crossword Puzzle No. 33

Clues

1. Do you . . . . the skins of potatoes or do you eat them 'skins and all'?

2. . . . . trees are often grown in orchards.

3. Trousers are described as . . . . s even if you buy only one.

4. It is illegal not to have a . . . . of headlights on your car.

5. What kind of tree did the partridge sit on in the song 'The twelve days of Christmas'?

peace / piece

(a) peace

(b) piece

Make **peace**, not war

Have a **piece** of pie

- <u>look</u> at the pictures; read each sentence aloud
- <u>say</u> homophone (a) and spell it out, aloud
- <u>cover</u> it
- <u>write</u> the word in the box below, while saying the letter names
- <u>check</u> the spelling; re-read the sentence
- <u>repeat</u> for homophone (b)

Section A

peace   piece

- Read the sentence
- Fill in the missing homophone and highlight it

1. I hope the _____ talks in Northern Ireland are successful.
2. We bought a _____ of land to build a house in Wales.
3. I wish you would turn off that music! I need some _____ and quiet.
4. We must live in _____ with others on our planet.
5. I ate a whole _____ of pie for supper last night.
6. A famous book written by the Russian novelist Tolstoy is *War and* _____.
7. Patchwork quilts are made by sewing odd _____s of fabric together.
8. A pie chart is a circle divided into parts; each _____ gives information in diagram form.
9. The UN often sends _____-keeping forces to prevent further fighting.
10. The US Government sends volunteers from the _____ Corps to help developing countries.

Section B

peace   piece

- read the passage
- copy it out below
- highlight the homophones
- write the passage to dictation

Hateful Henry was sitting in front of the television, eating a large piece of cake. 'Can I have a piece of that?' asked Horrible Harry.

'Go and get a piece yourself and leave me in peace for a moment,' moaned Hateful Henry. 'I want to watch this piece of news about the UN's Peace Plan for the Middle East,' he bawled.

_____

_____

_____

_____

_____

_____

_____

_____

_____

_____

_____

_____

_____

_____

_____

_____

_____

_____

_____

_____

_____

_____

_____

_____

Section C

Crossword Puzzle No. 34

Clues

1. May I have a . . . . . of pie?

2. The . . . . . Treaty of Versailles ended the First World War.

3. The poet William Butler Yeats escaped to the Isle of Innisfree to find some . . . . . there.

4. The Bible says 'Blessed are the . . . . . -makers'.

5. A . . . . . agreement was signed by the two governments.

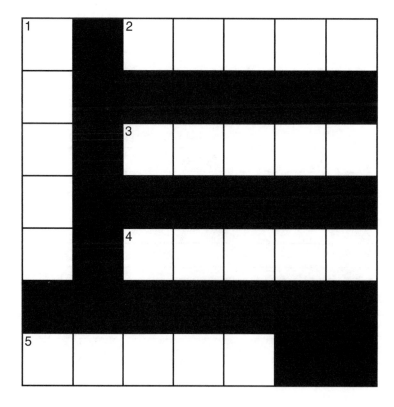

plain / plane

(a) plain

I like **plain** yoghurt

(b) plane

I want to go by **plane**

- <u>look</u> at the pictures; read each sentence aloud
- <u>say</u> homophone (a) and spell it out, aloud
- <u>cover</u> it
- <u>write</u> the word in the box below, while saying the letter names
- <u>check</u> the spelling; re-read the sentence
- <u>repeat</u> for homophone (b)

Section A

plain   plane

- Read the sentence
- Fill in the missing homophone and highlight it

1. Which type of _____ did he fly during the Second World War?
2. Cowboys ride on the _____s in the American West.
3. How many _____s are there in the RAF fleet?
4. Can I have the _____ chocolate bar please?
5. I saw a _____ high in the sky.
6. She made it very _____ that she was annoyed we were late.
7. Do you like _____ yoghurt or fruit-flavoured?
8. _____ lands have different names in different parts of the world, such as the prairies in Canada or the steppes in Russia.
9. The _____ English Society encourages the use of clear and simple language.
10. Some budget airline _____s have very little leg room.

Section B

plain   plane

- read the passage
- copy it out below
- highlight the homophones
- write the passage to dictation

Horrible Harry wanted to go to Spain by plane. 'We'll go on a private plane,' said Horrible Harry.
   'Don't be mad! we can't afford a private jet,' said Hateful Henry. 'A plain old plane will do me.'
   'I don't think I can take the strain on any old plane,' moaned Horrible Harry. 'What would we do if the plane came down on a plain in Spain?' he scoffed. 'We might drown because the rain in Spain stays mainly on the plain.'

_____

_____

_____

_____

_____

_____

_____

_____

_____

_____

_____

_____

_____

_____

_____

_____

_____

_____

_____

_____

_____

_____

_____

Section C

Crossword Puzzle No. 35

Clues

1. A . . . . . tree is a type of tall tree with burr-like fruits.

2. When a man does not have a title like Lord or Professor, he is just . . . . . Mister.

3. . . . . . Jane describes an ordinary-looking woman.

4. . . . . . flour is the opposite kind of flour to self-raising.

5. My granny often said that life is not always . . . . . sailing.

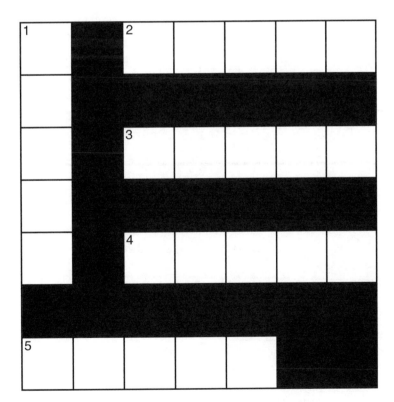

principal/principle

(a) principal

(b) principle

The school **principal** is the boss

It is a good **principle** to help the aged

- <u>look</u> at the pictures; read each sentence aloud
- <u>say</u> homophone (a) and spell it out, aloud
- <u>cover</u> it
- <u>write</u> the word in the box below, while saying the letter names
- <u>check</u> the spelling; re-read the sentence
- <u>repeat</u> for homophone (b)

Section A

principal   principle

- Read the sentence
- Fill in the missing homophone and highlight it

1. He is a person of strong _____s.
2. Have you no _____s, buying those stolen goods?
3. He is the _____ partner and most senior person in the firm.
4. He is the _____ shareholder of the company.
5. In _____ I understand how this computer works.
6. The _____ ingredient in wine is grapes.
7. The _____ roles in the film *Rainman* were played by Tom Cruise and Dustin Hoffman.
8. Nelson Mandela is widely admired for his _____s on racial equality in South Africa and was imprisoned for them.
9. The _____ ballet dancer is called the prima ballerina.
10. Bread-making needs an understanding of the _____ of using raising agents.

Section B

principal   principle

- read the passage
- copy it out below
- highlight the homophones
- write the passage to dictation

Hateful Henry was called to the principal's office. By mistake, he had left the office safe open all night. 'In principle, this is a good reason to give you the sack,' said the principal. He went on and said, 'You should be thrown out on your ear, in principle'. Horrible Harry burst out laughing in the next-door office. 'That's it!' said the principal, 'You twins are out on your ears'.

Section C

Crossword Puzzle No. 36

Clues

1. Martin Luther King, the Civil Rights leader, was admired for his . . . . .s.

2. Boston is the . . . . city of New England.

3. The judge told the fraudster that he had no morals or . . . .

4. The college . . . . had a great reputation because of his leadership.

5. It is a matter of honour to stand by one's . . . . despite peer pressure.

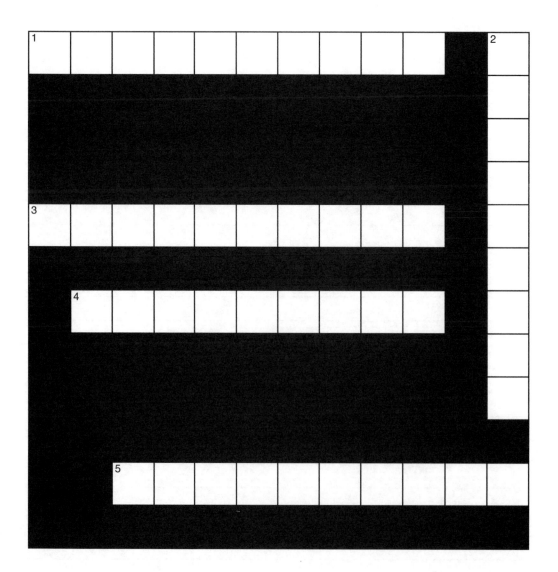

quiet/quite

These two are not really homophones – 'quiet' has two syllables, whereas 'quite' has only one – but it is easy to get them wrong.

(a) quiet

Ssh! Be **quiet**. Don't wake the baby!

(b) quite

It's **quite** cloudy

- <u>look</u> at the pictures; read each sentence aloud
- <u>say</u> homophone (a) and spell it out, aloud
- <u>cover</u> it
- <u>write</u> the word in the box below, while saying the letter names
- <u>check</u> the spelling; re-read the sentence
- <u>repeat</u> for homophone (b)

Section A

quiet   quite

- Read the sentence
- Fill in the missing homophone and highlight it

1. Be _____ and sit down, please!
2. I had _____ a lot of homework to finish off.
3. That is _____ enough fuss for one day.
4. I don't think this is _____ fair play.
5. Tom and Mary are _____ good friends.
6. There was a deathly hush and the whole place went _____ when the boss confessed that he had been fined for a drinking-and-driving offence.
7. He was told that he must settle down to a _____ life.
8. Madonna's appearance caused _____ a stir at the party.
9. I am not _____ sure whether I can come to your party or not.
10. In her own _____ way, Barbara was confident that she would get the part in the school play.

Section B

quiet   quite

- read the passage
- copy it out below
- highlight the homophones
- write the passage to dictation

Hateful Henry is quite quiet today. He must be ill because he is so quiet. He wanted to have a quiet day and went to bed. It was Horrible Harry's day off; he came banging up the stairs and turned on his CD player, making quite a din. The twins began to shout and yell at each other. 'There is no peace and quiet in this house ever,' wailed Hateful Henry. 'I might quite as well have gone to work'.

_____

_____

_____

_____

_____

_____

_____

_____

_____

_____

_____

_____

_____

_____

_____

_____

_____

_____

_____

_____

_____

_____

_____

_____

Section C

Crossword Puzzle No. 37

Clues

1. The headmaster was . . . . . decisive and said at once that the two boys would be suspended for smoking in school.

2. Deciding which car to buy is . . . . . a major decision for most people.

3. The eight-year-old violin player had . . . . . exceptional ability.

4. I need peace and . . . . . to complete this work.

5. My granny said that when her children were young she would have done anything for a . . . . . life.

rains / reigns / reins

(a) rains
(b) reigns
(c) reins

The heavy **rains** caused flooding

Queen Elizabeth **reigns** over the United Kingdom

She held the horse's **reins**

- <u>look</u> at the pictures; read each sentence aloud
- <u>say</u> homophone (a) and spell it out, aloud
- <u>cover</u> it
- <u>write</u> the word in the box below, while saying the letter names
- <u>check</u> the spelling; re-read the sentence
- <u>repeat</u> for homophones (b) and (c)

Section A

rains   reigns   reins

- Read the sentence
- Fill in the missing homophone and highlight it

1. Hold the _____ carefully: that horse is bad-tempered.
2. Torrential _____ fall during monsoons in certain countries.
3. Queen Beatrix of Holland _____ over the Dutch people.
4. The horse stood on the _____ and they broke.
5. The _____ of new kings and queens usually begin with their coronation.
6. The heavy _____ filled up the water tanks.
7. Tropical _____ often cause severe erosion.
8. The groom held the _____ as he led the racehorse to the starting line.
9. Queen Victoria had one of the longest _____ in British history.
10. Georgina and George were on leading _____ as they rode their Shetland ponies.

Section B

rains   reigns   reins

- read the passage
- copy it out below
- highlight the homophones
- write the passage to dictation

Hateful Henry likes to go from time to time for a ride with a pony and trap. One day there was a clap of thunder, heavy rains fell and the pony bolted. He hung on to the reins for dear life. Finally the pony stopped and he jumped down to the rain-soaked ground. When he got home, Horrible Harry said 'Serves you right! You should listen to the weather forecast'.

_____

_____

_____

_____

_____

_____

_____

_____

_____

_____

_____

_____

_____

_____

_____

_____

_____

_____

_____

_____

_____

_____

_____

_____

Section C

Crossword Puzzle No. 38

Clues

1. Mrs Thatcher held the . . . . . when she was Prime Minister.

2. The . . . . . . of many monarchs ended in warfare.

3. In tropical climates, when the . . . . . come, they can be very heavy.

4. The rider held on to the . . . . . when riding.

5. The cowboy . . . . . in the cattle on the ranch.

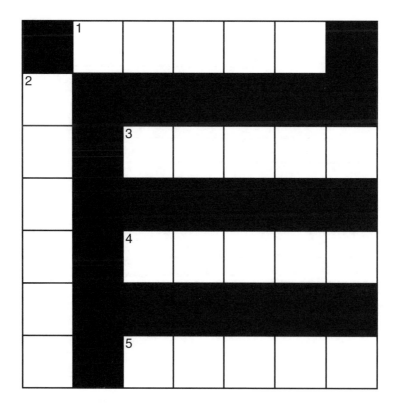

right/rite/wright/write

(a) right

(b) rite

(c) wright

(d) write

Turn **right** here

The Queen's coronation included many **rites**

Shakespeare is the world's best-known play **wright**

Always try to **write** neatly please

- <u>look</u> at the pictures; read each sentence aloud
- <u>say</u> homophone (a) and spell it out, aloud
- <u>cover</u> it
- <u>write</u> the word in the box below, while saying the letter names
- <u>check</u> the spelling; re-read the sentence
- <u>repeat</u> for homophones (b), (c) and (d)

Section A

right   rite   wright   write

- Read the sentence
- Fill in the missing homophone and highlight it

1. I like to _____ with an ink pen.
2. Can you _____ down the answer please?
3. Turn _____ at the bottom of the hill.
4. Is that the _____ way to the shops?
5. It is a good idea to _____ down telephone messages.
6. Different religions perform _____s, such as baptism for Christians or barmitzvah for Jews.
7. The Russian Tsar Peter the Great once worked as a ship_____.
8. His performance was given a very good _____-up by the critics.
9. The government had to _____ off Railtrack's debts.
10. Getting a bus pass is seen as a _____ of passage by many pensioners.

Section B

right   rite   wright   write

- read the passage
- copy it out below
- highlight the homophones
- write the passage to dictation

Horrible Harry felt that he knew his rights. 'There is a right of way through these fields,' he said.

'No, there is not!' said the farmer.

'I shall write to the council and complain,' interrupted Hateful Henry. Horrible Harry muttered, 'Ramblers have a right to roam.'

'Get off my land at once!' roared the farmer.

'We will write to the chairman of the Ramblers Association,' yelled the twins.

_____

_____

_____

_____

_____

_____

_____

_____

_____

_____

_____

_____

_____

_____

_____

_____

_____

_____

_____

_____

_____

_____

Section C

Crossword Puzzle No. 39

Clues

1. The majority of people use their . . . . . hand to write.

2. Tom Stoppard is well-known as a play . . . .

3. My granny always used to say that what you . . . . . remains.

4. Graphologists say they can tell people's characters when they examine how people . . . . . .

5. The guest of honour always sits on the host's . . . . . side.

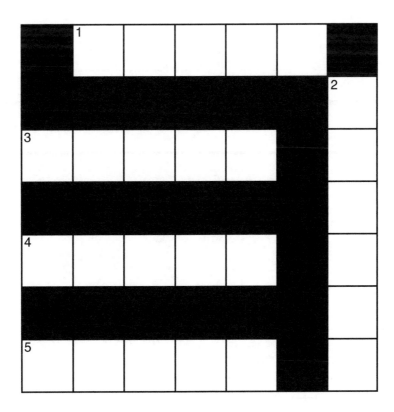

sea/see

(a) sea   (b) see

I do like to be beside the **sea**   We **see** with our eyes

- <u>look</u> at the pictures; read each sentence aloud
- <u>say</u> homophone (a) and spell it out, aloud
- <u>cover</u> it
- <u>write</u> the word in the box below, while saying the letter names
- <u>check</u> the spelling; re-read the sentence
- <u>repeat</u> for homophone (b)

| | |
| | |

Section A

sea   see

- Read the sentence
- Fill in the missing homophone and highlight it

1. I like to _____ my friends very often.
2. He fell over because he did not _____ the banana skin.
3. Do you _____ what I mean?
4. The Baltic is a very cold _____.
5. I don't always _____ the point of all this work.
6. He was very confused by the instructions and completely at _____ about what to do.
7. I must go and _____ what we are going to eat for supper.
8. The poet John Masefield wrote 'I must down to the _____s again'.
9. The doctor will call to _____ his patient today.
10. I was able to _____ through the lie he told, by the look of guilt on his face.

Section B

sea   see

- read the passage
- copy it out below
- highlight the homophones
- write the passage to dictation

Hateful Henry and Horrible Harry could not see eye to eye about where to go on holiday. 'I see that you want a hotel by the sea,' said Hateful Henry. 'I would much prefer to be able to see mountains and wild life from my bedroom window,' he said. 'Suit yourself. I've booked us in and paid for two weeks at Clacton-on-Sea,' smirked Horrible Harry.

Section C

Crossword Puzzle No. 40

Clues

1. Glass that is transparent is . . . -through.

2. My granny used to . . . red when we did not finish the food on our plates.

3. Rooms with a . . . view often cost more to rent.

4. The well-known song has a refrain 'I do like to be beside the . . . side.

5. A good chat-up line used to be to offer to . . . a girl home at the end of the evening.

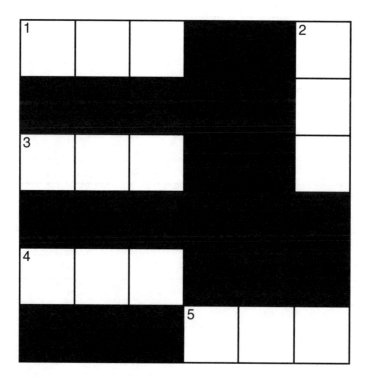

some/sum

(a) some

(b) sum

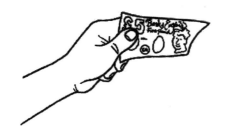

She gave me **some** money

He used his fingers to add up the **sum**

- <u>look</u> at the pictures; read each sentence aloud
- <u>say</u> homophone (a) and spell it out, aloud
- <u>cover</u> it
- <u>write</u> the word in the box below, while saying the letter names
- <u>check</u> the spelling; re-read the sentence
- <u>repeat</u> for homophone (b)

Section A

some   sum

- Read the sentence
- Fill in the missing homophone and highlight it

1. I had _____ lovely presents at Christmas.
2. Melanie sent me _____ flowers as a thank-you present.
3. He spent a large _____ of money.
4. How many _____s did you do in the maths test?
5. I saw _____ people smoking in the café.
6. Can you _____ up the main points of the argument?
7. I was left a small _____ of money in my granny's will.
8. _____ people never know how to behave.
9. The _____ total is that we are broke. We have spent all our cash.
10. He has _____ difficulties with spelling.

Section B

some   sum

- read the passage
- copy it out below
- highlight the homophones
- write the passage to dictation

Hateful Henry wanted some new curtains for the kitchen. He went and got some samples from the shops, but then he saw some ready-made ones in a sale. He bought these and when he got home, he showed them to Horrible Harry, who moaned, 'That is a huge sum of money to spend on some new curtains for the kitchen and I am not going to pay my half'.

    'Some help you are. You are a pain in the neck, because all you do is moan,' raged Hateful Henry.

_____

_____

_____

_____

_____

_____

_____

_____

_____

_____

_____

_____

_____

_____

_____

_____

_____

_____

_____

_____

_____

_____

_____

Section C

Crossword Puzzle No. 41

Clues

1. . . . . .how I must finish this coursework.

2. He won a large . . . of money in the lottery.

3. The . . . total of what he knows about cooking could be written on his thumb nail.

4. We had . . . . plum tart left over.

5. I cannot afford to buy a house in Devon: the . . . .s do not add up.

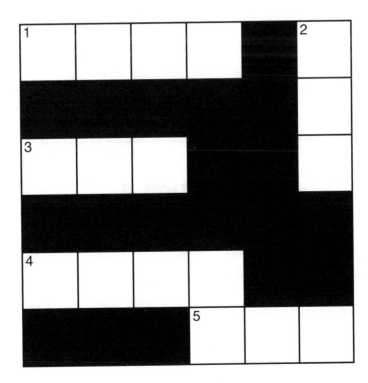

their/there/they're

(a) their

Where is **their** dog?

(b) there

Look **there**, please

(c) they're

They're dancing in the old-fashioned way

- <u>look</u> at the pictures; read each sentence aloud
- <u>say</u> homophone (a) and spell it out, aloud
- <u>cover</u> it
- <u>write</u> the word in the box below, while saying the letter names
- <u>check</u> the spelling; re-read the sentence
- <u>repeat</u> for homophone (b) and (c)

Section A

their   there   they're

- Read the sentence
- Fill in the missing homophone and highlight it

1. _____ are seven days in a week.
2. The children went to _____ grandmother for the day.
3. The golf ball is over _____, in a bush.
4. _____ school play will take place in May.
5. _____ eating a picnic lunch today.
6. _____ going to Florida for a holiday.
7. It was _____ own decision to enter the competition.
8. _____ is no way to foretell the future, except by chance.
9. The couple said that _____ neighbour's children were polite and friendly.
10. The head told the class she was proud of _____ achievement in the examination.

Section B

their   there   they're

- read the passage
- copy it out below
- highlight the homophones
- write the passage to dictation

Horrible Harry and Hateful Henry were going to visit their parents. 'They're going to be so glad to see us,' they told each other. Then there was a big row about their plans. 'There are sure to be lots of traffic jams on the way there, on Friday evening,' said Horrible Harry. 'They should leave their office early. Mum and Dad will be there waiting for us,' he said. 'They're expecting us to get there at six o'clock; that's when they have their meal'.

_____

_____

_____

_____

_____

_____

_____

_____

_____

_____

_____

_____

_____

_____

_____

_____

_____

_____

_____

_____

_____

_____

_____

_____

_____

_____

_____

Section C

Crossword Puzzle No. 42

Clues

1. The word '. . . . .' implies ownership or possession.

2. The word '. . . . .' is often repeated to comfort or console someone.

3. We often say '. . . . . and then', when a decision is made on the spot.

4. All her efforts to gain . . . . . support were in vain.

5. My granny used to point to a group of close-knit friends and say, '. . . . . . as thick as a bunch of thieves'.

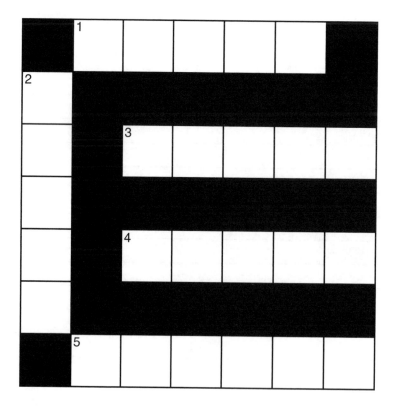

to / too (very) / too (as well as) / two

(a) to   (b) too (very)   (c) too (as well as)   (d) two

We go **to** school   The iron was **too** hot   I went for a walk and the dog came **too**   He has **two** cars

- <u>look</u> at the pictures; read each sentence aloud
- <u>say</u> homophone (a) and spell it out, aloud
- <u>cover</u> it
- <u>write</u> the word in the box below, while saying the letter names
- <u>check</u> the spelling; re-read the sentence
- <u>repeat</u> for homophones (b), (c) and (d)

Section A

to   too   two

- Read the sentence
- Fill in the missing homophone and highlight it

1. She was far _____ busy to check her e-mails before breakfast.
2. The Prime Minister brought his wife _____.
3. Only _____ of the Beatles pop group wrote their hit songs.
4. That car is beautiful, but it is _____ expensive for us.
5. Mother Teresa had _____ main aims: looking after the poor and feeding the hungry.
6. Donald Duck and Mickey Mouse are _____ of Disney's best-known characters.
7. Virginia Wade was the last Englishwoman _____ win the tennis championship at Wimbledon.
8. Sir Alex Ferguson threw David Beckham's boot _____ hard at him.
9. The Queen Mother lived _____ be a hundred.
10. The book *Harry Potter and the Order of the Phoenix* is _____ long for some readers.

Section B

to   too   two

- read the passage
- copy it out
- highlight the homophones
- write the passage to dictation

Horrible Harry and Hateful Henry like to play the piano. The two of them play duets. Sometimes they row because they cannot agree what tunes to play. They were asked to play in a concert. Hateful Henry played too fast. 'You silly fool, you have spoiled the tune too,' yelled Horrible Harry as he began to storm from the stage to the surprise of everyone. The conductor was too shocked to speak as Horrible Harry ran to the exit.

_____

_____

_____

_____

_____

_____

_____

_____

_____

_____

_____

_____

_____

_____

_____

_____

_____

_____

_____

_____

_____

_____

_____

Section C

Crossword Puzzle No. 43

Clues

1. . . . . much salt on food is bad for people's health.

2. When the telephone engineer comes . . connect us, we can use the phone.

3. Concorde had to be taken out of service because it was getting . . . old.

4. A starting gun is used . . begin sailing races.

5. The World Trade Centre in New York had . . . towers before 11 September 2001.

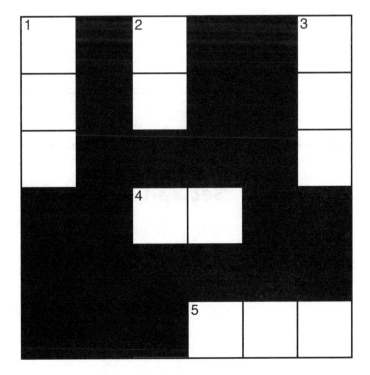

threw/through

(a) threw

(b) through

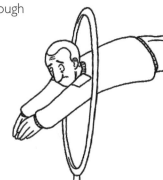

He **threw** the ball into the net

He jumped **through** the hoop

- <u>look</u> at the pictures; read each sentence aloud
- <u>say</u> homophone (a) and spell it out, aloud
- <u>cover</u> it
- <u>write</u> the word in the box below, while saying the letter names
- <u>check</u> the spelling; re-read the sentence
- <u>repeat</u> for homophone (b)

Section A

threw   through

- Read the sentence
- Fill in the missing homophone and highlight it

1. She was soaked _____ by the rain.
2. He came in _____ the back window last night, as he had lost the key.
3. She _____ the rubbish into the black bin-bag.
4. The fishermen _____ the small fish overboard.
5. I always go _____ all my notes when I revise.
6. He took a short cut _____ the woods.
7. The two-year-old toddler _____ a tantrum in the supermarket.
8. She _____ out all the old files and notes.
9. The parents had to sit _____ the school concert three evenings in a row because their three children performed on different evenings.
10. The angler _____ back the small trout he had caught.

Section B

threw   through

- read the passage
- copy it out below
- highlight the homophones
- write the passage to dictation

Hateful Henry was doing some spring-cleaning. He threw open the windows to let in some fresh air. While he was going through the bookcase, a crow flew in through the open window. Just at that moment, Horrible Harry came in through the door and was hit on the head by the silly crow's mess. He threw a fit and screamed, 'You stupid old crow!' 'Don't call me names!' yelled Hateful Henry. 'I am not speaking about you,' Horrible Harry bellowed as he threw off his coat.

_____

_____

_____

_____

_____

_____

_____

_____

_____

_____

_____

_____

_____

_____

_____

_____

_____

_____

_____

_____

_____

_____

_____

_____

_____

_____

_____

_____

Section C

Crossword Puzzle No. 44

Clues

1. It used to take ages to get . . . . to someone in Australia by telephone.

2. The bucking bronco . . . . . the rodeo rider to the ground.

3. Mothers are delighted when new-born babies sleep . . . . the night.

4. When someone looks at you and fails to acknowledge you, my granny says that they look . . . . you.

5. She . . . . . the empty bottles into the bin, so that they could be recycled.

weather/whether

(a) weather

(b) whether

What will the **weather** be like?

I am not sure **whether** I have a temperature

- <u>look</u> at the pictures; read each sentence aloud
- <u>say</u> homophone (a) and spell it out, aloud
- <u>cover</u> it
- <u>write</u> the word in the box below, while saying the letter names
- <u>check</u> the spelling; re-read the sentence
- <u>repeat</u> for homophone (b)

Section A

weather   whether

- Read the sentence then
- Fill in and highlight the missing word

1. The _____ is not too bad today.
2. What was the _____ like yesterday in Scotland?
3. The _____ forecast did not predict the storm.
4. She told me the _____ was always good in Spain in May.
5. I did not know _____ you wanted to come or not.
6. You have to pay taxes _____ you want to or not.
7. I do not know _____ he will accept the invitation or not.
8. An old-fashioned word for a barometer is a _____ glass.
9. According to the law, children must attend school _____ they like it or not.
10. Sailors always need to keep a _____ eye open when they sail.

Section B

weather   whether

- read the passage
- copy it out below
- highlight the homophones
- write the passage to dictation

Hateful Henry and Horrible Harry did not know whether to go to the football match at Wembley Stadium. The weatherman said that there would be snow in London. They argued about whether to drive up the night before or whether they should spend the night with Aunt Sally who lived in Acton. 'I'm not taking any chances with the weather,' said Hateful Henry, 'I'm leaving this evening while the weather is still fine, whether you are coming or not'.

Section C

Crossword Puzzle No. 45

Clues

1. Ulrika Johnson, the television presenter, used to be a . . . . presenter.

2. Bad-. . . . . . . warnings help people avoid or prepare for gales, floods, snow and ice.

3. Drivers in London must pay the Congestion Charge, ... they know about it or not.

4. There is a lot of debate about . . . . children should be given the triple vaccine for measles, mumps and rubella (MMR).

5. You must decide . . . . you are going to drink or drive.

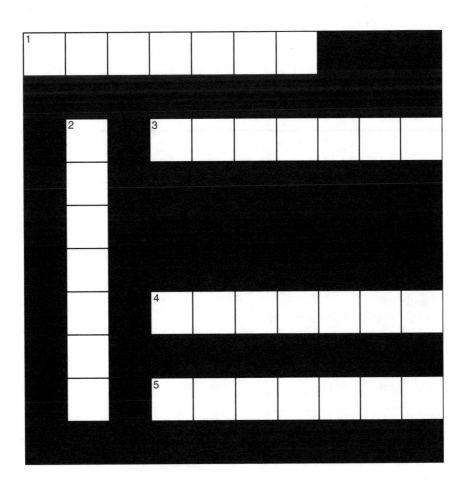

which/witch

(a) which

(b) witch

Which cake shall I eat?

This **witch** has a broomstick

- <u>look</u> at the pictures; read each sentence aloud
- <u>say</u> homophone (a) and spell it out, aloud
- <u>cover</u> it
- <u>write</u> the word in the box below, while saying the letter names
- <u>check</u> the spelling; re-read the sentence
- <u>repeat</u> for homophone (b)

Section A

which   witch

- Read the sentence
- Fill in the missing homophone and highlight it

1. _____ book did you read yesterday?
2. Did you see the _____ in the film last night?
3. The black cat lived with an old _____ in a cave.
4. A pen is something with _____ to write in ink.
5. I don't know _____ chocolate I should choose.
6. *Simon and the* _____ was a popular children's novel, _____ was later televised.
7. There was a _____ hunt to try to find those responsible for the outbreak of foot-and-mouth disease.
8. During an election it is sometimes difficult to decide _____ candidate to vote for.
9. In some countries in Africa, _____ doctors treat sick people.
10. There was a belief that a _____ could do magic by casting spells.

Section B

which   witch

- read the passage
- copy it out below
- highlight the homophones
- write the passage to dictation

Hateful Henry and Horrible Harry went climbing in Wales, which they thought would be fun. They got lost because they could not agree which path to take. They found a cave to shelter in and fell asleep. Hateful Henry had a dream in which he saw a witch with a horrid cat standing over him. He woke up in a cold sweat and there beside him was a big, black, wild cat which was staring at him. It scared him stiff.

_____

_____

_____

_____

_____

_____

_____

_____

_____

_____

_____

_____

_____

_____

_____

_____

_____

_____

_____

_____

_____

_____

_____

_____

Section C

Crossword Puzzle No. 46

Clues

1. The female form of wizard is a . . . . . .

2. Change the first letter of . . . . . to 'b' to make a female dog.

3. A . . . . . is often a character in children's books.

4. . . . . . country hosted the Football World Cup final in 2002?

5. A . . . . . without 'w' has an itch.

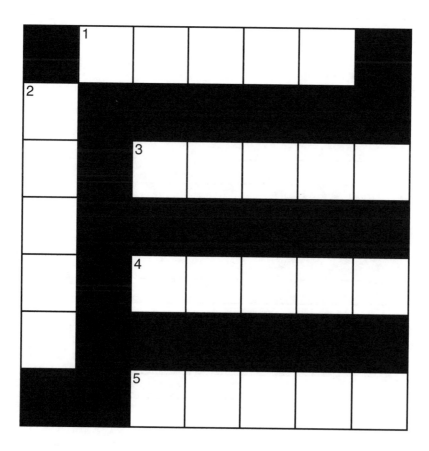

Crossword Puzzle Solutions

No. 14	**No. 15**	**No. 16**	**No. 17**	**No. 18**
1. allowed	1. eight	1. beans	1. blue	1. scent
2. allowed	2. eight	2. been	2. blue	2. sent
3. aloud	3. ate	3. beans	3. blew	3. sent
4. aloud	4. ate	4. bean	4. blue	4. cents
5. allowed	5. eight	5. been	5. blue	5. sent

No. 19	**No. 20**	**No. 21**	**No. 22**	**No. 23**
1. cereal	1. deer	1. flowers	1. grate	1. hare
2. serial	2. dear	2. flour	2. Great	2. hair
3. serial	3. dear	3. flowers	3. grate	3. hare
4. serial	4. dear	4. flour	4. Great	4. hair
5. cereal	5. dear	5. flowers	5. grate	5. hair

No. 24	**No. 25**	**No. 26**	**No. 27**	**No. 28**
1. hear	1. herd	1. hole	1. maid	1. meat
2. here	2. heard	2. hole	2. maid	2. meet
3. here	3. heard	3. whole	3. made	3. meet
4. here	4. herds	4. whole	4. made	4. meat
5. hear	5. heard	5. whole	5. made	5. meat

No. 29	**No. 30**	**No. 31**	**No. 32**	**No. 33**
1. new	1. no	1. off	1. one	1. pare
2. new	2. no	2. off	2. won	2. pear
3. knew	3. no	3. of	3. one	3. pair
4. new	4. know	4. off	4. won	4. pair
5. knew	5. know	5. off	5. won	5. pear

No. 34	**No. 35**	**No. 36**	**No. 37**	**No. 38**
1. piece	1. plane	1. principles	1. quite	1. reins
2. Peace	2. plain	2. principal	2. quite	2. reigns
3. peace	3. plain	3. principles	3. quite	3. rains
4. peace	4. plain	4. principal	4. quiet	4. reins
5. peace	5. plain	5. principles	5. quiet	5. reins

No. 39	**No. 40**	**No. 41**	**No. 42**	**No. 43**
1. right	1. see	1. some	1. their	1. too
2. wright	2. see	2. sum	2. there	2. to
3. write	3. sea	3. sum	3. there	3. too
4. write	4. sea	4. some	4. their	4. to
5. right	5. see	5. sum	5. they're	5. two

No. 44	**No. 45**	**No. 46**
1. through	1. weather	1. witch
2. threw	2. weather	2. witch
3. through	3. whether	3. witch
4. through	4. whether	4. which
5. threw	5. whether	5. witch

REVISION TESTS

How much have you remembered?

Use for dictation or as a copying exercise

Say it with flowers

(Grate/Great)-Aunt Marge lived in an old people's home with (ate/eight) other residents. Hateful Henry and Horrible Harry had not (bean/been) (allowed/aloud) to visit her because there had (bean/been) an outbreak of flu. They (cent/scent/sent) her (some/sum) (flours/flowers). When Horrible Henry was ordering them, Hateful Henry yelled, 'Be sure they are (blew/blue), because that's the old (dear/deer)'s favourite colour'.

There are 2 marks for each correct answer
The optimum score is 20

Your score

Use for dictation or as a copying exercise

Don't blame the Good Pub Guide

Horrible Harry said that he had (heard/herd) that the Old (Hair/Hare) pub served (grate/great) beer and good food. 'How do you (no/know) that?' barked Hateful Henry. 'I (made/maid) a point of looking it up in the *Good Pub Guide*. Look, (hear/here) it says that they have a (new/knew) chef and his toad in the (hole/whole) is the best in town'. 'It's closed on Mondays. Anyway, I fancy a home-(made/maid) (meat/meet) pie for my lunch,' whined Hateful Henry. 'Trust you to spoil all my plans, you rotten spoilsport!' bawled Horrible Harry.

There are 2 marks for each correct answer
The optimum score is 20

Your score

Use for dictation or as a copying exercise

The football incident

Hateful Henry and Horrible Harry go to football training whether it (rains/reign/reins) or shines. (One/won) weekend, the (pair/pare/pear) of them were chosen to play in a match on Salisbury (Plain/Plane), which was (quiet/quite) a way from home. (Right/rite/wright/write) away they began to argue whether they should go on the team coach or take (their/there/they're) car. 'In (principal/principle) we should go on the coach,' said Horrible Harry, 'but I suppose there will be no (peace/piece) if you don't get your own way'. 'Let's get ready and go (of/off) before the traffic gets bad,' concluded Hateful Henry.

There are 2 marks for each correct answer
The optimum score is 20

Your score ☐

Use for dictation or as a copying exercise

War and peace over a video

The (weather/whether) was dreadful. '(Their/There/They're) are a few videos I really want (to/too/two) (sea/see),' said Horrible Harry. They could not decide (which/witch) (one/won) they both wanted to watch. They went (threw/through) a list of popular films. I (quiet/quite) fancy seeing *Titanic* again,' said Horrible Harry.

'That's far (to/too/two) long and I (no/know) the story backwards,' grumbled Hateful Henry. 'Why don't we look at something (new/knew). I've (heard/herd) that *Lord of the Rings* is a (grate/great) film and that it (one/won) several Oscars,' moaned Horrible Harry hopefully.

'I've read the books several times and I am (blew/blue) in the face from reading Tolkien,' growled Hateful Henry.

'Oh, look! The (weather/whether) is improving. I am going out for a walk and for (some/sum) (peace/piece) and (quiet/quite) – if I'm (allowed/aloud) it.

There are 2 marks for each correct answer
The optimum score is 40

Your score ☐

Answers to revision tests

Say it with flowers

1. Great
2. eight
3. been
4. allowed
5. been
6. sent
7. some
8. flowers
9. blue
10. dear

Don't blame the Good Pub Guide

1. heard
2. Hare
3. great
4. know
5. made
6. here
7. new
8. hole
9. made
10. meat

The football incident

1. rains
2. One
3. pair
4. Plain
5. quite
6. Right
7. their
8. principle
9. peace
10. off

War and peace over a video

1. weather
2. There
3. to
4. see
5. which
6. one
7. through
8. quite
9. too
10. know
11. new
12. heard
13. great
14. won
15. blue
16. weather
17. some
18. peace
19. quiet
20. allowed

Total your scores to find out how well you managed the homophones

Your total:

100	excellent
99–80	very good
79–70	good
69–60	not bad
59–below	keep trying

5 How to Manage Root Words, Prefixes and Suffixes Skilfully

The aims of this chapter

Identifying root words and affixes helps to develop readers' awareness and ability with phonological skills. It heightens their consciousness of the beginning, middle and endings of words as well as the basic spelling elements and patterns. Those with good visual skills learn by grafting on affixes to root words and by memorising the word patterns. Strong verbalisers and those with good auditory and language skills deepen their understanding of word structure and spelling when using and learning the meanings of Anglo-Saxon, Greek and Latin derivatives. The use of multi-sensory strategies helps to compensate for poor visual skills, as well as helping those with poor phonological skills. Those who have good kinaesthetic skills learn by counting and dividing words into roots, prefixes and suffixes; they can then synthesise these syllables into words when reading and spelling.

Specific knowledge and understanding of affixes helps to lessen the fear of spelling long words, many of which follow a reliable sound-to-symbol match. Adding prefixes to words follows some clear-cut guidelines and rules.

Suffixes carry out many important functions, including grammatical and syntactic functions. The rules for adding suffixes are clear-cut, specific, reliable and frequently used. Studying them pays handsome dividends for all spellers, providing many opportunities to boost and enrich vocabulary. The Rose Review pointed out the importance of 'linguistic' comprehension which involves the interpretation of words, sentences and discourse' which each Section provides.

Keywords

The vowels are 'a' 'e' 'i' 'o' 'u'

'y' is sometimes a vowel, as in: sky, lady, tyre

There are two kinds of vowels: *Short vowels* say their sounds; *long vowels* say their names. *Digraphs* are two letters making one sound; there are consonant digraphs and vowel digraphs. *Diphthongs* are two vowels side by side, which glide together when pronounced in rapid succession. *Blends* are letters found next to each other; they sound separately but quickly to make the sound. *Assimilations* are nasal sounds (made down one's nose) and involve the letters 'm' and 'n'.

Affixes are a letter or a group of letters added to the beginning or end of a word to form another word:

duct   fresh

con<u>duct</u>ing   refresh<u>ment</u>

Root Words – sometimes called base words – are the main part or stem of a word. They can be words in themselves. They can take a prefix or suffix, or both. The root word here is 'sign':

re<u>sign</u>   <u>sign</u>al   de<u>sign</u>er

Prefixes are (groups of) letters that go at the beginning of a word and change its meaning:

<u>de</u>form   <u>in</u>form   <u>per</u>form   <u>re</u>form   <u>uni</u>form

Suffixes are (groups of) letters that go at the end of a word and change its meaning and the way it is used:

love<u>s</u>   lov<u>ed</u>   lov<u>ing</u>   lov<u>er</u>   love<u>able</u>

Differentiated activities

Most topics have three sections, with different levels of activities to match the individual's development and skills.

Section A: Using roots and prefixes

The learner inserts the missing root, prefix or syllable in a word, either by checking with the list of target words or from memory. He then uses it in a meaningful context in a sentence. He uses the proof-reading C-O-P-S to check for **c**apital letters, **o**missions, **p**unctuation and **s**pelling in the sentence. This is a visual and kinaesthetic reinforcement of the spelling.

Section B: Quiz questions

The learner:

- re-reads the target words
- reads the clues
- fills in the missing word in the quiz
- read the whole sentence
- underlines the target word

Practising with the target words is particularly effective for those with good auditory and oral language skills.

Section C: Seeing and hearing affixes

The teacher and learner read the passage through, to practise seeing and hearing the polysyllabic words with prefixes and suffixes in context.

The learner:

- re-reads the passage, sentence by sentence (longer sentences may need to be broken into short, meaningful phrases)
- copies out the passage
- uses the passage for dictation
- re-reads the passage using the proof-reading C-O-P-S
- highlights the polysyllabic target words, including the roots, prefixes and suffixes

Dictation can also be used by an individual without the help of a teacher/learning partner or parent, as follows.

The learner:

- reads the passage on to a cassette tape recorder or a minidisk recorder with playback facility
- plays it back, using headphones to listen to it sentence by sentence
- re-reads the passage, using the proof-reading C-O-P-S and checking with the original passage

How you can use these activities

These three sections use different learning strategies, a variety of tactics and different skills to teach, learn, rehearse and reinforce the use and meaning of root words, prefixes and suffixes. They represent differentiated levels of difficulty to match different spelling abilities.

Some learners will be able to tackle all the activities during the 20-minute segment of The Literacy Hour used 'for group or independent work', whereas others may work on just section A, or A and B. The keywords and strategies can be revised during the plenary session. Pupils can be asked to identify their 'best' strategy for remembering. Further examples can be noted during shared and guided text activities and added to an individual's personal 'spellofax'.

The various activities can also be used for one-to-one learning and teaching. An individual may do one sentence from the three activities every day, thus reinforcing spellings and the use of root words and affixes for five consecutive days to maximise learning.

Those who are strong auditorially will be helped to learn by remembering the meaning of each prefix or suffix when it is said. Kinaesthetic learners will find segmenting and highlighting the affixes and root words helpful. The simultaneous use of seeing, saying, learning the meanings and writing roots, prefixes and suffixes applies multi-sensory principles to segmenting words into meaningful chunks. This is an effective method for learning and remembering spelling patterns, as well as helping to reduce the memory load. Critics of multi-sensory teaching methods frequently derided the 'drill-and-skill' methods used and accused teachers of inducing 'death by workbook'. The criticism was valid when learners were given worksheets and just asked to fill in or copy out missing words on the page.

Constant repetition and the use of multi-sensory means will help to develop mastery and automatic recall, in order to manage root words, prefixes and suffixes successfully when reading and when doing independent writing.

Understanding and recall of keywords are significant factors for successful work on syllables. They can be established by using different strategies and a variety of tactics depending on preferred learning style. Many dyslexic learners have difficulties with word retrieval and word naming, so it is essential that teacher/learning partner and learner constantly revise and rehearse keywords, such as short and long vowel, consonant, blend, digraph, affix, root word, prefix, suffix and antonym. The teacher/learning partner and learner can discuss the aim of each activity, then review the list of keywords and look at the given examples. Further examples may be generated and these can be written on the board, on an overhead transparency (OHT) or on an interactive whiteboard to provide a computer printout. This can be filed in a personal 'Spellofax' for review and revision. Dictionary work will also play an important role as learners study meanings, derivations and the use of words.

Aim: To identify, understand and use words with Latin roots

Keywords to review:

A root word is the main part or stem of a word. It can take a prefix or suffix:

<u>port</u>er   re<u>port</u>er   de<u>port</u>ed

First, you need the checklist of useful Latin root words in front of you

- look at each word
- say the word
- learn its meaning
- read the examples
- highlight the root word within each example

Checklist of useful Latin root words

root	word origin	meaning	examples
audi	*audio*	hear	audible, audience, audition
ann	*annus*	year	anniversary, annual, annuity
cede	*cedere*	yield/admit	antecedent, precede, recede
clud, clus	*cludere, clusum*	shut	occlude, included, exclusive
cred	*credere*	believe	creditor, credence, incredible
loc	*locus*	place	allocate, dislocate, location
man	*manus*	hand	manipulated, manual, manuscript
port	*portare*	carry	deportation, import, portable
sci	*scire*	know	conscious, science, scientific
sign	*signum*	mark	insignia, signal, signature
spect	*spectare*	see	inspection, spectator, spectacles
struct	*structum*	assemble/build	construction, destruction, structure
terr	*terra*	land/earth	extraterrestrial, territory, terrain
urb	*urbs*	city	suburb, urban, urbanisation
vinc, vict	*vincere, victum*	conquer	invincible, victor, victorious
vid	*video, videre, visum*	see	evidence, television, video
viv	*vivere*	live	revival, survivor, vivid
vol	*volo, volens*	wish/be willing	voluntary, volunteer, malevolent
volv	*volvo, volvere*	roll	evolution, devolved, revolution,
vor	*vorare*	eat/devour	carnivorous, herbivore, voracious

Word list based on The National Literacy Strategy Key Stage 2 Spellingbank (DfEE, 1999)
The examples were chosen to show the use of both prefixes and suffixes, rather than listing every possibility.

Using Latin root words

- look at each word
- say the word
- highlight the root and say its meaning (you can use a dictionary)
- copy out the word
- use it in a sentence
- use the proof-reading C-O-P-S

1. audience_____

2. voluntary _____

3. location _____

4. television _____

5. survivor _____

6. territory _____

Checklist of useful Greek root words

Root	word origin	meaning	examples
aero	aer	air	aerial, aerobics, aerosol
arch	arche	power	archbishop, oligarchy, monarch
bio	bios	life	biography, biopsy, bionic
crat	cratos	rule	aristocrat, bureaucrat, democrat
chron	chronos	time	chronological, chronicle, chronology
cycl	kyklos	ring/circle	bicycle, cyclone, encyclopedia
dem	demos	people	democracy, demagogue, demographer
epi	epi	above/over	epicentre, epidemic, epilogue
gen	genos	race/kind	genealogy, genocide, progeny
gram	gramma	something written	grammar, monogram, telegram
graph	graphos	someone who writes/draws	autobiography, photograph, telegraph
hydr	hydr/hydro	water	dehydration, hydroelectricity, hydrant
path	pathos	feeling	empathy, pathetic, sympathetic
phon	phone	sound/voice	phonics, telephone, saxophone
photo	photo	light	photogenic, photography, photosynthesis
poli	polis	city	cosmopolitan, metropolitan, police
phys	physis	nature	physics, physiology, physique
psych	psyche	mind	psychology, psychiatrist, psychopath
scop	skopein	look at	microscope, stethoscope, telescope
therm	therme	heat	thermal, thermometer, thermostat

Word list based on The National Strategy Key Stage 2 Spellingbank (DfEE 1999)

The examples were chosen to show the use of both prefixes and suffixes, rather than listing every possibility.

ACTIVITY

Aim: To identify, understand and use words with Greek roots

Keywords to review:

A root word is the main part or stem of a word. It can take a prefix or suffix:

<u>port</u>er   re<u>port</u>er   de<u>port</u>ed

First, you need the checklist of useful Greek root words in front of you

Using Greek root words

- Look at each word
- Say the word
- Highlight the root word say its meaning (you can use a dictionary)
- Copy out the word
- Use it in a sentence
- use the proof-reading C-O-P-S

1. tricycle _____

2. aerosol _____

3. metropolitan _____

4. thermometer _____

5. psychiatrist _____

6. autobiography _____

Section A

- have the checklists of Latin and Greek roots in front of you
- fill in the missing letters (below) to complete the word
- then make a sentence for each word

1. ....ible _____

2. ....acles _____

3. ....versary _____

4. ....phone _____

5. de.........ation _____

6. ....genic _____

7. ....terrestrial _____

8. ....script _____

9. ....ature _____

10. ....ostat _____

Section B – Quiz 1

Complete the quiz by using words from the Latin and Greek root checklists

1. The name of an American political party. At one time Bill Clinton was one of the best known members of the . . . . party.

2. A doctor uses a . . . . to check a patient's lungs and chest.

3. The Nazis committed . . . . against the Jews.

4. Roald Dahl called his . . . . *Going Solo.*

5. Encarta is the name of an online . . . .

6. The doctor carried out a . . . . on the kidney removed from the patient.

7. Most jazz bands have a . . . . in their line-up.

8. Dr Rowan Williams is the . . . . of Canterbury.

9. . . . . is an activity often carried out in the gym.

10. Desert travellers often suffer from . . . . because they have too little water.

Section C

- read the passage
- copy it out
- write the passage to dictation
- highlight the roots
- re-read, using the proof-reading C-O-P-S

The Mastermind competition

Hateful Henry and Horrible Harry fancied their chances in the competition. 'I am good enough to be on television,' boasted Horrible Harry on the telephone to the producer. He was told to come for an audition. He went on his bicycle from the suburb where they lived. He chose natural history as his specialist subject and felt that he was invincible. He got the highest score and was told he would have to perform in a studio before a live audience.

Hateful Henry sat in the audience. It had been a voluntary decision to be there. 'I hope you have turned on the video at home, so I have evidence of my performance tonight,' whispered Horrible Harry. The studio lights were turned up. He sat in the black chair. He answered questions on the physique of animals and the eating habits of carnivorous and herbivorous animals. The competition was a dead heat. The final question was to give the name of the lion in the film *The Lion King*.

He got it wrong. Horrible Harry smirked. 'Everyone knows it was King Louis.'

PREFIXES

It is useful to divide prefixes into categories for easy reference; it also helps to lighten the load for learners when subjects are broken down into more manageable pieces of information. The initial objective should be to show how prefixes work. Then their usefulness can be explained in an interactive manner. Prefixes can be illustrated by examples showing how helpful they can be for everyone, especially poor spellers. Use root words such as 'form', 'port' and 'tend', with a computer graphics package, to make a family tree diagram.

Then brainstorm to generate new words orally: try to make as many different words as possible. Use colour for the prefix, to heighten the visual impact when they are written. Revise and rehearse the meaning and spelling of common prefixes.

Useful Tip

The *Oxford Spell-it-Yourself Dictionary* lists over 8,000 root words, gives the derivations and highlights the root in bold.

Aim: To identify, understand and use words with Latin prefixes

Keywords to review:

A prefix is a letter or group of letters that goes at the beginning of a root word. A prefix changes the meaning of the word.

The vowels are 'a' 'e' 'i' 'o' 'u' (and sometimes 'y')

The consonants are all the other letters in the alphabet

HANDY HINT

The following are the most common prefixes:

   'com' 'con' 'de' 'dis' 'ex' 'im' 'in' 'pre' 'pro' 're' 'un'

Source: **Becker, Dixon and Anderson-Inman's (1980) analysis of 26,000 high-frequency words**

First, you need the checklist of useful Latin prefixes in front of you

- look at each word
- say the word
- learn its meaning
- read the examples
- highlight the prefix within each example

Checklist of useful Latin prefixes

prefix	meaning	examples
ab	from	abandon, abstain, absent
ac	to go forwards	accede, accelerate,
ambi	on both sides	ambidextrous, ambiguity, ambivalent
ante	before	antenatal, ante-post, anteroom
circa	around	circulate, circumference, circumlocution
co	together/with	coeducational, co-exist, cohabiting
contra	against	contraception, contradictory, contraflow
de	down/opposite	deflate, detoxify, devalue
dis	lack of	disabled, disapproval, disinterested
inter	among/between	international, intercom, Internet
non	not	non-alcoholic, non-stick, non-smoking
omni	all	omnibus, omnipotent, omnivorous
per	through/by means	perforation, perennial, pervade
post	after	postgraduate, post-mortem, postscript
re	again	recapture, remake, retake
retro	backwards	retrocede, retrograde, retrospection
sub	under	submarine, subterranean, subway
super	above	superglue, superpower, supermarket
trans	across	transatlantic, transfer, transcribed
ultra	beyond/very	ultimatum, ultrasound, ultraviolet
uni	one/single	uniformity, unisex, unison

ACTIVITY

Using Latin prefixes

- look at each word
- say the word
- highlight the prefix and say its meaning
  (you can use a dictionary)
- copy out the word
- use it in a sentence
- use the proof-reading C-O-P-S

1. ambidextrous _____

2. circumference_____

3. unison_____

4. postscript _____

5. omnivorous _____

6. intercom_____

Section A

- have the checklist of Latin prefixes in front of you
- fill in the missing prefixes (below) to complete the word
- then make a sentence for each word

1. .... mortem _____

2. ....national _____

3. ....toxify_____

4. ....graduate _____

5. ....glue _____

6. ....andoned _____

7. ....way _____

8. ....educational _____

9. ....vade _____

10. ....atlantic _____

Section B – Quiz 2

Complete the quiz by using words from the Latin prefix checklist

1. The umpire or referee must not support either team: he must be . . . .

2. At Buckingham Palace there is an . . . . before the Throne Room.

3. Roman emperors were . . . . : they had the power of life and death over their citizens.

4. A . . . . of the inner tube of the tyre caused the puncture.

5. The underground train system in New York is called the . . . .

6. A . . . . examination was carried out on the accident victims.

7. Fathers sometimes now attend . . . . classes with pregnant mothers.

8. The . . . . fee for David Beckham to Real Madrid broke many records.

9. Candidates who fail examinations are sometimes allowed to . . . . them.

10. That man is . . . . : he writes with his right hand, but uses his left hand to bat when playing cricket.

Section C

- read the passage
- copy it out
- write the passage to dictation
- highlight the prefixes
- re-read, using the proof-reading C-O-P-S

A hospital visit

Hateful Henry and Horrible Harry had been to a party. It was Hateful Henry's turn to drive. He had been drinking non-alcoholic beer all evening. On the way home he did not see that there was a traffic contraflow. Half a mile from home he began to accelerate, because he wanted to watch the rugby international match live on television. There was an almighty bang as he hit an on-coming dustcart.

They had to abandon the car and were taken to the local hospital. The nurse looked at him in disapproval as she bandaged his bleeding head and broken leg. 'I suppose we will have to let you detoxify before the doctor can treat you'. He sat up in the bed and screamed indignantly at her, 'I am not a Saturday night drunk, I am stone-cold sober.'

Horrible Harry was in the next cubicle. He shouted out, 'Serves you right for being so stupid, not reading the road signs and not looking where you were going'.

Aim: To identify, understand and use words with Greek prefixes

Keywords to review:

A prefix is a letter or group of letters that goes at the beginning of a root word. A prefix changes the meaning of the word.

The vowels are 'a' 'e' 'i' 'o' 'u' (and sometimes 'y')

The consonants are all the other letters in the alphabet

First, you need the checklist of useful Greek prefixes in front of you

- look at each word
- say the word
- learn its meaning
- read the examples
- highlight the prefixes in the examples.

Checklist of useful Greek prefixes

Prefix	Meaning	Examples
a	not/without	apathy, asymmetry, aversion
aero	air	aerobics, aeroplane, aerosol
ana	backwards/again	anachronism, anagram, anathema
anti	from/against	antipathy, antipodes, antonym
auto	self	autobiography, autograph, automatic
dys	bad/difficulty	dyscalculia, dyslexia, dyspraxia
ex	out	excavation, excerpt, extractor
hetero	one or the other	heterogeneous, heterosexual
hydro	water	hydrofoil, hydrogen, hydrotherapy
hyper	excessive	hyperactive, hyperbole, hypermarket
hypno	sleep	hypnosis, hypnotherapy, hypnotism
hypo	under	hypochondriac, hypocrisy, hypothermia
meta	between/among	metacarpal, metamorphosis, metaphor
micro	little	microclimate, microlight, microphone
mono	single	monologue, monoplane, monosyllabic
optic	seen/visible	optical, optician, optometry
peri	around	peripatetic, peripheral, periscope
photo	light	photocopy, photography, photostat
poly	many	polychrome, polygamy, polyglot
syn	with/together	synchronise, syndicate, syndrome
tele	far/far off	telephone, telescope, televise

ACTIVITY

Using Greek prefixes

First, you need the checklist of useful Greek prefixes in front of you

- look at each word
- say the word
- highlight the prefix and say its meaning
  (you can use a dictionary)
- copy out the word
- use it in a sentence

1. autograph _____

2. hydrofoil _____

3. synchronise _____

4. optician _____

5. microlight _____

6. monologue _____

Aim: To identify, understand and use words with Anglo-Saxon prefixes

Keywords to review:

A prefix is a letter or group of letters that goes at the beginning of a root word. A prefix changes the meaning of the word.

The vowels are 'a' 'e' 'i' 'o' 'u' (and sometimes 'y')

The consonants are all the other letters in the alphabet

First, you need the checklist of useful Anglo-Saxon prefixes in front of you, see p. 358

- look at each word
- say the word
- learn its meaning
- read the examples
- highlight the prefixes in the examples.

Checklist of useful Anglo-Saxon prefixes

prefix	meaning	examples
a	with	aback, aground, aloud
afore	before/previously	aforesaid, aforementioned, aforethought
all	all, completely	almighty, altogether, always
be	all around	bedecked, bedevilled, befriend
by	next to/to the side	byroads, bystander, bypass
fore	before	forecast, foresee, forehead
mid	middle	midnight, midriff, midwife
mis	wrongly/badly	misfit, misjudged, mislay
out	out/openly	outlandish, outlaw, outward
over	above/beyond	overdo, overrated, overthrow
self	self	self-assurance, self-fulfilling, self-winding
un	not	unbearable, uncleanliness, unfold
up	upper	upbringing, uphill, upright
wel, well	competent/skilful	welcome, well-bred, well-wisher
with	away/back	withdraw, without, withstand

ACTIVITY

Using Anglo-Saxon prefixes

- look at each word
- say the word
- highlight the prefix and say its meaning (you can use a dictionary)
- copy out the word
- use it in a sentence

1. forehead _____

2. midnight _____

3. bypass _____

4. overrun _____

5. unclean _____

6. self-assured _____

Section A

- Have the checklists of Greek and Anglo-Saxon prefixes in front of you
- Fill in the missing prefix (below) to complete the word
- Then make a sentence for each word

1. ....carpal_____

2. ....thermia _____

3. ....-fulfilling _____

4. ....lay _____

5. ....bole_____

6. ....roads _____

7. ....draw _____

8. ....climate_____

9. ....calculia_____

10. ....law_____

Section B – Quiz 3

Complete the quiz by using words from the Greek and Anglo-Saxon checklists

1. The judges had to . . . . their watches before the competition began.

2. Some old people suffer from . . . . in cold winters.

3. Stoke Mandeville Hospital has a . . . . pool for its patients.

4. Giant supermarkets are called . . . . , especially in France.

5. The Arctic is the . . . . of the Antarctic.

6. During the summer, the heat was . . . . in the London Underground.

7. The music teacher/learning partner's job was . . . . as she taught at three different schools.

8. The plot in the Harry Potter book . . . . gradually to keep the reader's interest.

9. Some people give up smoking by using . . . .

10. A . . . . is a nurse who helps to deliver babies and care for pregnant women.

Section C

- read the passage
- copy it out
- write the passage to dictation
- highlight the prefixes
- re-read, using the proof-reading C-O-P-S

A trip across the English Channel

One day Hateful Henry and Horrible Harry decided to take the hydrofoil to France. They wanted to see whether bargain shopping was overrated. They checked the prices of beer and wine at their nearest supermarket so they could compare them with prices at a hypermarket in Calais.

All went well on the outward trip until they missed their turning off the bypass. 'Your job is to foresee where I have to turn off when you are map-reading,' grumbled Hateful Henry. They rolled down the window and asked directions from a bystander. His answer was in monosyllabic English because the twins did not speak much French.

They stacked their shopping trolleys up to the brim and all was well until they were given the bill at the checkout. They had misjudged the number of euros to the pound and their forecast for savings took a nosedive. A row broke out as the twins squabbled in the shop. The manager came over and said that their behaviour was outlandish. They abandoned their trolleys, ran out of the shop and had a punch-up in the car park.

_____

_____

_____

_____

_____

_____

_____

_____

_____

_____

_____

_____

_____

_____

_____

_____

_____

_____

_____

Guidelines for odd-bod spellings of prefixes

Aim: To read and spell words with the prefix 'all'

When 'all' is added before a very common word, they are usually joined and one 'l' is squeezed out:

almost   already   also   altogether   although   always

An exception is 'all right', which stays as two words – though you will sometimes see it spelt 'alright'.

One other exception is 'allspice', which is always one word, but keeps 'double l'.

When 'all' is used to make a compound word, it usually keeps double 'l':

all-purpose   all-night   all-risks   all-rounder   all-star   all-time

- look at all the words above
- say each word (or pair of words)
- learn its meaning

HANDY HINT

A prefix such as 'all' sometimes drops the second 'l' when it is added to a root word:

also   although   always

Section B – Quiz 4

Fill in the gaps, using the target words above

1. We have an . . . . insurance policy.

2. I am on the penultimate page and have . . . . finished reading *Lord of the Rings*.

3. . . . . I did not hear the alarm clock, I still managed to be on time for work.

4. . . . . is one of the ingredients in Christmas pudding.

5. That cricketer can bat, bowl and field well: he is an . . . .

6. Winston Churchill is regarded as one of the . . . . great Britons.

7. . . . . , there were a hundred guests at the party.

8. Paper towels are an . . . . cleaning material.

9. I . . . . had a copy of the Three Tenors video.

10. Some supermarkets now offer . . . . shopping.

CONTINUED

Make a sentence for each of the target words on p. 361

1. _____

2. _____

3. _____

4. _____

5. _____

6. _____

7. _____

8. _____

9. _____

10. _____

Aim: To read and spell words with the prefix 'well'

When 'well' is used before an adjective made from a verb, it makes a compound adjective. If this is followed a noun, it is hyphenated:

well-behaved (child)   well-educated (person)
well-groomed (girl)   well-informed (student)
well-known (personality)   well-timed (arrival)
well-read (teenager)

Here are some more:

well-built
well-done
well-heeled
well-knit
well-oiled
well-stacked
well-balanced
well-bred
well-dressed
well-loved
well-matched
well-prepared
well-spoken

If they are not followed by a noun, they are not hyphenated:

She is well prepared for the test
He is well dressed

There are also a few compound nouns made with 'well' – some are hyphenated:

well-being   well-wisher

Some drop one 'l' and become one word:

welfare   welcome

There are a few other compounds with 'well' and these are hyphenated:

well-nigh   well-to-do

Section B – Quiz 5

Fill in the gaps, using the target words on p. 363

1. Cilla Black is a . . . . television personality.

2. The bride and groom were . . . . : they had a lot of common interests.

3. Our local library always has . . . . shelves of novels.

4. Our dog Wellington is . . . . ; he is registered by the Kennel Club as a Cavalier King Charles spaniel.

5. The child was very . . . . in the restaurant

6. Their neighbours are . . . . ; they have a Rolls-Royce and a Porsche.

7. Members of the Royal Family are always . . . . when they attend public functions.

8. A . . . . diet is essential for everyone, especially children.

9. I do not like . . . . steak; I prefer mine rare.

10. The student was . . . . about the company before he went to the interview.

Make a sentence for each of the target words.

1. _____

2. _____

3. _____

4. _____

5. _____

6. _____

7. _____

8. _____

9. _____

10. _____

Aim: To read and spell words beginning 'ill'

When 'in' is used as a prefix to a root word beginning with 'l', it becomes 'il':

illegal	illegible	illegitimate	illiberal
illogical	illuminate	illusion	illustration

When the word 'ill' is used to make a compound adjective, it is hyphenated:

ill-advised	ill-equipped
ill-bred	ill-natured
ill-mannered	ill-treated
ill-gotten	ill-humoured

The word 'ill' is not usually hyphenated in compound nouns:

ill feeling	ill health	ill humour	ill will

- look at the words above
- say each word (or pair of words)
- learn its meaning (you can use a dictionary)
- highlight the prefix

Section B – Quiz 6

Fill in the gaps, using the target words above

1. She used an . . . . to show what she meant.

2. His handwriting was . . . . , so the letter had to be typed.

3. Basil Fawlty was often . . . . with his guests.

4. There has been some . . . . in Middle East about the Gulf War.

5. They had to apply for planning permission to . . . . the restaurant sign at night.

6. . . . . immigrants are sometimes smuggled into Britain.

7. The climbers were . . . . for their trip to Glencoe.

8. . . . . behaviour is not acceptable in car parks.

9. King George IV had a family of . . . . children.

10. Under-age drinking is . . . . in pubs.

CONTINUED

Make a sentence for ten of the target words on p. 365

1. _____

2. _____

3. _____

4. _____

5. _____

6. _____

7. _____

8. _____

9. _____

10. _____

Aim: To read and spell words with the prefixes 'im', 'in' and 'ir'

When 'in' is used as a prefix to a root word beginning with 'm', 'b' or 'p', it becomes 'im':

immaterial	immaturity	immediate	immensely	immersion
immigrant	imminent	immobile	immoderate	immunise
imbalance	imbibe	impact	impatient	import

CONTINUED

When 'in' is used as a prefix to a root word beginning with 'n', the word has a double 'nn':

innards	innate	inner	innermost	innings
innocent	innocuous	innovative	innuendo	innumerable

When 'in' is used as a prefix to a root word beginning with 'r', it becomes 'ir':

irreconcilable	irredeemable	irrefutable
irregular	irrelevant	irreligious
irremovable	irreplaceable	irrigate

- look at the words above
- say each word
- learn its meaning (you can use a dictionary)
- highlight the prefix

Section B – Quiz 7

Fill in the gaps, using the target words above

1. An . . . . heater is very useful for hot water.

2. The police had . . . . evidence because the burglar had left his fingerprints at the scene of the crime.

3. The French language has many . . . . verbs.

4. The information he gave was . . . . , so it was unhelpful.

5. She has an . . . . collection of old postcards.

6. . . . . bowel syndrome is a common medical complaint.

7. The stroke victim was . . . . and so was confined to a wheelchair.

8. The Mona Lisa painting is . . . . valuable.

9. The cricketer made a good . . . . and helped his team win the match.

10. Britain has to . . . . bananas from overseas.

Make a sentence for ten of the target words listed in the above box.

1. _____

2. _____

CONTINUED

3. _____

4. _____

5. _____

6. _____

7. _____

8. _____

9. _____

10. _____

SUFFIXES

Review the grammatical uses of suffixes by a brainstorming session with the learner(s). Include the following:

- Regular plurals adding 's' – such as pig, pigs or cup, cups
- Apostrophe 's to denote belonging – as in dog's paws and dogs' paws
- Past tense of verbs adding 'ed' – such as walk, walked or mend, mended
- Present tense of verbs adding 'ing' – as in look, looking or like, liking
- Contractions adding 'n't' – such as don't and won't
- Comparatives and superlatives of adjectives adding 'er' and 'est' – as in quick, quicker, quickest

Checklist of useful Latin and French suffixes

suffix	meaning	examples
able	knowledge/power	capable, fashionable, payable
age	collection/set of	baggage, orphanage, wreckage
al	related/action of doing	arrival, parental, emotional
ate	like/related to	affectionate, compassionate, passionate
ee	person who is or has something	absentee, employee, payee
ese	related to a country/place	Burmese, Chinese, Japanese
ess	female of type/class	duchess, lioness, tigress
ian	relating/similar to	beautician, optician, musician
ism	ideas/principles	alcoholism, feminism, socialism
ist	believer in/practitioner of	anarchist, novelist, tourist
ive	quality/feeling	creative, effective, supportive
ol	derived from	alcohol, ethanol, methanol
ose	possession of a certain quality	bellicose, morose, verbose
osis	condition	hypnosis, metamorphosis, psychosis
ous	quality/character	adventurous, jealous, marvellous
tude	disposition/state of mind	attitude, gratitude, solitude

Using Latin and French suffixes

Aim: To identify, understand and learn how to use words with Latin or French suffixes

Keywords for review:

A suffix is a letter or group of letters that goes at the end of a root word. A suffix usually changes the way the word is used.

First, you need the checklist of useful Latin and French suffixes in front of you, see p. 368.

- look at each word
- say the word
- learn its meaning
- read the examples
- highlight the suffix within each example

Using Latin and French suffixes

- look at each word
- say the word
- highlight the suffix and say its meaning (you can use a dictionary)
- copy out the word
- use it in a sentence
- use the proof-reading C-O-P-S

1. employee _____

2. lioness _____

3. jealous _____

4. gratitude_____

5. fashionable _____

6. effective _____

7. jealous _____

8. gratitude_____

9. fashionable _____

10. effective _____

Section A

- have the checklist of Latin and French suffixes in front of you, see p. 368
- fill in the missing suffix to complete the word
- then make a sentence for each word

1. orphan.......... _____

2. pay............. _____

3. employ........... _____

4. beautic........... _____

5. marvell......... _____

6. alcoh........ _____

7. sol........ _____

8. duch........ _____

9. bagg........ _____

10. parent........ _____

Section B – Quiz 8

Complete the quiz by using words from the checklist of Latin and French suffixes on p. 368.

1. She went to the . . . . for an eye test.
2. Charlotte Bronte was a famous . . . .
3. . . . . takeaways are popular meals.
4. The film had to have . . . . guidance.
5. Dogs can be . . . . companions.
6. The caterpillar underwent . . . . to become a butterfly.
7. The mortgage on the house is . . . . in monthly instalments.
8. The dress designer is a very . . . . person.
9. That woman is very . . . . : she uses six long words where one short word would do.
10. Mother Theresa was very . . . . towards the poor.

Section C

- read the passage
- copy it out
- write the passage to dictation
- highlight the suffixes
- re-read, using the proof-reading C-O-P-S

The trip to a video store that did not provide emotional comfort

Horrible Harry and Hateful Henry were feeling in a morose mood because their dog had died. Rover had been very affectionate and an important part of their lives. They had taken him to the vet, a most compassionate man, who said there was no effective treatment for the creature because he had had a bad seizure. They had to have poor Rover put down.

They both needed some solace, so they went to the video shop to get a video to help them forget their emotional state. They watched *The Bridge on the River Kwai*. 'This was a bad choice,' groaned Hateful Henry. 'I'm more depressed than ever, watching those poor prisoners-of-war building that railway line.' 'Don't you dare switch it off,' shrieked Horrible Harry, 'I want to know the ending'.

_____
_____
_____
_____
_____
_____
_____
_____
_____
_____
_____
_____
_____
_____
_____
_____
_____
_____
_____
_____
_____

Checklist of useful Greek suffixes

suffix	origin	meaning	examples
ide	*ides*	chemical/compound	chloride, fluoride, peroxide
ism	*isma*	beliefs/principles/prejudices	agnosticism, Buddhism, vandalism
ist	*istes*	believer in	communist, feminist, pacifist
ite	*ites*	group	anthracite, dynamite, granite
itis	*itis*	name of disease/condition	appendicitis, conjunctivitis, tonsillitis
ology	*logos*	science/word/reason	ecology, biology, neurology
phobia	*phobos*	fear	agoraphobia, claustrophobia, xenophobia

Checklist of useful Anglo-Saxon suffixes

suffix	meaning	examples
ed	denotes past tense of verbs	looked, talked, spilled
en	denotes past participles of verbs	broken, fallen, written
er	someone who does something	baker, singer, teacher
er	comparative degree of adjectives	happier, longer, sharper
est	superlative degree of adjectives	funniest, hottest, sunniest
ful	being full of some quality	forgetful, graceful, merciful
hood	condition of being	childhood, fatherhood, priesthood
ing	denotes present tense/present participle of verbs	driving, loving, running
ish	slightly/fairly	babyish, reddish, fiftyish
le	names of tools/diminutives	handle, kettle, thimble
less	lacking	breathless, homeless, tasteless
like	similar/resembling	ladylike, lifelike, warlike
ly	used to form adverbs/manner of	happily, quickly, slowly
ness	quality/condition	greediness, kindness, ugliness
ship	position/rank	apprenticeship, premiership, scholarship
ward	direction of/towards	forward, homeward, upward

Aim: To identify, understand and learn how to use words with Greek and Anglo-Saxon suffixes

Keywords for review:

A suffix is a letter or group of letters that goes at the end of a root word. A suffix usually changes the way the word is used.

First, you need the checklists of useful Greek and Anglo-Saxon suffixes in front of you, see p. 372.

- look at each word
- say the word
- learn its meaning
- read the examples
- highlight the suffix within each example

Using Greek and Anglo-Saxon suffixes

- look at each word
- say the word
- highlight the suffix and say its meaning (you can use a dictionary)
- copy out the word
- use it in a sentence
- use the proof-reading C-O-P-S

1. vandalism _____

2. appendicitis _____

3. scholarship _____

4. babyish _____

5. priesthood _____

6. funniest _____

Section A

- have the checklists of Greek and Anglo-Saxon suffixes in front of you, see p. 372
- fill in the missing suffix to complete the word
- use a dictionary if necessary
- then make a sentence for each word

1. bi .... _____

2. gran............... _____

3. apprentice............... _____

4. vandal............... _____

5. fluor............... _____

6. tonsill......... _____

7. hott......... _____

8. writt......... _____

9. home......... _____

10. greedi......... _____

Section B – Quiz 9

Complete the quiz by using words from the checklist of Greek and Anglo-Saxon suffixes

1. . . . . is a substance sometimes used to dye hair blond.

2. A highly contagious eye infection is called . . . .

3. . . . . is a fear of being in confined spaces.

4. . . . . should be a happy, carefree time for children.

5. A . . . . is used to protect one's fingers when sewing.

6. Some sculptures have a . . . . expression.

7. . . . . is used as an explosive substance.

8. Top football clubs like Arsenal and Liverpool are in the . . . . Division.

9. . . . . people sometimes sleep in doorways.

10. Don't regret something in the past because there is no good in crying over . . . . milk.

Section C

- read the passage
- copy it out
- write the passage to dictation
- highlight the suffixes
- re-read and use the proof-reading C-O-P-S

The jumble sale

Horrible Harry and Hateful Henry went to a jumble sale in the village hall on the sunniest day of the year. Hateful Henry browsed through all the items that reminded him of his childhood. He bought a box of lifelike Beatrix Potter animals and some Dinky cars. Catching sight of him, Horrible Harry yelled out, 'What a lot of babyish junk!'

   He went to the bookstall where he bought books about neurology and agnosticism, and a study of the priesthood. He then began to feel unwell as the crowd grabbed and pulled at all the goods on sale on the tables. He screamed, 'Get me out of here fast; the dust is giving me conjunctivitis and I can feel an attack of claustrophobia coming on'. 'It's your own fault for your greediness and for pushing to the front and grabbing all the bargains,' sniggered Hateful Henry.

The Seven Seriously Super Suffixing Rules

Keywords to review:

- The vowels are a e i o u (and sometimes y)
- Short vowels say their sounds
- The consonants are all the other letters in the alphabet
- A syllable is a beat
- A suffix is a letter or a group of letters that go at the end of a word and change its use

Suffixing: Rule One

Aim: To learn and apply the One-One-One Rule

The One-One-One Rule says:

When a word has <u>one</u> syllable, <u>one</u> short vowel and ends in <u>one</u> consonant, the consonant is doubled before adding a suffix beginning with a vowel

fat   fatter, fatted, fattest, fattening, fatty
wet   wetter, wetted, wettest, wetting

If the root word ends in a long vowel, do not double the final consonant – for example:

| ow̄ | **blow** | blowed, blowing, blowy |
| āi | **wait** | waited, waiter, waiting |

If the root word ends in a consonant digraph, do not double the final consonant – for example:

| sh | **wish** | wished, wishing, wishy-washy |
| ch | **punch** | puncher, punchier, punchiest, punched, punching |

HANDY HINT

Common suffixes beginning with a vowel include:

    er   ed   est   en   ing   ish   ous   y

Section A

Aim: To add suffixes beginning with a vowel

- look at the word
- say the root word and the suffix
- apply the One-One-One Rule and add the suffix
- copy out the word
- read the word
- use ten of the words in sentences, using the proof-reading C-O-P-S

1. run – er_____
2. mop – ed _____
3. long – est _____
4. stop – ing _____
5. stiff – en _____
6. soft – y _____
7. blend – er _____
8. drift – ing_____
9. ham – er _____
10. hand – y _____

11. pot – y_____
12. drag – ing _____
13. slip – er _____
14. wish – ed_____
15. bunch – ing _____
16. win – er_____
17. tall – est_____
18. flat – en_____
19. clap – ing_____
20. wet – er _____

1. _____

2. _____

3. _____

4. _____

5. _____

6. _____

7. _____

8. _____

9. _____

10. _____

Section A

To add suffixes beginning with a vowel – further practice

- look at the word
- say the root word and the suffix
- apply the One-One-One Rule and add the suffix
- copy out the word
- read the word
- use six of the words in sentences, using the proof-reading C-O-P-S

1. big – er _____

2. mud – y _____

3. rent – ing _____

4. lick – ing _____

5. slow – ish _____

6. sip – ing _____

7. smack – ed _____

8. red – ish _____

9. kick – ing _____

10. dust – y _____

11. rob – ed _____

12. tank – er _____

1. _____

2. _____

3. _____

4. _____

5. _____

6. _____

Section A

Aim: To add suffixes beginning with a consonant

- look at the word
- say the root word and the suffix
- apply the One-One-One Rule and add the suffix
- copy out the word
- read the word
- use six of the words in sentences, using the proof-reading C-O-P-S

HANDY HINT

Common suffixes beginning with consonants include:

ful   less   ly   ment   ness   some

1. cup – ful _____

2. harm – less _____

3. whole – some _____

4. plate – ful _____

5. glad – ness _____

6. mad – ness _____

7. tire – some _____

8. enjoy – ment _____

9. dim – ly _____

10. home – ly _____

11. hot – ly _____

12. wet – ness _____

1. _____

2. _____

3. _____

4. _____

5. _____

6. _____

Section A

Aim: To add suffixes beginning with vowels or consonants

- look at the word
- say the root word and the suffix
- apply the One-One-One Rule and add the suffix
- copy out the word
- read the word
- use six of the words in sentences, using the proof-reading C-O-P-S

1. wed – ing _____

2. pack – er _____

3. pad – ed _____

4. blush – ing _____

5. dig – ing _____

6. swift – ly _____

7. cold – er _____

8. nod – ing _____

9. tap – ed _____

10. set – er _____

11. grip – ing _____

12. ill – ness _____

1. _____

2. _____

3. _____

4. _____

5. _____

6. _____

Suffixing: Rule Two

Aim: To learn and apply the Lazy 'e' Rule – part one

The Lazy 'e' Rule says:

Drop the 'e' before you add a suffix **beginning** with a **vowel**

race	racer, raced, racing, racy
slope	sloped, sloping, slopy
stone	stonier, stoniest, stony, stoned, stoning

Exceptions: fire, fiery; joke, jokey; size, sizeable

Section A

Apart from those two special cases, the following are rule-breakers and keep 'e' when adding a suffix beginning with a vowel:

acre	acreage	hoe	hoeing	singe	singeing
canoe	canoeing	mile	mileage	tinge	tingeing
dye	dyeing	shoe	shoeing	toe	toeing

Aim: To practise adding suffixes beginning with a vowel to words ending in 'e'

- look at the word
- say the root word and the suffix
- apply the Lazy 'e' Rule - part one
- copy out the word, including the suffix
- read the word
- use six of the words in sentences, and use the proof-reading C-O-P-S

HANDY HINT

Common suffixes beginning with vowels include:

al   ance   ed   er   est

1. ride – er _____

2. fine – est _____

3. stripe – ed _____

4. like – en _____

5. arrive – ing _____

6. dive – ed _____

7. slope – ing _____

8. five – er _____

9. brave – est _____

10. hire – ing _____

11. pure – est _____

12. hole – ed _____

1. _____

2. _____

3. _____

4. _____

5. _____

6. _____

Suffixing: Rule Three

Aim: To learn and apply the Lazy 'e' Rule – part two

The Lazy 'e' Rule also says:

Keep the 'e' before you add a suffix beginning with a consonant

name	nameless, namely, namelessly, namelessness
use	useful, useless, usefulness, uselessly

HANDY HINT

Common suffixes beginning with consonants include:

ful   hood   ment   ness   th

Exceptions: 'judgement' (opinion or understanding) follows the rule, but 'judgment' (court verdict) does not.

The following are rule-breakers, which drop 'e' when adding a suffix beginning with a consonant:

awe	awful	nine	ninth	subtle	subtly
due	duly	true	truly	whole	wholly

Section A

Aim: To add suffixes beginning with a consonant to words ending in 'e'

- look at the word
- say the root word and the suffix
- apply the Lazy 'e' Rule - part one
- copy out the word, including the suffix
- read the word
- use six of the words in sentences, and use the proof-reading C-O-P-S

1. hate – ful _____

2. home – less _____

3. acknowledge – ment _____

4. care – less _____

5. wakeful – ness _____

6. time – less _____

7. lone – some _____

8. time – ly _____

9. due – ly _____

10. acute – ly _____

11. judge – ment _____

12. true – ly _____

1. _____

2. _____

3. _____

4. _____

5. _____

6. _____

Suffixing: Rule Four

Aim: To learn and apply the Lazy 'e' Rule – part three

The Lazy 'e' Rule also says:

Keep the 'e' in words ending 'ce' or 'ge' before you add the suffixes 'able', 'ade' and 'ous'

dance	danceable
peace	peaceable
orange	orangeade
change	changeable
marriage	marriageable
courage	courageous

Section A

Aim: To practise adding the suffixes 'able', 'ade' or 'ous' to words ending in 'e'

- look at the word
- say the root word and the suffix
- apply the Lazy 'e' Rule – part three
- copy out the word, including the suffix
- read the word
- use the words in sentences, and use the proof-reading C-O-P-S

1. courage- _____
2. trace- _____
3. change- _____

4. advantage- _____
5. orange- _____
6. outrage- _____

1. _____

2. _____

3. _____

4. _____

5. _____

6. _____

Suffixing: Rule Five

Aim: To learn and apply the 'y' Rule – part one

The 'y' Rule says:

Change 'y' to 'i' before adding most suffixes

memory	memorial
defy	defiance
friendly	friendliness
try	trier
busy	busiest
beauty	beautiful
likely	likelihood
weary	weariness

Exceptions: shy, shyer; shyest; drier (weather) but a (tumble) dryer

Section A

Aim: To practise adding suffixes to words ending in 'y'

- look at the word
- say the root word and the suffix
- apply the 'y' Rule – part one
- copy out the word, including the suffix
- read the word
- use six of the words in sentences, and use the proof-reading C-O-P-S

1. hardy – ness _____

2. ceremony – al _____

3. dreary – ness _____

4. lively – hood _____

5. beauty – ful _____

6. apply – ance _____

7. weary – ness _____

8. testimony – al _____

9. fancy – ful _____

10. cry – ed _____

11. dry – ed _____

12. tiny – est _____

1. _____

2. _____

3. _____

4. _____

5. _____

6. _____

Suffixing: Rule Six

Aim: To learn and apply the 'y' Rule – part two

The 'y' Rule also says:

Keep 'y' when adding the suffixes 'ing', 'ish' and 'ist'

    cry   crying   **baby**   babyish   **copy**   copyist

HANDY HINT

Keep 'y' when adding suffixes beginning with 'i' because we never have double 'i' in English spelling

Section A

Aim: To practise adding the suffixes 'ing', 'ish' and 'ist' to words ending in 'y'

- look at the word
- say the root word and the suffix
- apply the 'y' Rule – part two
- copy out the word, including the suffix
- read the word
- use the six words in sentences, and use the proof-reading C-O-P-S

1. carry – ing _____

2. grey – ish _____

3. play – ing _____

4. dry – ing _____

5. tomboy – ish _____

6. clarify – ing _____

1. _____

2. _____

3. _____

4. _____

5. _____

6. _____

Suffixing: Rule Seven

Aim: To learn and apply the 'y' Rule – part three

The 'y' Rule also says:

When adding any suffix, **keep 'y'** if there is a **vowel before** it

| **boy** | boyish, boys |
| **destroy** | destroyed, destroyer, destroying, destroys |

Exceptions: The following are rule-breakers that drop 'y' from the root word before adding a suffix:

| day | daily | lay | laid | say | said |
| gay | gaily | pay | paid | slay | slain |

Section A

Aim: To add suffixes to words with a vowel before 'y'

- look at the word
- say the root word and the suffix
- apply the 'y' Rule – part three
- copy out the word including the suffix
- read the word
- use six of the words in sentences, and use the proof-reading C-O-P-S

1. employ – able _____

2. holiday – ing _____

3. monkey – s _____

4. buoy – ant _____

5. trolley – s _____

6. employ – ee _____

7. gangway – s _____

8. play – er _____

9. pay – ment _____

10. pay – able _____

11. boy – hood _____

12. bray – ing _____

1. _____

2. _____

CONTINUED

3. _____

4. _____

5. _____

6. _____

Section A

Aim: To add suffixes, applying the three 'y' rules with the exceptions

- look at the word
- say the root word and suffix
- apply the 'y' rules, with their exceptions
- copy out the word including the suffix
- read the word
- use six of the words in sentences, and use the proof-reading C-O-P-S

1. multiply – ing _____

2. easy – est _____

3. lucky – er _____

4. shy – ness _____

5. portray – ed _____

6. gloomy – est _____

7. busy – ness _____

8. day – ly _____

9. rely – ing _____

10. notice – able _____

11. journey – ed _____

12. alley – s _____

1. _____

2. _____

3. _____

4. _____

5. _____

6. _____

HANDY HINT

Words of two syllables, with the stress on the final syllable – double the final consonant:

begin-	beginner, beginning
prefer-	preferred, preferring

Words of two syllables, with the stress on the first syllable – do not double the final syllable:

en-ter	entered, entering
hap-pen	happened, happening

Words of two syllables, ending in 'l' – double the 'l' no matter where the stress is:

equal	equalled, equalling
rebel	rebelled, rebelling

Mix-and-match revision of all the suffixing rules

Section A – Mix-and-Match

- fill in any missing letters when adding the suffix
- write the word, correctly spelt
- then make a short sentence for each word

1. plan – er _____   _____
   – ed _____   _____
   – ing _____   _____

2. help – ing _____   _____
   – ful _____   _____
   – ed _____   _____

3. wit – ness _____   _____
   – y _____   _____
   – less _____   _____

4. sun – y _____   _____
   – ing _____   _____
   – less _____   _____

CONTINUED

5. fit – est _____

    – ful _____ _____

    – ness _____ _____

6. thin – ly _____ _____

    – er _____ _____

    – ish _____ _____

7. brim – less _____ _____

    – ed _____ _____

    – ing _____ _____

8. rub – er _____ _____

    – ed _____ _____

    – ing _____ _____

9. slip – ed _____ _____

    – er _____ _____

    – ing _____ _____

10. flat – ly _____ _____

    – ness _____ _____

    – er _____ _____

Section B – Mix-and-Match

- re-read the target words in section A
- fill in the missing words in the quiz
- read the whole sentence
- highlight the target word

1. On . . . . days, we use blinds to exclude strong sunlight.

2. New buildings usually need . . . . permission.

3. Cinderella lost one of her glass . . . . s at the ball.

4. A friend gives you a . . . . hand when you are struggling.

5. You can remove pencil marks with a . . . .

6. She . . . . on the ice and broke her hand.

7. He goes to the gym to do . . . . training.

8. The cup was too full, so the tea was . . . . over.

9. The child was patting down the top of the mud pie to make it . . . .

10. The . . . . gave evidence to the police about the accident.

Section C

- read the passage
- copy it out
- write the passage to dictation
- highlight the suffixes
- re-read and proof-read with the C-O-P-S

The tale of the red setter puppy

Hateful Henry and Horrible Harry decided to buy a new puppy. They hunted high and low and tramped all over the place to find a red setter. They argued about calling him Bobby or Slippers. 'Let's call him Slippers as last night he made the biggest hole possible in my best slippers. I found them hidden under my bed in a dusty corner,' moaned Horrible Harry.

Hateful Henry was in the kitchen, wearing rubber gloves. He had been mopping up the floor after Slippers. His hands were dripping as he ran to answer the doorbell. Slippers darted out of the open door barking at the postman, who was running down the garden path by now.

Horrible Harry ran across the tiled kitchen floor and skidded on the wet as he tried to grab the silly puppy. He fell hitting his head and smashed his glasses. 'Oh! That red setter is as mad as a hatter. Whose idea was it to choose that breed of dog? Not mine!' he muttered, as he swept up the shattered glass.

_____

_____

_____

_____

_____

_____

_____

_____

_____

_____

_____

_____

_____

_____

_____

_____

_____

_____

_____

_____

_____

_____

_____

Section A – Mix-and-Match

- fill in any missing letters when adding the suffix
- write the word, correctly spelt
- then make a short sentence for each word

1. happy – er _____ _____
   – ly _____ _____
   – est _____ _____

2. easy – ness _____ _____
   – ly _____ _____
   – est _____ _____

3. rely – ed _____ _____
   – able _____ _____
   – ing _____ _____

4. pay – ed _____ _____
   – ing _____ _____
   – er _____ _____

5. obey – ed _____ _____
   – ing _____ _____
   – s _____ _____

6. apply – ed _____ _____
   – ance _____ _____
   – es _____ _____

7. dye – es _____ _____
   – ed _____ _____
   – ing _____ _____

8. change – ed _____ _____
   – able _____ _____
   – ing _____ _____

9. size – able _____ _____
   – ed _____ _____
   – es _____ _____

10. try – ing _____ _____
    – er _____ _____
    – es _____ _____

Section B – Mix-and-Match

- re-read the target words in Section A
- read the clues
- fill in the missing words in the quiz
- read the whole sentence
- highlight the target word

1. Electrical . . . . include washing machine and radios.

2. . . . . machines never break down.

3. He made a bad mistake; he . . . . the price.

4. Noisy children can be very . . . .

5. He had ten shops; it was a . . . . business.

6. I don't want a large one or a small one; I would like a middle- . . . . one.

7. They got . . . . and went swimming.

8. In the army, orders must be . . . .

9. My favourite place is the garden; that's where I'm . . . .

10. You can become a blonde by . . . . your hair.

Section C

- read the passage
- copy it out
- write the passage to dictation
- highlight the suffixes in the target words
- re-read and proof-read with the C-O-P-S

An action-packed day in the snow

Horrible Harry and Hateful Henry stayed at home, displaying smug satisfaction that they had wisely not driven to work on the icy motorway. At lunchtime, Hateful Henry remarked casually to his twin, 'I am relying on you to take Slippers the dog for a walk as I still have a lot of soreness in my broken ankle'.

Flurries of snow blew in his face as he carried out this tiresome task. He was truly amazed at how intensely the snow was falling. He tried to find the easiest path in the snow. He hurried home, relieved to have finished this chore.

As he opened the door he was greeted by Hateful Henry calling out. 'That was a short walk'.

'It is the last time I will go out in this foul weather, you spineless, lazy lout! You will be taking the dog out tonight,' shrieked an exhausted Horrible Harry.

Section A – Mix-and-Match

- fill in any missing letters when adding the suffix
- write the word, correctly spelt
- then make a short sentence for each word

1. lone – some _____   _____
   – ly _____   _____
   – er _____   _____

2. spray – er _____   _____
   – ed _____   _____
   – ing _____   _____

3. busy – er _____   _____
   – ing _____   _____
   – est _____   _____

4. copy – ed _____   _____
   – er _____   _____
   – es _____   _____

5. pray – ed _____   _____
   – ing _____   _____
   – er _____   _____

6. carry – ing _____   _____
   – ed _____   _____
   – er _____   _____

7. display – ed _____   _____
   – s _____   _____
   – ing _____   _____

8. employ – er _____   _____
   – able _____   _____
   – ing _____   _____

9. empty – ed _____   _____
   – ness _____   _____
   – ier _____   _____

10. load – ed _____   _____
    – er _____   _____
    – ing _____   _____

Section B – Mix-and-Match

- re-read all the target words in Section A
- read the clues
- fill in the missing words in the quiz
- read the whole sentence
- highlight the target word

1. The government sent an aircraft . . . . to the conflict.

2. Age Concern helps many . . . . old people who have no family.

3. The farmer . . . . his crops with fertiliser.

4. Have you . . . . the dishwasher?

5. The swimming pool . . . . as soon as it started to rain.

6. His . . . . sacked him because he was always late for work.

7. Hyde Park corner is one of the . . . . places in London.

8. 'I am . . . . for good weather for the picnic', said the priest.

9. The bird of paradise . . . . the most beautiful feathers .

10. The photo . . . . in our office has stopped working.

Section C

- read the passage
- copy it out
- write the passage to dictation
- highlight the root words
- re-read using the proof-reading C-O-P-S

The Forty Pound Ice Cream Incident

Horrible Harry and Hateful Henry were enjoying a lovely sunny summer's day. 'I am dying for an ice cream,' said Hateful Henry. 'Let's pull in here – we can easily dash over to that ice-cream van. We don't need to bother paying for a parking ticket'. When they arrived at the van they were dismayed that there was a long queue. They were annoyed when they had to wait for ten minutes. They went hurrying back to their car and began panicking about the traffic warden they had just seen lurking about.

As they came around the corner they were annoyed to see the warden sticking a parking ticket on their windscreen. They ranted and raved, and begged to be let off for illegal parking. The warden said that a forty-pound fine was payable on the spot.

Horrible Harry said, 'You can pay: it was all your idea to buy ice cream. I am certainly enjoying this forty-pound ice cream'.

_____

_____

_____

_____

_____

_____

_____

_____

_____

_____

_____

_____

_____

_____

_____

_____

_____

_____

_____

_____

_____

_____

Answers to activities and quizzes

Section A Page 350

1. incredible
2. spectacles
3. anniversary
4. telephone
5. dehydration
6. photogenic
7. extraterrestrial
8. postscript
9. signature
10. thermostat

Section B – Quiz 1 Page 350

1. Democratic
2. stethoscope
3. genocide
4. autobiography
5. encyclopaedia
6. biopsy
7. saxophonist
8. archbishop
9. aerobics
10. dehydration

Section A Page 354

1. post mortem
2. international
3. detoxify
4. postgraduate
5. superglue
6. abandoned
7. subway
8. co-educational
9. pervade
10. transatlantic

Section B – Quiz 2 Page 354

1. impartial
2. anteroom
3. omnipotent
4. perforation
5. subway
6. post mortem
7. antenatal
8. transfer
9. retake
10. ambidextrous

Section A Page 359

1. metacarpal
2. hypothermia
3. self-fulfilling
4. mislay
5. hyperbole
6. byroads
7. withdraw
8. microclimate
9. dyscalculia
10. outlaw

Section B – Quiz 3 Page 359

1. synchronise
2. hypothermia
3. hydrotherapy
4. hypermarkets
5. antipodes
6. unbearable
7. peripatetic
8. unfolded
9. hypnotherapy
10. midwife

Quiz 4 Page 361

1. all-risks
2. almost
3. although
4. allspice
5. all-rounder
6. all-time
7. altogether
8. all-purpose
9. already
10. all-night

Quiz 5 Page 364

1. well-known
2. well matched
3. well-stacked
4. well bred
5. well behaved
6. well heeled
7. well dressed
8. well-balanced
9. well-done
10. well informed

Quiz 6 Page 365

1. illustration
2. illegible
3. ill mannered
4. ill feeling
5. illuminate
6. illegal
7. ill equipped
8. ill-mannered
9. illegitimate
10. illegal

Quiz 7 Page 367

1. immersion
2. irrefutable
3. irregular
4. irrelevant
5. irreplaceable
6. irritable
7. immobile
8. immensely
9. innings
10. import

Section A Page 370

1. orphanage
2. payable
3. employee
4. beautician
5. marvellous
6. alcoholism
7. solitude
8. duchess
9. baggage
10. parental

Section B – Quiz 8 Page 370

1. optician
2. novelist
3. Chinese
4. parental
5. affectionate
6. metamorphosis
7. payable
8. creative
9. verbose
10. compassionate

Section A Page 374

1. biology
2. granite
3. apprenticeship
4. vandalism
5. fluoride
6. tonsillitis
7. hottest
8. written
9. homeless
10. greediness

Section B – Quiz 9 Page 374

1. peroxide
2. conjunctivitis
3. claustrophobia
4. childhood
5. thimble
6. lifelike
7. dynamite
8. premiership
9. homeless
10. spilled (or spilt)

Section A Page 377

1. runner
2. mopped
3. longest
4. stopping
5. stiffen
6. softly
7. blender
8. drifting
9. hammer
10. handy
11. potty
12. dragging
13. slipper
14. wished
15. bunching
16. winner
17. tallest
18. flatten
19. clapping
20. wetter

Section A Page 378

1. bigger
2. muddy
3. renting
4. licking
5. slowish
6. sipping
7. smacked
8. reddish
9. kicking
10. dusty
11. robbed
12. tanker

Section A Page 379

1. cupful
2. harmless
3. wholesome
4. plateful
5. gladness
6. madness
7. tiresome
8. enjoyment
9. dimly
10. homely
11. hotly
12. wetness

Section A Page 380

1. wedding
2. packer
3. padded
4. blushing
5. digging
6. swiftly
7. colder
8. nodding
9. tapped
10. setter
11. gripping
12. illness

Section A Page 381

1. rider
2. finest
3. striped
4. liken
5. arriving
6. dived
7. sloping
8. fiver
9. bravest
10. hiring
11. purest
12. holed

Section A Page 382

1. hateful
2. homeless
3. acknowledgement
4. careless
5. wakefulness
6. timeless
7. lonesome
8. timely
9. duly
10. acutely
11. judgement
12. truly

Section A Page 384

1. courageous
2. traceable
3. changeable
4. advantageous
5. orangeade
6. outrageous

Section A Page 385

1. hardiness
2. ceremonial
3. dreariness
4. livelihood
5. beautiful
6. appliance
7. weariness
8. testimonial
9. fanciful
10. cried
11. dried
12. tiniest

Section A Page 386

1. carrying
2. greyish
3. playing
4. drying
5. tomboyish
6. clarifying

Section A Page 387

1. employable
2. holidaying
3. monkeys
4. buoyant
5. trolleys
6. employee
7. gangways
8. player
9. payment
10. payable
11. boyhood
12. braying

Section A Page 388

1. multiplying
2. easiest
3. luckier
4. shyness
5. portrayed
6. gloomiest
7. business
8. daily
9. relying
10. noticeable
11. journeyed
12. alleys

Section A
Mix-and-Match Page 389

1. planner
   planned
   planning
2. helping
   helpful
   helped
3. witness
   witty
   witless
4. sunny
   sunning
   sunless
5. fittest
   fitful
   fitness
6. thinly
   thinner
   thinnish
7. brimless
   brimmed
   brimming
8. rubber
   rubbing
   rubbed
9. slipped
   slipper
   slipping
10. flatly
    flatness
    flatter

Section B
Mix-and-Match Page 390

1. sunny
2. planning
3. slipper
4. helping
5. rubber
6. slipped
7. fitness
8. brimming
9. flatter
10. witness

Section B
Mix-and-Match Page 393

1. appliances
2. reliable
3. paid
4. trying
5. sizeable
6. sized
7. changed
8. obeyed
9. happiest
10. dyeing

Section A
Mix-and-Match Page 392

1. happier
   happily
   happiest
2. easiness
   easily
   easiest
3. relied
   reliable
   relying
4. paid
   paying
   payer
5. obeyed
   obeying
   obeys
6. applied
   appliance
   applies
7. dyeing
   dyed
   dyes
8. changed
   changeable
   changing
9. sized
   sizes
   sizeable
10. tries
    trier
    trying

Section A
Mix-and-Match Page 395

1. lonesome
   lonely
   loner
2. sprayer
   sprayed
   spraying
3. busier
   busying
   busiest
4. copied
   copier
   copies
5. prayed
   praying
   prayer
6. carrying
   carried
   carrier
7. displayed
   displays
   displaying
8. employer
   employable
   employing
9. emptied
   emptiness
   emptier
10. loaded
    loader
    loading

Section B
Mix-and-Match Page 396

1. carrier
2. lonely
3. sprayed
4. loaded
5. emptied
6. employer
7. busiest
8. praying
9. displayed
10. copier

Affixes – Revision and attainment test

The teacher/learning partner reads out each word twice; the learner writes the word in the box.

1. antecedent	2. import	3. extraterrestrial	4. television	5. voluntary
6. tricycle	7. grammar	8. photography	9. police	10. microscope
11. circumference	12. disabled	13. submarine	14. postscript	15. superglue
16. disapproval	17. aerobics	18. dyslexia	19. metaphor	20. photograp
21. forehead	22. mislay	23. outward	24. fulfilling	25. without
26. although	27. well-behaved	28. illegal	29. immigrant	30. innings
31. irregular	32. payable	33. duchess	34. alcohol	35. leisure
36. visible	37. collage	38. forgettable	39. communism	40. biology
41. funniest	42. babyish	43. ugliness	44. scholarship	45. forward
46. fattening	47. beginner	48. equalled	49. mileage	50. ninth
51. forty	52. married	53. awful	54. wholly	55. usefulness
56. sincerely	57. courageous	58. knowledgeable	59. busiest	60. beautiful
61. appliance	62. supplier	63. defiance	64. handy	65. edible
66. colourful	67. realise	68. advertisement	69. tries	70. boyish
71. payer	72. gaily	73. daily	74. employable	75. laziest
76. reliant	77. gloomiest	78. diaries	79. payable	80. notice
81. simplification	82. obeying	83. happiness	84. carried	85. buyer
86. thinnish	87. sunning	88. easiness	89. dyeing	90. bullying
91. notify	92. obscurity	93. disadvantageous	94. disagreement	95. discouraging
96. employee	97. outrageous	98. respectable	99. serviceable	100. visible

1. _____

2. _____

3. _____

4. _____

5. _____

6. _____

7. _____

8. _____

9. _____

10. _____

11. _____

12. _____

13. _____

14. _____

15. _____

16. _____

17. _____

18. _____

19. _____

20. _____

21. _____

22. _____

23. _____

24. _____

25. _____

26. _____

27. _____

28. _____

29. _____

30. _____

31. _____

32. _____

33. _____

34. _____

35. _____

36. _____

37. _____

38. _____

39. _____

40. _____

41. _____

42. _____

43. _____

44. _____

45. _____

46. _____

47. _____

48. _____

49. _____

50. _____

51.
52.
53.
54.
55.
56.
57.
58.
59.
60.
61.
62.
63.
64.
65.
66.
67.
68.
69.
70.
71.
72.
73.
74.
75.
76.
77.
78.
79.
80.
81.
82.
83.
84.
85.
86.
87.
88.
89.
90.
91.
92.
93.
94.
95.
96.
97.
98.
99.
100.

There is 1 mark for each correct answer

The optimum score is 100

100	Excellent
99–80	Very Good
79–70	Good
69–60	Not Bad
59 or less	Keep Trying